I Am Your Sister

COLLECTED AND UNPUBLISHED WRITINGS OF AUDRE LORDE

Edited by
RUDOLPH P. BYRD
JOHNNETTA BETSCH COLE
BEVERLY GUY-SHEFTALL

OXFORD
UNIVERSITY PRESS

OXFORD
UNIVERSITY PRESS

Oxford University Press, Inc., publishes works that further
Oxford University's objective of excellence
in research, scholarship, and education.

Oxford   New York
Auckland   Cape Town   Dar es Salaam   Hong Kong   Karachi
Kuala Lumpur   Madrid   Melbourne   Mexico City   Nairobi
New Delhi   Shanghai   Taipei   Toronto

With offices in
Argentina   Austria   Brazil   Chile   Czech Republic   France   Greece
Guatemala   Hungary   Italy   Japan   Poland   Portugal   Singapore
South Korea   Switzerland   Thailand   Turkey   Ukraine   Vietnam

Copyright © 2009 by Oxford University Press, Inc.

First issued as an Oxford University Press paperback, 2011

Published by Oxford University Press, Inc.
198 Madison Avenue, New York, New York 10016
www.oup.com

Oxford is a registered trademark of Oxford University Press

Library of Congress Cataloguing-in-Publication Data
Lorde, Audre.
  I am your sister ; collected and unpublished writings of Audre Lorde / edited by
Rudolph P. Byrd, Johnnetta Betsch Cole, Beverly Guy-Sheftall.
     p. cm. -- (Transgressing boundaries)
  Includes bibliographical references and index.
  ISBN 978-0-19-534148-5 (hardcover); 978-0-19-984645-0 (pbk. : alk. paper) 1. Feminism.
2. Lesbianism I. Byrd, Rudolph P. II. Cole, Johnnetta B. III. Guy-Sheftall, Beverly. IV.
Title.
  PS3562.O75I3 2009
  814'.54--dc22
2009002083

I AM YOUR SISTER

TRANSGRESSING BOUNDARIES

Studies in Black Politics and Black Communities
Cathy Cohen and Fredrick Harris, Series Editors

We dedicate this book to the friendship the three of us enjoy. It is a friendship that keeps us on each other's minds and in each other's hearts; gives us permission to critique each other's work; and is strengthened by the belief we share with Audre Lorde that "it is not difference that immobilizes us but silence."

ACKNOWLEDGMENTS

We wish to express our gratitude to the following institutions for their support and encouragement as we brought *I Am Your Sister: Collected and Unpublished Writings of Audre Lorde* to publication: the Spelman College Archives; the Estate of Audre Lorde; the Audre Lorde Collection of the Lesbian Herstory Archives; the Spelman College Women's Research and Resource Center; and the Raymond Danowski Poetry Library of the Manuscript, Archive, Rare Book Library of Emory University.

Permission to reprint the following selections is also gratefully acknowledged: "The Transformation of Silence into Language and Action" (Ten Speed Press); and "Sexism: An American Disease in Blackface" (Aunt Lute Books).

We also would like to acknowledge the generosity of three special friends who granted permission to reprint their works in this volume: bell hooks for "Lorde: The Imagination of Justice"; Gloria I. Joseph for "Remembering Audre Lorde"; and Alice Walker for "Audre's Voice."

I Am Your Sister is published as part of Oxford University Press's series Transgressing Boundaries, which was conceived and is very ably edited by Cathy J. Cohen and Frederick Harris. We are indebted to them for their support of a collection that will generate new scholarship and teaching on Audre Lorde.

Finally, we would like to express our gratitude to our partners, friends, and colleagues who advanced this project in vital and significant ways: Brenda Banks, Cecelia Corbin Hunter, Lydia English, Jeffrey B. Leak, Henry A. Leonard, Ingrid Saunders Jones, Cynthia N. Spence, Taronda Spencer, and James D. Staton, Jr.

CONTENTS

PART III.   DIFFERENCE AND SURVIVAL

PART IV.   REFLECTIONS

CREDITS

Part I. From *Sister Outsider* and *A Burst of Light*

"The Transformation of Silence into Language and Action." Paper delivered at the Modern Language Association's Lesbian and Literature panel, Chicago, Illinois, December 28, 1977. Published in *Sinister Wisdom* 6 (1978); *The Cancer Journals* (Spinsters, Ink, 1980); and *Sister Outsider: Essays and Speeches by Audre Lorde* (Crossing Press, 1984).

"Sexism: An American Disease in Blackface." First published as "The Great American Disease," *Black Scholar* 10, no. 9 (May–June 1979), in response to Robert Staples, "The Myth of Black Macho: A Response to Angry Black Feminists," *Black Scholar* 10, no. 8 (March–April 1979); and subsequently published as "Sexism: An American Disease in Blackface," in *Sister Outsider: Essays and Speeches by Audre Lorde* (Crossing Press, 1984).

"Sadomasochism: Not About Condemnation." An earlier version of this interview appeared in *Against Sadomasochism: A Radical Feminist Analysis*, ed. Robin Ruth Linden, Darlene R. Pagano, Diana E. H. Russell, and Susan Leigh Star (Frog in the Well, 1982). Subsequently published in *A Burst of Light: Essays by Audre Lorde* (Firebrand, 1988).

"I Am Your Sister." First published in pamphlet form along with "Apartheid U.S.A." (Kitchen Table: Women of Color Press, 1985). Subsequently published in *A Burst of Light: Essays by Audre Lorde* (Firebrand, 1988).

"Apartheid U.S.A." First published in pamphlet form along with "I Am Your Sister" (Kitchen Table: Women of Color Press, 1985). Subsequently published in *A Burst of Light: Essays by Audre Lorde* (Firebrand Books, 1988).

"Turning the Beat Around: Lesbian Parenting 1986." First published in *Politics of the Heart: A Lesbian Parenting Anthology*, ed. Sandra Pollack and Jeanne Vaughn (Firebrand Books, 1987). Subsequently published in *A Burst of Light: Essays by Audre Lorde* (Firebrand Books, 1988).

"A Burst of Light: Living with Cancer." First published as *A Burst of Light: Essays by Audre Lorde* (Firebrand Books, 1988).

Part II. My Words Will Be There

"*Eva's Man* by Gayl Jones: A Review." We have found no record that Lorde's review of Gayl Jones, *Eva's Man* (Random House, 1976), was ever published. Audre Lorde Papers, Box 8, Spelman College Archives.

"Self-Definition and My Poetry." Paper delivered at the Modern Language Association meeting, New York, NY, December 1976. Audre Lorde Papers, Box 8, Spelman College Archives.

"Introduction: *Movement in Black* by Pat Parker." Originally published in *Movement in Black: The Collected Poetry of Pat Parker* (Diana Press, 1978).

"My Words Will Be There." First published in *Black Women Writers (1950–1980): A Critical Evaluation*, ed. Mari Evans (Anchor Press/Doubleday, 1983).

"Introduction to *Farbe bekennen: Afro-deutsche Frauen auf den Suren ihrer Geschichte.*" Originally published in *Farbe bekennen*, ed. Katharina Oguntoye, May Opitz, and Dagmar Schultz (Orlanda Frauenverlag, 1986). The English edition, *Showing Our Colors: Afro-German Women Speak Out*, trans. Anne V. Adams, was published by the University of Massachusetts Press in 1992.

"Preface to a New Edition of *Need: A Chorale for Black Woman Voices.*" The poem was first written in 1979. This preface was first published in 1989 by Kitchen Table: Women of Color Press.

"Poet as Teacher—Human as Poet—Teacher as Human." Undated manuscript published here for the first time. Audre Lorde Papers, Box 8, Spelman College Archives.

"Poetry Makes Something Happen." Undated manuscript published here for the first time. Audre Lorde Papers, Box 8, Spelman College Archives.

"My Mother's Mortar." This version was first published in *Sinister Wisdom* 8 (1977): 54–61.

Part III. Difference and Survival

"Difference and Survival: An Address at Hunter College." Undated address published here for the first time. Audre Lorde Papers, Box 8, Spelman College Archives.

"The First Black Feminist Retreat: July 6, 1977." Published here for the first time. Audre Lorde Papers, Box 8, Spelman College Archives.

"When Will the Ignorance End? Keynote Address at the First National Third World Lesbian and Gay Conference." Delivered in Washington, D.C., on October 13, 1979. A condensed version of this speech was published in *Off our backs* 9, no. 10 (November 1979). The complete version is published here for the first time. Audre Lorde Papers, Box 8, Spelman College Archives.

"Litany of Commitment: An Address Delivered at the March on Washington (1983)." Published here for the first time, Lorde delivered this address on August 27, 1983. Audre Lorde Papers, Box 8, Spelman College Archives.

"Commencement Address: Oberlin College." Delivered on May 29, 1989, and published here for the first time. Audre Lorde Papers, Box 8, Spelman College Archives.

"There Is No Hierarchy of Oppression." First published in *Interracial Books for Children Bulletin* 14, no. 3 (1983). Subsequently published in *Dangerous Liaisons: Blacks, Gays and the Struggle for Equality*, ed. Eric Brandt (New Press, 1999).

"What Is at Stake in Lesbian and Gay Publishing Today: The Bill Whitehead Award Ceremony, 1990." Published here for the first time. Audre Lorde Papers, Box 8, Spelman College Archives.

"Is Your Hair Still Political?" Audre Lorde Papers, Box 8, Spelman College Archives. Subsequently published in *Go Girl! The Black Woman's Book of Travel and Adventure*, ed. Elaine Lee (Portland, OR: Eighth Mountain Press, 1997).

I AM YOUR SISTER

You cannot, you cannot use someone else's fire. You can only use your own. And in order to do that, you must first be willing to believe that you have it. —Audre Lorde

CREATE YOUR OWN FIRE

Audre Lorde and the Tradition of Black Radical Thought

Rudolph P. Byrd

During her lifetime, Audre Lorde struggled to ignite and tend her own fire, notwithstanding the efforts of many to extinguish it. Born Audrey Geraldine Lorde in Harlem, New York, on February 18, 1934, the black, lesbian, feminist, poet, mother, warrior, and sister outsider was the third and last child of Linda Belmar and Frederick Byron Lorde from Grenada. Born during the Great Depression, Lorde's childhood and early adult experiences were shaped not only by the collapse of the American economy, but also by such global events as World War II and the rise of McCarthyism during the 1950s. Educated in the parochial schools of Harlem, Lorde graduated from Hunter High School in 1951. She enrolled at Hunter College in the same year. As a result of a sojourn in Mexico and financial setbacks, Lorde would not graduate from Hunter College until 1959. In that same year, she entered the master of arts program in Library Science at Columbia University. After completing her studies in library science, Lorde found employment as a librarian in the New York City public library system. In her adolescence and youth, Lorde was a shy, deeply thoughtful young woman who was both a rebel and an experimentalist. While Lorde was active as a lesbian in her adolescence, she was married to Edwin Rollins from 1962 to 1970 and became the mother of two children, Elizabeth and Jonathan. Following her divorce from Rollins, Lorde developed significant relationships with women including Frances Clayton, with whom she was involved from 1968 to 1988. Lorde's last major relationship was with Gloria I. Joseph, whom she met in 1981. Following the dissolution of her relationship with Clayton in 1984, Joseph and Lorde were companions until her death in 1992.

Lorde wrote and published poetry in a range of journals and magazines. In 1968, Lorde published *The First Cities*, the first of eleven volumes of poetry. *From a Land Where Other People Live*, her third volume of poetry, which was published in 1973, was nominated for a National Book Award. A librarian and teacher, Lorde held faculty appointments at Tougaloo College, Herbert H. Lehman College, John Jay College of Criminal Justice, and Hunter College while concurrently developing a national reputation as a leader in the women's movement, the civil rights movement, and the gay and lesbian movement. She was diagnosed with breast cancer in 1977 and liver cancer in 1984. Lorde died of cancer in 1992, only a year after being named New York State Poet Laureate: the first woman and African American to be so honored. The dynamism of Lorde's life as a black lesbian feminist and the complex subjectivities each of these identities evoked are mapped in *I Am Your Sister: Collected and Unpublished Writings of Audre Lorde*.

I Am Your Sister had its genesis in a shared commitment on the part of the editors of this volume to accomplish several important goals. The first is to honor the life and legacy of Audre Lorde, a major figure in American poetry, culture, and politics. The second is to elevate the importance of Lorde's published essays and speeches, which have served as a foundation and catalyst for theorizing by scholars and activists in relation to questions of identity, difference, power, social movements, and social justice for more than twenty-five years. The third goal is to publish selections from the unpublished writings by Lorde. With the arrival of the Audre Lorde archive at Spelman College in 1995 and the opening of the archive to scholars in 2009, we were presented with an extraordinary opportunity to publish for the first time a rare body of Lorde's speeches and essays. These texts reveal striking points of continuity with Lorde's published writings, as well as efforts on her part to chart an ever more radical course of thought and action, which situates her within specific traditions in women's history and African American history. Fourth and finally, we are committed to recovering some of Lorde's prose writings that have been out of print. *I Am Your Sister* contains the complete text of *A Burst of Light*, along with selections from Lorde's prose writings *Sister Outsider* and *The Cancer Journals*, and marks the first publication of these writings since the 1990s.

I Am Your Sister introduces new and vital perspectives on the depth and range of Lorde's intellectual interests and her commitment to progressive social change. These perspectives include Lorde's relationship to the vibrant tradition of black feminist thought and the women's movement; the particular value she placed upon the erotic and issues related to women's health; and her insights on difference and oppression, which culminated in a new critical social theory that is central to several fields and disciplines but in particular to gay and lesbian studies and black queer studies. It is our hope that this volume will catalyze new research and scholarship on a major poet and intellectual whose thinking and writing left a deep imprint upon an era marked by significant change in the domains of art, culture, and politics.

Throughout this introduction, I will refer to Lorde as a black lesbian feminist and also as the sister outsider. The latter term fulfills certain strong functions. This term recalls Lorde's *Sister Outsider*, a landmark collection of essays, some of the most important of which are reprinted here. The term also highlights Lorde's status as an outsider in the often contested realm of social relations. Above all, the term sister outsider illustrates the ways in which Lorde reclaimed and transformed overlapping, discredited, and marginalized identities—black, lesbian, feminist—into a powerful, radical, and progressive standpoint.

"It is not easy for me to speak here with you as a Black Lesbian feminist, recognizing that some of the ways in which I identify myself make it difficult for you to hear me,"[1] observed Audre Lorde in an address delivered at the Women's Center of Medgar Evers College entitled "I Am Your Sister: Black Women Organizing Across Sexualities." Lorde, in characteristic fashion, publicly self-identified as a "Black Lesbian feminist."[2]

In identifying herself in this manner, Lorde wished to stress that she possessed multiple identities. In the process, she positioned herself in a particular tradition of black radical thought and activism and indicated the ways in which she adds to and further radicalizes this evolving tradition. Our insistence that Lorde's corpus of published essays and speeches reveals her allegiances to particular traditions within American and African American history, and the brilliant, intrepid manner in which she expands, complicates, and revitalizes these traditions, constitutes one important claim of this volume. Co-equal with this claim is another which posits that there is a powerful synergy and continuity of thought between Lorde's previously published essays and speeches and those unpublished writings that appear in this volume for the first time. Above all, "I Am Your Sister," an address whose title also serves as the title of this collection, is a useful point of entry into an anthology that underscores Lorde's importance and influence as both a theorist and an activist whose life and writings challenge us to adopt more expansive views of the women's movement, the civil rights movement, and the gay and lesbian movement. Equally as important, as pioneering works in the domains of difference and sexuality, Lorde's essays and speeches prepared the ground for the emergence of a new form of critical social theory focusing upon difference, oppression, and sexuality.

In "I Am Your Sister," Lorde spoke of herself as a black feminist. As such, she located herself in a tradition of black feminist thought inaugurated in the 1830s by Maria W. Stewart who, according to scholar Marilyn Richardson, was the first American-born woman to speak before a public audience.[3] In Stewart's historic speech, which she delivered before a so-called promiscuous audience, that is, an audience composed of men and women, in Boston's Franklin Hall in 1832, she, a free black woman from Hartford, Connecticut, called for the abolition of slavery and championed women's rights and equality. In her landmark pamphlet, *Religion and the Pure Principles of Morality: The Sure Foundation on Which We Must Stand* (1831), and in her speeches, Stewart denounced white supremacy, which led, in her view, to "prejudice, ignorance and poverty."[4] She also underscored the urgency for the creation of black educational and cultural institutions; bravely criticized the sexist, patriarchal practices within black secular and religious institutions; and insisted that African American men assume a greater leadership role in their communities. "And, my brethren," she asked at the conclusion of the now well-known 1832 speech in Franklin Hall, "have you made a powerful effort?"[5] It was this last question with its implied criticism of African American men that doubtless led to her expulsion from Boston.

Lorde is also part of a tradition of black feminist thought that includes such heroic nineteenth-century figures as Sojourner Truth. In "Woman's Rights" (1851), Truth revealed both the peculiar degradations endured by black women and the possibilities that black and white women embodied in their united opposition to patriarchy and white supremacy. This complexity is captured in the famous interrogative that functions, for the abolitionist and pioneering figure in black feminism, as both a call to action and a shaming critique: "And a'n't I a woman?"[6] Certainly, Truth's powerful question would resonate with Lorde and other black lesbian feminists who, because of their particular species of difference, were regarded, among many things, as abnormal, as a threat to the survival of the race, as apolitical, and, above all, as the final break in black womanhood. Or, put another way, as the sign and coefficient for what black womanhood is not.

Certainly, Lorde is heir to a tradition of black feminist thought that includes Frances E. W. Harper, an abolitionist, advocate for women's rights, national figure in the temperance movement, poet, and fiction writer. In "Our Greatest Want" (1859), Harper argued, "Our greatest need is not gold or silver, talent or genius, but true men and women. . . . We need men and women whose hearts are the homes of a high and lofty enthusiasm, and a noble devotion to the cause of emancipation, who are ready and willing to lay time, talent and money on the altar of universal freedom."[7] Having written this in the period before the Civil War and the abolition of slavery, Harper envisioned a broad, progressive coalition of black men and women committed to the cause of "universal freedom."

It must be understood that, as an advocate for women's rights as well as an advocate for the race, Lorde is part of a nineteenth-century tradition that includes "race women" who, as scholar Beverly Guy-Sheftall has argued, "are also early feminists, though they would not have used this terminology."[8] She reminds us that these foremothers include Josephine St. Pierre Ruffin, Fannie Barrier Williams, Mary Ann Shadd Cary, and Sarah Redmond.[9] According to Guy-Sheftall, what emerges from the collective efforts of these "race women" is a vision of race progress that is marked by a "sensitivity to race and gender issues, though they tend not to question their culturally prescribed roles as wives and mothers. They demand equal access to education, the removal of barriers which would prohibit their work in the public domain, and a greater voice in the political arena." "They also acknowledge," argues Guy-Sheftall, "the extraordinary accomplishments of black women in a variety of professions, despite restrictive cultural attitudes within and without the black community."[10]

This nineteenth-century tradition of black feminist thought and activism assumes a particular force and significance in the writings of Anna Julia Cooper. A fierce and uncompromising commitment to gender equality in all aspects of civil society in nineteenth-century America is one of the hallmarks of Cooper's writings, and it is a commitment Lorde carried forward into the late twentieth century. Cooper's enunciation of a black feminist standpoint is on full display in her now canonical work *A Voice from the South* (1892).[11] In "Womanhood: A Vital Element in the Regeneration and Progress of a Race," Cooper argued for the autonomy and self-determination of black women, and in so doing revealed the manner in which the elevation of black women also elevates the race: "Only the Black Woman can say 'when and where I enter,' in the quiet, undisputed dignity of my womanhood, without violence and without suing or special patronage, then and there the whole *Negro race enters with me*."[12] Cooper had a special concern and disdain for African American men who were progressive on race and other issues, while also holding retrograde views on gender: "It seems hardly a gracious thing to say, but it strikes me as true, that while our men seem thoroughly abreast of the times on almost every other subject, when they strike the woman question they drop back into sixteenth century logic."[13]

Turning now to the twentieth century, this dynamic tradition of black feminist thought and activism is expressed very powerfully in the lives and writings of such figures as Elsie Johnson McDougald, Alice

Dunbar-Nelson, Amy Jacques Garvey, and Lorraine Hansberry, the last of whom was a contemporary of Lorde.

In "The Task of Negro Womanhood," McDougald provided an examination of the changing social and economic position of African American women during the period of the New Negro movement, or Harlem Renaissance, of the 1920s. In Harlem, McDougald claimed, "the Negro woman is free from the cruder handicaps of primitive household hardships and the grosser forms of sex and race subjugation. Here, she has considerable opportunity to measure her powers in the intellectual and industrial fields of the great city."[14] In her survey of vocations, McDougald documented the economic opportunities and growing economic independence among African American women and the obstacles that remained in their paths. In *Warrior Poet: A Biography of Audre Lorde*, Alexis de Veaux wrote that Lorde's parents, Frederick Byron Lorde and Linda Belmar, arrived in Harlem in 1925.[15] As a working-class immigrant from Grenada, Belmar, de Veaux tells us, had a "strong work ethic, inculcated by the women on her mother's side of the family."[16] To be sure, Linda Belmar was part of the social and economic formation that McDougald documented in her essay. Belmar passed on to Lorde, the last of three daughters, the values of economic success and self-sufficiency which undergirded the lives of the black West Indian immigrant women of her generation. Notwithstanding the marked sense of "multiple jeopardy"[17] that stained the life of Belmar and other women, McDougald's landmark essay concludes on an optimistic note: "We find the Negro woman, figuratively [and doubtless literally] struck in the face daily by contempt from the world about her. . . . [Nevertheless, she] is measuring up to the needs of her family, community and race, and radiating a hope throughout the land."[18]

A contemporary of McDougald, Alice Dunbar-Nelson, teacher, clubwoman, journalist, writer, and, for a very brief period, the wife of poet Paul Lawrence Dunbar, was an unwavering advocate for gender equality and racial uplift. This commitment was reflected in the positions she held in such organizations as the League of Colored Republican Women and the national leadership she provided in the effort, led by James Weldon Johnson of the National Association for the Advancement of

Colored People, to make lynching a federal crime through the passing of the Dyer Anti-Lynching Bill, which did not become law because of insufficient votes in the U.S. Senate. In her essay "The Negro Woman and the Ballot" (1926), Dunbar-Nelson expressed disappointment in African American women's exercise of the franchise six years after the adoption of the Nineteenth Amendment. In her own words, "the Negro woman has by and large been a disappointment in her handling of the ballot."[19] This criticism notwithstanding, Dunbar-Nelson was confident that, over time, the African American woman would become a political force to be reckoned with when "she will strike off the political shackles she has allowed to be hung upon her, and win the economic freedom of her race."[20]

As a black feminist, Amy Jacques Garvey placed the social, political, and economic position of African American women of her generation in a global context. Decades later, Lorde would advance this perspective in her efforts to build alliances with black women in South Africa, Europe (in particular, Germany), and the Caribbean. In "Our Women Getting into the Larger Life," Jacques Garvey argued, "Negro women of the United States share equally in the larger life which has come to women of other race groups, and [they have] met every test in the home, in bread winning, in church and social upbuilding, in charitable uplift work, and in the school room which could have been expected of [them] reasonably."[21] Predictably and justifiably, she reserved high praise for the women of Marcus Garvey's United Negro Improvement Association. Confidently and without apologies, Jacques Garvey closed her essay with the assertion: "The success of the Negro race thus far has been largely due to the sympathy and support which our women have given to the cause."[22]

Like Jacques Garvey, Lorraine Hansberry advanced in considerable ways an evolving black and global feminism in the classic American drama *A Raisin in the Sun* (1959). Through her art, Hansberry dramatized the spirit of what would become the second wave of American feminism and an advanced black feminism in her complex portrayal of the institution of marriage, her sympathetic view of abortion, the manner in which she emphasized the need for black women to be educated and independent, and her insistence that black women cultivate a global, Pan-Africanist perspective. These perspectives are embodied in the character of Beneatha Younger. Hansberry also reflected her commitment to black feminism in "Simone de Beauvoir and *The Second Sex*: An American Commentary," an unfinished essay. In this essay, Hansberry expressed great praise for what she described as de Beauvoir's "revolutionary treatment of the 'woman question.'" Beyond her examination of de Beauvoir's text and its reception, Hansberry offered incisive commentary on the dangers women invite upon themselves when they limit themselves to the domestic sphere:

> [S]ociety tells woman from cradle to the grave that her husband, her home, her children will be the source of all rewards in life, the foundation of all true happiness. And women believe it and they plunge into marriages; wrap themselves in their husbands and their children—and continue to constitute one of the most neurotic sections, no doubt, of our entire population.[23]

This survey of the American tradition of black feminist thought and activism is meant to be suggestive, not comprehensive. My intention is to indicate the particular tradition of thought and action that constitutes the expanding floor for Lorde's own theorizing and activism. She extended and magnified the commitment to gender equality championed by black feminists while emphasizing the particularity of the lived experience of black women. Like her foremothers, she rejected the confinement of African American women to the domestic sphere, and through her example of radical engagement redefined the role of African American women in the public sphere. For Lorde, the sister outsider, this engagement in the public sphere encompassed both national and international politics and struggle. And like her foremothers, Lorde was concerned always with the specificity of the lived experience of black women. This deep concern with the lived experience of black women, wherever they are, derived from her recognition that the personal is political.

In "Sexism: An American Disease in Blackface," Lorde asserted, "Black feminism is not white feminism in blackface. Black women have particular and legitimate issues which affect our lives as Black women, and addressing those issues does not make us any less Black."[24] In "I Am Your Sister," Lorde further explained her terms of self-definition: "When I say I am a Black feminist, I mean I recognize that my power as well as my primary oppressions come as a result of my Blackness as well as my womanness, and therefore my struggles on both of these fronts are inseparable."[25] Like Maria Stewart, Anna Julia Cooper, Amy Jacques Garvey, and her other foremothers, Lorde was grounded in the specificity of the lived experience of black women in both national and global contexts, and it is from this location that she set out to address the many setbacks in the contemporary juncture and to work toward a livable future free of gender oppression. But what did the sister outsider add to this rich and dynamic tradition, which is now almost two centuries old? In what particular ways did she expand and complicate a progressive and radical tradition whose goal is the liberation of women and men? Are there particular perspectives that Lorde introduced to this evolving discourse? What new ideas and stances did she bring to the kitchen table, as it were?

To begin, Lorde brought the perspective of a Black lesbian radicalized within the civil rights movement, the black power movement, the second wave of the U.S. women's movement, and the gay and lesbian movement. She was among the first black feminists to publicly self-identify as a lesbian and to position lesbianism as a legitimate and powerful standpoint from which to enunciate a radical and progressive politics of struggle. This accounted, in part, for the rock-star following and iconic status she enjoyed during her lifetime. While Lorde was not the first black lesbian feminist, she was among the first to live her life and to practice her politics in the public domain, that is to say, out of the closet. Other black lesbian feminists who came before Lorde in this tradition and who publicly self-identified as lesbian were activist Ruth Ellis and novelist Ann Shockley. Contemporaneous with Lorde were writers and activists Barbara Smith and Pat Parker. The lesbianism of such black feminists as Alice Dunbar-Nelson and Angelina Weld Grimké was perhaps an open secret in some circles, but during their lifetimes it was not public knowledge. As a result of the scholarship of Gloria Hull, Erlene

Stetson, Cheryl Wall, and others, we now know that these pioneering black feminists possessed complex identities. Lorde had a special affection for Grimké, about whom she wrote in *A Burst of Light* (1988):

> I often think of Angelina Weld Grimké dying alone in an apartment in New York City in 1958 while I was a young Black Lesbian struggling in isolation at Hunter College, and I think of what it could have meant in terms of sisterhood and survival for each one of us to have known of the other's existence: for me to have had her words and her wisdom, and for her to have known I needed them![26]

As the sister outsider to so many, Lorde always made a point of publicly self-identifying as a black lesbian feminist because she wished to make visible the often invisible existence of women who occupy this sexual, social, and political location. Relatedly, her objective was to reduce the isolation and fear that often define the lives of such women. In a diary entry in *A Burst of Light*, Lorde reflected upon the desired utility and outcome of this political practice following a talk in East Lansing on October 25, 1985: "I explained that I identified myself as [a black feminist lesbian poet] because if there was one other Black Feminist Lesbian poet in isolation somewhere within the reach of my voice, I wanted her to know she was not alone."[27]

While Lorde's brave acts of public self-identification were meant to make visible and to empower other black lesbians, her words had a similar impact upon black gay men. The sister outsider first encountered a new generation of radical black gay men when she attended the first National Third World Gay and Lesbian Conference in Washington, D.C., on October 12, 1979, where she delivered the keynote address, reprinted here, entitled "When Will the Ignorance End?" As biographer Alexis de Veaux reminds us, Lorde was also in the nation's capital to participate in the first National March on Washington for Lesbian and Gay Rights, whose purpose was to commemorate the tenth anniversary of the Stonewall Rebellion. She delivered an address at the rally on the mall on October 14, two days after her keynote address and meetings with the organizers of the National Third World Gay and Lesbian Conference.

Lorde felt empowered and affirmed as a consequence of her involvement in the conference. In particular, she felt a new and special affinity for certain black gay men in attendance there. Writing in her journal, Lorde remembered them in this way: "I felt a connection to certain men I'd never found before—black men I never knew existed. I'd like to send Jonathan [Lorde's son] off to some of them. . . . They were saying things I'd never heard any men say before, about the fatherland."[28]

While Lorde did not name these black gay men, de Veaux suggests that they were Essex Hemphill and Joseph Beam. Poet, essayist, fiction writer, anthologist, and activist Hemphill was based in Washington, D.C. Beam lived in Philadelphia and was a columnist and contributing editor to a number of gay publications. Their activism and commitment to make visible the lives and writings of black gay men would make them friends and, in a rather short period of time, national figures in an emerging scholarly field in which Lorde was clearly a revered ancestral figure. Beam was the editor of *In the Life: A Black Gay Anthology* (Alyson, 1986), the first compilation of its kind in American literature. Hemphill subsequently edited *Brother to Brother: New Writings by Black Gay Men* (Alyson, 1991). The latter project was conceived by Beam, but he died before the anthology was completed. In memory of their friendship, Hemphill brought the project to fruition. The commitment of Beam and Hemphill to chart, excavate, and document a tradition of black gay male writing and to map the emergence of a black gay male subjectivity positions them, without question, as among the founding figures of a new field of critical inquiry that some now call black queer studies.[29]

Beam and Hemphill valued Lorde's example and appreciated her encouragement of their efforts. On the occasion of Beam's death in 1989, Lorde paid tribute to him in "Dear Joe." The poem opens with these evocative lines: "How many other dark young men at 33 / left a public life becoming legend."[30] When Lorde died in 1992, Hemphill remembered the sister outsider in the following manner: "Your powerful, sky-soaring, heart-piercing, soul-stirring words will forever resonate with commitment, integrity, and responsibility. . . . You gave us words we could use wisely. Words we could depend on."[31] Lorde, Hemphill, Beam, and many others advanced gay and lesbian studies, and they constitute, through their writings and activism, the founding figures of black queer studies.

As a national figure in the gay and lesbian movement, Lorde was among the first to name, define, and denounce the toxic forms of discrimination experienced by gays and lesbians. In "I Am Your Sister," the sister outsider was mainly concerned with "heterosexism and homophobia, two grave barriers to organizing among Black women."[32] Lorde defined *heterosexism* and *homophobia* in the following manner:

> *Heterosexism*—a belief in the inherent superiority of one form of loving over all others and thereby the right to dominance.
> *Homophobia*—a terror surrounding feelings of love for members of the same sex and thereby a hatred of those feelings in others.

After defining her terms, Lorde named the various stereotypes attributed to black lesbians:

> I have heard it said—usually behind my back—that Black Lesbians are not normal. . . . I have heard it said that Black Lesbians are a threat to the Black family. . . . I have heard it said that Black Lesbians will mean the death of the race. . . . I have heard it said that Black Lesbians are not political, that we have not been and are not involved in the struggles of Black people.

In naming these stereotypes, Lorde also identified their origin: "The terror of Black Lesbians is buried in that deep inner place where we have been taught to fear all difference—to kill or ignore it."[33]

Having decisively rejected the notion that black lesbians are some kind of *tertium quid*, Lorde indicated the ways in which the accusation of lesbianism can destabilize even the strongest of black women committed to social change:

> If someone says you're Russian and you know you're not, you don't collapse into stunned silence. Even if someone calls you a bigamist, or a childbeater, and you know you're not, you don't crumple into bits. You say it's not true and keep on printing the posters. But let anyone, particularly a Black man, accuse a straight Black woman of being a Black *Lesbian*, and right away

that sister becomes immobilized, as if that is the most horrible thing she could be, and must at all costs be proven false. That is homophobia. It is a waste of woman energy, and it puts a terrible weapon into the hands of your enemies to be used against you to silence you, to keep you docile and in line. It also serves to keep us isolated and apart.[34]

Lorde was eloquent and insightful in her examination of the ways in which homophobia is painful to individual heterosexual women, as well as destructive of the radical and progressive work that women may choose to undertake together across sexualities. While in this passage Lorde highlighted the homophobia practiced by black heterosexual men who are threatened by the power and independence of black women, in an unpublished version of "Scratching the Surface: Some Notes on Barriers to Women and Loving," she addressed the ways in which homophobia is corrosive to the relationships between black women:

In the same way that the existence of the self-defined black woman is no threat to the self-defined black man, the black lesbian is an emotional threat only to those black women who are unsure of, or unable to express, their feelings of kinship and love for other black women in any meaningful way. Yet within this country, for so long, we, as black women, have been encouraged to view each other with suspicion and distrust; as eternal competitors for the scarce male; or as the visible face of our own self-rejection.[35]

If black women are to build a meaningful sisterhood then, as Lorde suggested, particular forms of socialized behavior must be unlearned.

At the conclusion of "I Am Your Sister," Lorde constructed an analogy based upon racist stereotypes and described a practice that might lead to an antihomophobic standpoint:

Even if you *do* believe any of these stereotypes about Black Lesbians, begin to practice *acting* like you don't believe them. Just as racist stereotypes are the problem of the white people who believe them, so also are homophobic stereotypes the problem of the heterosexuals who believe them. In other words, those stereotypes are yours to solve, not mine, and they are a terrible and wasteful barrier to our working together. I am not your enemy. . . .

I am a Black Lesbian, and I *am* your sister.[36]

In providing us with a useful, potentially liberating practice, Lorde also reminds us that antihomophobic work, like antiracist work, is the work of the homophobe and the racist. She suggests that everyone, finally, is responsible for his or her own development. This is important to remember, for one's survival may depend upon such an insight.

Along with naming and defining homophobia and heterosexism and highlighting what will be lost if we fail to struggle against them, another important contribution that Lorde made to the tradition of black feminist thought was an emphasis upon the erotic. "There are many kinds of power, used and unused, acknowledged or otherwise," wrote Lorde. "The erotic is a resource within each of us that lies in a deeply female and spiritual plane, firmly rooted in the power of our unexpressed or unrecognized feeling."[37] So opens "Uses of the Erotic: The Erotic as Power," perhaps Lorde's most anthologized essay. In it, she theorizes about the power of the erotic: what is lost when it is devalued; its origins; why it is feared by men; how it is often confused with its opposite, pornography; its vital functions; how it can be a vehicle for sharing rather than using; and the various ways in which it can be a resource for women. "Our erotic knowledge empowers us, becomes a lens through which we scrutinize all aspects of our existence, forcing us to evaluate those aspects honestly in terms of their relative meaning within our lives." According to Lorde, "this is a grave responsibility, projected from within each of us, not to settle for the convenient, the shoddy, the conventionally expected, nor the merely safe."[38] Lorde insisted that women must not fear "the yes" within themselves. Alice Walker would build upon Lorde's revelations on the erotic in "Coming Apart," a fable, and in such novels as *The Color Purple* and *By the Light of My Father's Smile*. In these works, Walker reveals the ways in which the erotic can be the source of an empowering self-knowledge and liberation from the most debased forms of desire.

Published in 1978, "Uses of the Erotic" appeared at a particular cultural and political moment. Against the background of the Vietnam War, in August 1970, the U.S. House of Representatives had passed the Equal Rights Amendment while the Senate deliberated on this historic legislation. In the same year, Toni Cade Bambara published her landmark anthology *The Black Woman* (1970). In her essay "On the Nature of Roles," Bambara rejected the traditional heterosexual model and the ways in which it blinds both men and women to a more expansive vision of human relationships. In 1971, the National Women's Political Caucus was founded by Bella Abzug, Shirley Chisholm, Betty Friedan, Gloria Steinem, and others with the mission to inject a feminist perspective into the electoral process. In July 1972, the first issue of *Ms.* magazine was published, and Flo Kennedy and Shirley Chisholm ran for president on, respectively, the Feminist Party ticket and the Democratic Party ticket. In January 1973, the Supreme Court in *Roe v. Wade* allowed for first-trimester abortions and nullified restrictions in places that provided abortions. In the same year, the National Black Feminist Organization was established. Also in 1973, Toni Morrison published *Sula*, her second novel, which treated friendship between African American women, sexuality, and forms of the erotic. In 1974, the Combahee River Collective held its first meetings, and three years later its members published the now canonical "Black Feminist Statement." In 1975, *Signs*, a scholarly journal on gender, began publication, and Ntozake Shange's *for colored girls who have considered suicide/when the rainbow is enuf* made its Broadway debut. In 1976, the National Alliance of Black Feminists was established. Also that year, Alice Walker published her second novel, *Meridian*, a meditation on literary ancestry, black feminism, and the modern civil rights movement. Meridian Hill, Walker's heroine, embodied the new freedoms of the women who came of age during the era of "the pill" and social movements committed to the eradication of barriers based on race, gender, and sexuality. In 1977, the first National Women's Conference took place, creating a feminist agenda that addressed a range of issues, including domestic abuse, rape, and sexual preference. It is against this cultural and political background that Lorde's meditation on the erotic must be read. It is this configuration of cultural and political events within the evolving tradition of American feminism, in all of its complexity, that informed her assertion that "the power of the erotic within our lives can give us the energy to pursue genuine change within the world, rather than merely settling for a shift of characters in the same weary drama."[39] The very fact that Lorde could make this claim is proof of the distance that black feminism had traveled since the nineteenth century when, according to scholar Darlene Clark Hine, "black women, as a rule, developed and adhered to a cult of secrecy, a culture of dissemblance, to protect the sanctity of inner aspects of their lives."[40] Hine's insightful commentary is a useful framework for examining not only the lived experience of African American women of the nineteenth century, but also their descendants in the twentieth century and into the present.

In addition to an elevation of the importance of the erotic, Lorde introduced to black feminism a heightened awareness of issues related to women's health. In the classic essay "The Transformation of Silence into Language and Action" (1977), *The Cancer Journals* (1980), and *A Burst of Light* (1988), Lorde documented the impact of her diagnosis first with breast cancer in November 1977 and then with liver cancer in February 1984. As a trilogy, these works constitute the first public reflections by an African American woman, and specifically a black lesbian feminist, on the nature of health, disease, mortality, and social struggle. Without question, these texts are among the most eloquent and inspiring treatments available to us of what it means to live with cancer.

In *A Burst of Light*, Lorde documented, through what she termed "prose monologues," the first three years of her valiant struggle against liver cancer. She was diagnosed with what she termed the "cold disease" for the second time only two weeks before her fiftieth birthday. At the outset, Lorde was resolute and defiant: "The struggle with cancer now informs all my days, but it is only another face of that continuing battle for self-determination and survival that Black women fight daily, often in triumph."[41] In the early stages, Lorde saw her liver cancer as a struggle like any other, and she bravely did not turn away from it. Then, somewhat later, she revealed in a memorable entry her fears and her efforts not to be overtaken by them: "Dear goddess! Face-up again against the renewal of vows. Do not let me die a coward, mother. Nor forget how to sing. Nor forget song is a part of mourning as light is a part of sun."[42]

In her effort to maintain some sense of control in a medical culture where patients often feel they must surrender to those who are, presumably, more knowledgeable, Lorde rightly insisted upon the authority of her own individual experience: "I just know I must not surrender my body to others unless I completely understand and agree with what they think should be done to it. I've got to look at all of my options carefully, even the ones I find distasteful. I know I can broaden the definition of winning to the point where I can't lose."[43] Starkly confronted with the reality of time and mortality, Lorde asserted that the "accuracy of that diagnosis has become less important than how I use the life I have."[44]

In the final pages of *A Burst of Light*, Lorde emphasized, in many places, how her cancer diagnosis introduced a marked sense of urgency to her life. The following passage is representative of this pattern of thought:

> This is no longer a time of waiting. It is a time for the real work's urgencies. It is a time enhanced by an iron reclamation of what I call a burst of light—that inescapable knowledge, in the bone, of my own physical limitation. Metabolized and integrated into the fabric of my days, that knowledge makes the particulars of what is coming seem less important. When I speak of wanting as much good time as possible, I mean time over which I maintain some relative measure of control.[45]

Like AIDS and other terminal disorders, cancer introduces a marked sense of urgency to living. This Lorde felt deeply as well as an awareness—"a burst of light"—of her own mortality, which she described as "that inescapable knowledge . . . of my own physical limitation." Along with these insights, Lorde was conscious of time, of which there is never enough, and her cancer diagnosis endowed her with a special perspective on time. For Lorde, time did not mean only the clock and the calendar, but rather the amount and quality of control one exercises over one's life as one lives the hours in each day. At the age of fifty-eight, Lorde's battle with cancer ended on November 17, 1992. In *A Burst of Light* and other writings, she bravely and generously offered her own life as an example of how to live one's life when confronted hourly with one's own mortality. In the process, Lorde brought even greater national awareness to the several urgencies which mark women's health.

The final contribution that Lorde made to the vibrant tradition of black feminist thought was a new critical social theory that provides us with the grammar and vocabulary to describe and define difference and the complex nature of oppression. We are now keenly aware of difference. Some of us are weary of it. Many of us today take this discourse for granted. However, when in the 1970s Lorde began theorizing difference from the perspective of a black lesbian feminist, we encountered an entirely new intellectual phenomenon.

Lorde's theorizing on difference emerged during the period that scholar Henry Louis Gates, Jr., termed the "culture wars," that period in the 1970s and 1980s when we witnessed the emergence of what some derisively dismiss as identity politics and political correctness as well as the beginnings of a national backlash against affirmative action.[46] During this period and afterward, we witnessed advances in the institutionalization in the academy of such fields as African American studies, women's studies, and gay and lesbian studies. This expansion in the curricula of American colleges and universities engendered new debates over such matters as the canon and the epistemology of knowledge, which in turn spawned an often contentious national debate on American pluralism or multiculturalism. On the Right, this debate was led by such figures as William Bennett, Arthur M. Schlesinger, Jr., and Dinesh D'Souza; on the Left, this debate was led by Gates, Manning Marable, Cornel West, Johnnetta B. Cole, Earl Lewis, and others. The national debate on multiculturalism, identity politics, political correctness, and attacks on affirmative action is also part of the background against which Lorde's theorizing on difference and oppression must be read and understood.

The sister outsider introduced a necessary precision and specificity to the national discourse on race and culture, which was dominated by facile, oversimplified readings of difference as evidenced in the civil rights movement and the black power movement. Regarding the limitations of both of these social movements, Lorde remarked:

> The civil rights and Black power movements rekindled possibilities for disenfranchised groups within this nation. Even though we fought common enemies, at times the lure of individual solutions made us careless of each other. Sometimes we could not bear the face of each other's differences because of what we feared those differences might say about ourselves.[47]

Similarly, Lorde challenged the women's movement to move beyond the notion that white womanhood was the national pattern and paradigm into which to incorporate the histories and lived experiences of women of color in the United States and abroad. "The failure of academic feminists," wrote Lorde, "to recognize differences as a crucial strength is a failure to reach beyond the first patriarchal lesson. In our world, divide and conquer must become define and empower."[48] Perhaps Lorde's most withering critique of this blindness among white feminists was her open letter to Mary Daly, author of the celebrated *Gyn/Ecology: The Metaethics of Radical Feminism*, published in 1978. In her critique of the limitations of the scope and focus of Daly's research, Lorde pointed to the consequences of such narrow forms of feminist scholarship:

> Mary, I ask that you be aware of how this serves the destructive forces of racism and separation between women—the assumption that the herstory and myth of white women is the legitimate and sole herstory and myth of all women to call upon for power and background, and that nonwhite women and our herstories are noteworthy only as decorations, or examples of female victimization. . . . When radical lesbian feminist theory dismisses us, it encourages its own demise.[49]

Writing this almost ten years after the Stonewall Rebellion in 1969 in New York's Greenwich Village, which marks for many the beginning of the gay and lesbian movement in the United States, here again Lorde insisted upon the integration of perspectives and histories and challenged the mistaken notion that the experiences of white gay men should be accepted as both normative and universal (thus rendering invisible the experiences of gays and lesbians who do not occupy this social category). In an unpublished essay, Lorde denounced the homophobia in the civil rights movement and the racism in the gay and lesbian movement:

> So there are voices in the Black community such as the *Bay State Banner*, a Boston Black newspaper, saying that gays belong in the closet, that we cannot equate the struggles for gay liberation and Black liberation, because one is the expression of a legitimate minority, and the other is legalizing a perversion.
>
> There are voices in the lesbian and gay community such as appeared in *Gay Community News* in the summer of 1979 after Eleanor Johnson and Beverly Smith's moving speeches in the Lesbian and Gay Pride Rally. These voices term racism and classism and sexism as a "collection of peripheral issues" and saw the discussion of these crucial issues in the gay community . . . as "co-opting our rally." Yet after we exclude Black, working class, ethnic and religious minority concerns from gay politics, who will be left to define "our" considerations?
>
> Yet the time is long past when any of us can afford the luxury of exclusive oppression.[50]

Plainly, as a black lesbian feminist, she embodied the complexities that she insisted become a part of the discourses of the social movements of which she was a shaping figure. One of the few black men in the black power movement who shared Lorde's progressive, expansive view of liberation movements was Huey P. Newton, the founder and supreme commander of the Black Panther Party. In "A Letter from Huey to the Revolutionary Brothers and Sisters About the Women's Liberation and Gay Liberation Movements," Newton called for the Black Panther Party to establish alliances with the women's movement and the gay liberation movement:

> Whatever your personal opinion and your insecurities about homosexuality and the various liberation movements among homosexuals and women (and I speak of the homosexuals and women as oppressed groups) we should try to unite with them in a revolutionary fashion. . . . Homosexuals are not enemies of the people. . . . We should try to form a working coalition with the Gay Liberation and Women's Liberation groups.[51]

Whether addressing racism, sexism, or homophobia, Lorde was concerned always with complexity and the sense of possibility that the discourse of difference invokes. This conception of difference is a hallmark of Lorde's writings. In "The Master's Tools Will Never Dismantle the Master's House," Lorde defined difference as a dialect and a resource:

> Difference must not be merely tolerated, but seen as a fund of necessary polarities between which our creativity can spark like a dialectic. Only then does the necessity for interdependency become unthreatening. Only within that interdependency of different strengths, acknowledged and equal, can the power to seek new ways of being in the world generate, as well as the courage and sustenance to act where there are no charters.
>
> Within the interdependence of mutual (nondominant) differences lies that security which enables us to descend into the chaos of knowledge and return with true visions of our future, along with the concomitant power to effect those changes which can bring that future into being. Difference is that raw and powerful connection from which our personal power is forged.[52]

In theorizing difference as a "fund of necessary polarities" and as that "raw and powerful connection from which our personal power is forged," Lorde cast difference as the starting point for both individual and collective action. Difference becomes an essential property in a mode of being that makes us courageous and open even in the absence of what she terms "charters," that is, signposts, guides, and road maps.

Lorde offered elaborations that added depth and complexity to her definition of difference in "Difference and Survival," an address published here for the first time. In this speech, she asserted that it "is within our differences that we are both most powerful and most vulnerable, and some of the most difficult tasks of our lives are the claiming of differences and learning to use those differences for bridges rather than as barriers between us." She also stressed that it is vital for us to develop a critical apparatus to examine the range of differences among us, which have been misnamed and distorted by the dominant society. In a later passage, Lorde emphasized again the importance of self-definition and the danger of abdicating that function to someone else: "What does this mean for each of us? I think it means that I must choose to define my difference as you must choose to define yours, to claim it and use it as creative before it is defined for you and used to eradicate any future, any change."[53]

In a series of public addresses delivered between 1976 and 1979, Lorde continued to expand and refine her robust theory of difference. In remarks delivered at the Black Writers' Conference at Howard University in April 1976 to an audience not always receptive to what some would regard as deviant forms of difference, Lorde made this assertion: "We cannot love 'our people' unless we love each of us ourselves, unless I love each piece of myself, those I wish to keep and those I wish to change—for survival is the ability to encompass difference, to encompass change without destruction."[54] During a period when black cultural nationalism was the dominant ideology in the arts and literature, an ideology which defined gays and lesbians as deviant and outside of "the black community," Lorde spoke of the value of self-love and its relationship to difference, survival, and change.

In a paper delivered at the Modern Language Association convention in December 1977, "The Transformation of Silence into Language and Action," Lorde took as the point of departure her diagnosis of breast cancer and its profound impact upon her life: "I was forced to look upon myself and my living with a harsh and urgent clarity that has left me still shaken but much stronger."[55] In this groundbreaking essay, reprinted here, Lorde wrote eloquently of the importance of breaking silence, of coming to voice: two very important objectives of the second wave of the women's movement and of black feminism. The sister outsider also made an insightful observation about the relationship between the breaking of silence and difference: "The fact that we are here and that I speak these words is an attempt to break that silence and bridge some of those differences between us, for it is not difference which immobilizes us, but silence. And there are so many silences to be broken."[56] Lorde maintained that it is not difference which is a barrier to progressive mobilization, but rather silence: our mute response to difference.

In a keynote address entitled "When Will the Ignorance End?" delivered at the first National Third World Gay and Lesbian Conference in Washington, D.C., on October 12, 1979, Lorde emphasized again the urgency of redefining difference in positive terms. At this historic gathering, the sister outsider insisted upon both honesty and creativity as we approach the many questions related to difference: "And it is upon our ability to look honestly upon our differences, to see them as creative rather than divisive, that our future success may lie."[57] Reprinted here in its entirety for the first time, "When Will the Ignorance End?" not only contains further evidence of Lorde's efforts to codify her theorizing on difference, but the address also marks the deepening of her involvement in the black lesbian and gay movement.

In an undated and unpublished address before a different audience, Lorde asserted that a creative approach to difference promises to advance in vital ways the gay and lesbian movement:

> Yet now more than ever, we need the cross-pollination of vision which our many differences can offer each other, if we can overcome conditioning to view differences as creative rather than as a reason for destruction or ignoring.
>
> As lesbian and gay men we have come together because of what we share in common; now can we come together to learn what we can from our differences? To do this we must first see our common enemy.
>
> Too often we pour energy needed for relating across difference in[to] pretending these differences are insurmountable barriers, or that these differences do not exist. For we have never been allowed to develop tools for using human difference as a springboard for progress within our lived consciousness. The time is now. Our survival as lesbians and gay men requires that we pull together all of the other communities of which we are a part, recognizing that liberation, like freedom, is not indivisible. . . .
>
> For it is within the poetry and vision of acknowledged difference that we form new and creative alternatives for genuine social change. . . .
>
> We need to root out the pieces of the oppressor which are planted deeply within each of us, otherwise as lesbians and gay men, we will only be switching places in the same old weary

drama. But together, the strength of our differences can illuminate our politics with a skill and passion born of survival, and we can transform the very meaning of power within our lives.[58]

Lorde stressed again and again that the survival of lesbians and gay men is dependent upon their ability "to use difference for something other than destruction."[59] In using the metaphor of cross-pollination, she introduced again her vital theme of "the interdependency of different strengths." If the gay and lesbian movement is to have a wide, far-reaching impact, Lorde insisted that it must think of difference as creative rather than divisive and to know and see clearly the common enemy: heterosexist patriarchal white supremacist culture. As the sister outsider, she argued that "genuine social change" requires vision and clarity of purpose, otherwise lesbians and gay men will contribute to the maintenance of the status quo. Ever undaunted, Lorde believed that lesbians and gay men possess the potentiality to transform, in alchemical fashion, "the meaning of power within [their] lives."

In fine, Lorde theorized difference as a "fund of necessary polarities" that provides us with the "courage and sustenance to act where there are no charters. . . . [and], within that interdependency of different strengths, difference is that raw and powerful connection from which our personal power is forged." She insisted that it is within our differences "that we are both most powerful and most vulnerable . . . and [that it is our task to use our differences] as bridges rather than as barriers between us." Lorde tells us that it is not our differences that keep us apart but rather silence and the ways in which our differences have been "misnamed" and deployed against us in an illegitimate fashion. It is vital, according to Lorde, to name our differences before they are misnamed by others. Ultimately, our survival depends upon our capacity for self-love and the ability to "encompass difference" and to see our differences as "creative rather than divisive." Lorde reminds us that our survival also depends upon our ability to see "our common enemy" through the cultivation of vision, for what is at stake is a livable future and "genuine social change."

In theorizing difference in this manner, Lorde also had insightful observations to make about the nature of oppression. She argued in many places that racism, sexism, and homophobia are inseparable, that is, they are all similar injuries by the same hand. Lorde's signal contribution to theories of difference and oppression was her belief that oppressions cannot be ranked, numbered, or prioritized. Through her theorizing, she helped us to understand that oppressions are interlocking and, equally as important, that they are not hierarchical but rather intersectional.

Lorde's insight regarding the interlocking nature of oppression was perhaps first expressed in "Sexism: An American Disease in Blackface." In this essay, which illuminated the black sexism debate set in motion by Robert Staples' "The Myth of Black Macho: A Response to Angry Black Feminists," Lorde refuted Staples' claim that only race and black male privilege matter and called for the cultivation of a new consciousness among black men:

> But the Black male consciousness must be raised to the realization that sexism and woman-hating are critically dysfunctional to his liberation as a Black man because they arise out of the same constellation that engenders racism and homophobia. Until that consciousness is developed, Black men will view sexism and the destruction of Black women as tangential to Black liberation rather than as central to that struggle. This continued blindness between us can only serve the oppressive system within which we live.[60]

Lorde argued that sexism emerges from the same "constellation" of social, political, and economic factors that give rise to racism and homophobia. In other words, these are interlocking oppressions and our "continued blindness" to this historical and contemporary fact makes us vulnerable to further exploitation by patriarchal white supremacy.

This theory of oppression achieved its most mature expression in "There Is No Hierarchy of Oppression" (1983). In this short but dense essay, reprinted here, Lorde carefully defined sexism, homophobia, and racism and asserted, "among those of us who share the goals of liberation and a workable future for our children, there can be no hierarchies of oppression."[61] Offering her own life experience as an example,

Lorde revealed the ways in which sexism, racism, and homophobia are inextricable:

> Within the lesbian community I am black, and within the black community I am a lesbian. Any attack against black people is a lesbian and gay issue, because I and thousands of other black women are part of the lesbian community. Any attack against lesbians and gays is a black issue, because thousands of lesbians and gay men are black. There is no hierarchy of oppression.

By theorizing oppression in this complex and nuanced manner, Lorde made an original and significant contribution to critical social theory. In so doing, she prepared the ground for the emergence, some years later, of Deborah King's theory of multiple jeopardy and Kimberlee Crenshaw's theory of intersectionality.

Audre Lorde made brilliant, original, and far-reaching contributions to the discourse of black feminist thought. In her writings, she situated the lived experience of African American women within a particular historical, political, and cultural context that is both national and global. As the sister outsider, she brought a theory and a praxis that advanced black feminism, gay and lesbian studies, black queer studies, and African American studies. But what, ultimately, was the purpose and function of Lorde's theorizing, which maps the complex subjectivities of black feminists and black gay men and lesbians? Is there a particular kind of intellectual labor performed by this mapping of subjectivities? Lorde's observations on the function of poetry may provide us with an answer to these questions:

> Ultimately it comes down to making yourself and the people who can share it with you, in some way, more themselves, to make you more yourself, to make human beings more themselves, and therefore, by extension, better, stronger, more real. Isn't this the function of all art? I mean, get out of the Western bag, out of the "art for art's sake," out of the perfect circle. A perfect circle is a point. It moves not at all. It's stationary. Let's get out of that. The function of any art is to move, more deeply, to make us more whoever we are.[62]

As one function of her poetry is to "make human beings more themselves" and thus "better, stronger, more real," I would like to suggest that this is likewise one function of Lorde's nonfiction writings, one outcome of her labors in this domain. As a black lesbian feminist, Lorde was motivated by two objectives. The first was to create a corpus that would endure, and the second was to advance, through this corpus, social justice. This, I believe, the sister outsider succeeded in doing.

We return again and again to Lorde's nonfiction writings, whether speeches or essays, for a variety of reasons. Certainly, the concepts are enduring, powerfully rendered, and prescient. There is also the wisdom born of experience and an engagement with ideas and the social movements that she defined—that also defined her era—and that we need now more than ever. Just as Lorde possessed a distinctive spoken voice, as Alice Walker tells us in "Audre's Voice," an essay reprinted here, so the sister outsider also possessed a distinctive written voice. It is also the power of Lorde's written voice that draws us back to her corpus. I return again to her observations on poetry as a way to advance this claim:

> There are words, the energy that surrounds words is something
> we use all the time. Now I'm not talking about connotative
> meanings. I'm talking about the shared kind of raw energy, hav
> ing to do with sound, having to do with the hundred associa
> tions some of which we share, some of which we don't share.
> But a feeling, a sense of that energy surrounding words is some
> thing that you come to use over and over again in your poetry.[63]

Certainly, Lorde's special gift to summon and channel the "energy surrounding words," whether in poetry or in prose, is one of the distinguishing features of her art. It is this unique quality that inspires us and that enables us to recognize her written voice, to not mistake it for someone else's. In every way, the sister outsider's now canonical prose is an exemplary model in the genre of nonfiction writing. In their totality, these writings, many of the most important and influential of which are represented in this volume, also point the way to a livable, humane, democratic future. To the ways we can and must create our own fire.

I Am Your Sister contains a representative collection of Lorde's published essays, speeches, and diaries and selections from her unpublished writings in the Audre Lorde Collection of Spelman College. Divided into four parts, this volume contains some of Lorde's best nonfiction as well as commentary about her life and writings by some of the leading figures in black feminist thought: scholars Johnnetta B. Cole, bell hooks, Gloria I. Joseph, and Beverly Guy-Sheftall and writer Alice Walker.

Part I is composed of groundbreaking essays from *Sister Outsider* and the complete text of *A Burst of Light*. Reprinted here in chronological order, the essays from *Sister Outsider* are "The Transformation of Silence into Language and Action" and "Sexism: An American Disease in Blackface." These two essays, widely taught and the subject of much scholarly inquiry, reveal Lorde as a substantive theorist concerned with questions related to women's health; the achievement of voice; sexism, racism, and homophobia in African American communities; and the interlocking nature of these oppressions. These essays span the period 1977–1979.

Also in part I is the complete text of *A Burst of Light*, Lorde's third volume of nonfiction prose. The collection is composed of four essays and a series of journal entries that chart the first three years of Lorde's struggle with liver cancer. Encompassing the years between 1984 and 1987, this volume offers insightful commentary on controversial sexual practices in lesbian communities; the lost opportunities for coalition building among black feminists as a result of homophobia; the points of intersection of apartheid as practiced in the United States and in South Africa; the joys and jeopardy of lesbian parenting in a white supremacist patriarchal society; and the continued struggle for meaning and direction when confronted with a terminal disease.

Part II of this volume, "My Words Will Be There," contains a collection of Lorde's published and unpublished nonfiction writings spanning the period 1976–1989. This section is composed of nine selections, four of which are published for the first time here. The essays, book reviews, and speeches reveal Lorde's sustained commitment to the intellectual and activist project of a national and global black feminism; her support of an emerging generation of women writers associated with the renaissance in African American women's writings of the 1970s; and her active involvement in the teaching of the art and craft of poetry. Of special importance to readers is Lorde's "My Mother's Mortar." The version reprinted here first appeared in *Sinister Wisdom* in 1977. "My Mother's Mortar" is not to be regarded as fiction, but as a splendid example of creative nonfiction prose. It is an essay which, in my estimation, stands alongside such essays in the African American literary tradition as W. E. B. Du Bois's "The Passing of the First Born," James Baldwin's "Notes of a Native Son," and Alice Walker's "In Search of Our Mothers' Gardens."

"Difference and Survival," part III of *I Am Your Sister*, contains selections that provide us with evidence of Lorde's deepening involvement in the three social movements of which she was a pioneering figure: the movements for civil rights, women's rights, and gay and lesbian rights. Of special importance to many readers of this volume will be "The First Black Feminist Retreat." Published here for the first time, Lorde's remarks were delivered at the first retreat of black feminists and activists in 1977 who were members of Boston's Combahee River Collective. The broad audience for this volume also will be interested in "An Address Delivered at the March on Washington," which was given on August 27, 1983. This address signals, in a way that the 1963 March on Washington did not, the manner in which the gay and lesbian movement is organically related to and extends the modern civil rights movement. While I could highlight several other selections in this section, I will mention only one more: "Difference and Survival: An Address at Hunter College," published for the first time here. The scholars and activists who have been chronicling Lorde's theoretical practices will find, I predict, her theorizing on difference in this speech to be both compelling and substantive.

"Reflections," the fourth and final part of *I Am Your Sister*, contains a range of writings that sheds new light upon several different aspects of Lorde's art and humanity. In "Audre Lorde: My Shero, My Teacher, My Sister Friend," Johnnetta B. Cole reflects upon her long friendship with Lorde and the manner in which the sister outsider challenged Cole to interrogate even more closely matters related to the institutionalization of women's studies and homophobia. Among other things, Cole documents the important role she played in persuading Lorde to deposit her archive at Spelman College. In "Audre's Voice," Alice Walker recalls the special and memorable aspects of Lorde's spoken voice. bell hooks's "The Imagination of Justice" is an address that was delivered at Spelman College on the occasion of the twenty-fifth anniversary of the Women's Research and Resource Center established by Beverly Guy-Sheftall. In this address, hooks challenges us to reflect upon the power and possibilities of what Lorde termed "the dark and ancient and divine within ourselves." In "Remembering Audre Lorde," Gloria I. Joseph provides us with a meditation on her long and important friendship with Lorde. Delivered on the same twenty-fifth anniversary occasion, Joseph reflects upon Lorde's final years in St. Croix, U.S. Virgin Islands, as well as the genesis for Lorde's "Is Your Hair Still Political?" The volume closes with Beverly Guy-Sheftall's epilogue, in which she documents further the circumstances of Lorde's first visit to Spelman College and her impact on the center's evolving mission. Guy-Sheftall also recalls the twenty-fifth anniversary celebration of the Women's Research and Resource Center, a celebration that marked the pending arrival of the Lorde Papers at Spelman and the continuing importance of Lorde for scholars from a range of disciplines and fields in the academy.

Notes

1. "I Am Your Sister: Black Women Organizing Across Sexualities," in *A Burst of Light* (Ithaca, N.Y.: Firebrand, 1988), 19–20.

2. I am aware that, over time, Lorde frequently introduced herself as a Black Lesbian Feminist Poet Mother, but for the purposes of this introduction I will use the identifier that appears in "I Am Your Sister." My intention is not to be disrespectful of Lorde's multiple identities, but rather to achieve economy in the introduction.

3. Preface in Marilyn Richardson, ed., *Maria W. Stewart: America's First Black Woman Political Writer: Essays and Speeches* (Bloomington: Indiana University Press, 1987), xiii.

4. Ibid., 49.

5. Ibid.

6. "Woman's Rights" (1851), in *Words of Fire: An Anthology of African American Feminist Thought*, ed. Beverly Guy-Sheftall (New York: New Press, 1995), 36.

7. "Our Greatest Want," in *A Brighter Coming Day: A Frances Ellen Watkins Harper Reader*, ed. Frances Smith Foster (New York: Feminist Press, 1990), 103–104.

8. Guy-Sheftall, *Words of Fire*, xv.

9. Ibid.

10. Ibid.

11. I am indebted to Patricia Hill Collins for the application of standpoint theory to black feminist discourse. See Hill Collins's *Fighting Word: Black Women and the Search for Justice* (Minneapolis: University of Minnesota Press, 1998), 193–195.

12. Anna Julia Cooper, "Womanhood: A Vital Element in the Regeneration and Progress of a Race," in *A Voice from the South*, ed. Henry Louis Gates, Jr. (1892; New York: Oxford University Press, 1988), 31.

13. Cooper, "The Higher Education of Women," in *A Voice from the South*, 75.

14. Elsie Johnson McDougald, "The Task of Negro Womanhood," in *The New Negro*, ed. Alain Locke (1925; New York: Touchstone, 1997), 369.

15. Alexis de Veaux, *Warrior Poet: A Biography of Audre Lorde* (New York: Norton, 2004), 10.

16. Ibid., 7.

17. I reference here the multiple and intersecting points of oppression for black women as theorized by Deborah K. King in "Multiple Jeopardy, Multiple Consciousness: The Context for Black Feminist Ideology," in Guy-Sheftall, *Words of Fire*, 294–317.

18. Ibid., 382.

19. Alice Dunbar-Nelson, "The Negro Woman and the Ballot," in Guy-Sheftall, *Words of Fire*, 87.

20. Ibid., 88.

21. Amy Jacques Garvey, "Our Women Getting into the Larger Life," in Guy-Sheftall, *Words of Fire*, 92.

22. Ibid.

23. Lorraine Hansberry, "Simone de Beauvoir and *The Second Sex*: An American Commentary," in Guy-Sheftall, *Words of Fire*, 140–141.

24. Audre Lorde, "Sexism: An American Disease in Blackface," in *Sister Outsider* (Trumansburg, N.Y.: Crossing, 1984), 60.

25. "I Am Your Sister," 20.

26. *A Burst of Light* (Ithaca, N.Y.: Firebrand, 1988), 73.

27. Ibid.

28. De Veaux, *Warrior Poet*, 256.

29. See *Black Queer Studies*, ed. E. Patrick Johnson and Mae Henderson (Durham, N.C.: Duke University Press, 2005).

30. Audre Lorde, "Dear Joe," *Gay Community News* 16, no. 41 (May 7–13, 1989): 7, in Audre Lorde Collection, Lesbian Herstory Archives, Brooklyn, N.Y.

31. Essex Hemphill, "Dear Audre," an addendum to the Audre Lorde Memorial Program Journal, January 18, 1993, in Audre Lorde Collection, Lesbian Herstory Archives, Brooklyn, N.Y.

32. "I Am Your Sister," 20–22.

33. Ibid., 21.

34. Ibid., 22.

35. Audre Lorde, untitled essay, Audre Lorde Papers, Box 16, Spelman College Archives.

36. "I Am Your Sister," 25–26.

37. Audre Lorde, "Uses of the Erotic: The Erotic as Power," in *Sister Outsider*, 53.

38. Ibid., 57.

39. Ibid., 59.

40. Darlene Clark Hine, "Rape and the Inner Lives of Black Women in the Middle West: Preliminary Thoughts on the Culture of Dissemblance," in *Hine Sight: Black Women and the Re-Construction of American History* (Brooklyn, N.Y.: Carlson, 1994), 41.

41. *A Burst of Light*, 49.

42. Ibid., 55.

43. Ibid., 61.

44. Ibid., 112.

45. Ibid., 121.

46. Henry Louis Gates, Jr., *Loose Canons: Notes on the Culture Wars* (New York: Oxford University Press, 1992).

47. "Learning from the 60s," in *Sister Outsider*, 136.

48. "The Master's Tools Will Never Dismantle the Master's House," in *Sister Outsider*, 112.

49. "An Open Letter to Mary Daly," in *Sister Outsider*, 69.

50. Audre Lorde Papers, Box 8, Spelman College Archives.

51. Huey P. Newton, "A Letter from Huey to the Revolutionary Brothers and Sisters About the Women's Liberation and Gay Liberation Movements," in *Traps: African American Men on Gender and Sexuality*, ed. Rudolph P. Byrd and Beverly Guy-Sheftall (Bloomington: Indiana University Press, 2001), 281–283.

52. "The Master's Tools Will Never Dismantle the Master's House," in *Sister Outsider*, 111–112.

53. "Difference and Survival," Audre Lorde Papers, Box 8, Spelman College Archives.

54. "Survival," Audre Lorde Papers, Box 8, Spelman College Archives.

55. "The Transformation of Silence into Language and Action," in *Sister Outsider*, 40.

56. Ibid., 44.

57. "When Will the Ignorance End?" Audre Lorde Papers, Box 8, Spelman College Archives.

58. Untitled and undated address, Audre Lorde Papers, Box 8, Spelman College Archives.

59. "The Dream of Europe," Audre Lorde Papers, Box 8, Spelman College Archives.

60. "Sexism: An American Disease in Blackface," in *Sister Outsider*, 64.

61. "There Is No Hierarchy of Oppression," in *Dangerous Liaisons: Blacks, Gays and the Struggle for Equality*, ed. Eric Brandt (New York: New Press, 1999), 306.

62. Audre Lorde, "Notes from Audre Lorde Discussion at Cazenovia Women Writers Center," 2, Audre Lorde Papers, Box 16, Spelman College Archives.

63. Ibid., 5.

FROM *SISTER OUTSIDER* AND
A BURST OF LIGHT

THE TRANSFORMATION OF SILENCE
INTO LANGUAGE AND ACTION

I have come to believe over and over again that what is most important to me must be spoken, made verbal and shared, even at the risk of having it bruised or misunderstood. That the speaking profits me, beyond any other effect. I am standing here as a Black lesbian poet, and the meaning of all that waits upon the fact that I am still alive, and might not have been. Less than two months ago I was told by two doctors, one female and one male, that I would have to have breast surgery, and that there was a 60 to 80 percent chance that the tumor was malignant. Between that telling and the actual surgery, there was a three-week period of the agony of an involuntary reorganization of my entire life. The surgery was completed, and the growth was benign.

But within those three weeks, I was forced to look upon myself and my living with a harsh and urgent clarity that has left me still shaken but much stronger. This is a situation faced by many women, by some of you here today. Some of what I experienced during that time has helped elucidate for me much of what I feel concerning the transformation of silence into language and action.

In becoming forcibly and essentially aware of my mortality, and of what I wished and wanted for my life, however short it might be, priorities and omissions became strongly etched in a merciless light, and what I most regretted were my silences. Of what had I *ever* been afraid?

Paper delivered at the Modern Language Association's Lesbian and Literature panel, Chicago, Illinois, December 28, 1977. First published in *Sinister Wisdom* 6 (1978) and *The Cancer Journals* (San Francisco, Calif.: Spinsters, Ink, 1980).

To question or to speak as I believed could have meant pain, or death. But we all hurt in so many different ways, all the time, and pain will either change or end. Death, on the other hand, is the final silence. And that might be coming quickly, now, without regard for whether I had ever spoken what needed to be said, or had only betrayed myself into small silences, while I planned someday to speak, or waited for someone else's words. And I began to recognize a source of power within myself that comes from the knowledge that while it is most desirable not to be afraid, learning to put fear into perspective gave me great strength.

I was going to die, if not sooner then later, whether or not I had ever spoken myself. My silences had not protected me. Your silence will not protect you. But for every real word spoken, for every attempt I had ever made to speak those truths for which I am still seeking, I had made contact with other women while we examined the words to fit a world in which we all believed, bridging our differences. And it was the concern and caring of all those women which gave me strength and enabled me to scrutinize the essentials of my living.

The women who sustained me through that period were Black and white, old and young, lesbian, bisexual, and heterosexual, and we all shared a war against the tyrannies of silence. They all gave me a strength and concern without which I could not have survived intact. Within those weeks of acute fear came the knowledge—within the war we are all waging with the forces of death, subtle and otherwise, conscious or not—I am not only a casualty, I am also a warrior.

What are the words you do not yet have? What do you need to say? What are the tyrannies you swallow day by day and attempt to make your own, until you will sicken and die of them, still in silence? Perhaps for some of you here today, I am the face of one of your fears. Because I am woman, because I am Black, because I am lesbian, because I am myself—a Black woman warrior poet doing my work—come to ask you, are you doing yours?

And of course I am afraid, because the transformation of silence into language and action is an act of self-revelation, and that always seems fraught with danger. But my daughter, when I told her of our topic and my difficulty with it, said, "Tell them about how you're never really a whole person if you remain silent, because there's always that one little piece inside you that wants to be spoken out, and if you keep ignoring it, it gets madder and madder and hotter and hotter, and if you don't speak it out one day it will just up and punch you in the mouth from the inside."

In the cause of silence, each of us draws the face of her own fear—fear of contempt, of censure, or some judgment, or recognition, of challenge, of annihilation. But most of all, I think, we fear the visibility without which we cannot truly live. Within this country where racial difference creates a constant, if unspoken, distortion of vision, Black women have on one hand always been highly visible, and so, on the other hand, have been rendered invisible through the depersonalization of racism. Even within the women's movement, we have had to fight, and still do, for that very visibility which also renders us most vulnerable, our Blackness. For to survive in the mouth of this dragon we call america, we have had to learn this first and most vital lesson—that we were never meant to survive. Not as human beings. And neither were most of you here today, Black or not. And that visibility which makes us most vulnerable is that which also is the source of our greatest strength. Because the machine will try to grind you into dust anyway, whether or not we speak. We can sit in our corners mute forever while our sisters and our selves are wasted, while our children are distorted and destroyed, while our earth is poisoned; we can sit in our safe corners mute as bottles, and we will still be no less afraid.

In my house this year we are celebrating the feast of Kwanza, the African-american festival of harvest which begins the day after Christmas and lasts for seven days. There are seven principles of Kwanza, one for each day. The first principle is Umoja, which means unity, the decision to strive for and maintain unity in self and community. The principle for yesterday, the second day, was Kujichagulia—self-determination—the decision to define ourselves, name ourselves, and speak for ourselves, instead of being defined and spoken for by others. Today is the third day of Kwanza, and the principle for today is Ujima—collective work and responsibility—the decision to build and maintain ourselves and our communities together and to recognize and solve our problems together.

Each of us is here now because in one way or another we share a commitment to language and to the power of language, and to the reclaiming of that language which has been made to work against us. In the transformation of silence into language and action, it is vitally necessary for each one of us to establish or examine her function in that transformation and to recognize her role as vital within that transformation.

For those of us who write, it is necessary to scrutinize not only the truth of what we speak, but the truth of that language by which we speak it. For others, it is to share and spread also those words that are meaningful to us. But primarily for us all, it is necessary to teach by living and speaking those truths which we believe and know beyond understanding. Because in this way alone we can survive, by taking part in a process of life that is creative and continuing, that is growth.

And it is never without fear—of visibility, of the harsh light of scrutiny and perhaps judgment, of pain, of death. But we have lived through all of those already, in silence, except death. And I remind myself all the time now that if I were to have been born mute, or had maintained an oath of silence my whole life long for safety, I would still have suffered, and I would still die. It is very good for establishing perspective.

And where the words of women are crying to be heard, we must each of us recognize our responsibility to seek those words out, to read them and share them and examine them in their pertinence to our lives. That we not hide behind the mockeries of separations that have been imposed upon us and which so often we accept as our own. For instance, "I can't possibly teach Black women's writing—their experience is so different from mine." Yet how many years have you spent teaching Plato and Shakespeare and Proust? Or another, "She's a white woman and what could she possibly have to say to me?" Or, "She's a lesbian, what would my husband say, or my chairman?" Or again, "This woman writes of her sons and I have no children." And all the other endless ways in which we rob ourselves of ourselves and each other.

From *Sister Outsider* and *A Burst of Light*

We can learn to work and speak when we are afraid in the same way we have learned to work and speak when we are tired. For we have been socialized to respect fear more than our own needs for language and definition, and while we wait in silence for that final luxury of fearlessness, the weight of that silence will choke us.

The fact that we are here and that I speak these words is an attempt to break that silence and bridge some of those differences between us, for it is not difference which immobilizes us, but silence. And there are so many silences to be broken.

2

SEXISM

An American Disease in Blackface

Black feminism is not white feminism in blackface. Black women have particular and legitimate issues which affect our lives as Black women, and addressing those issues does not make us any less Black. To attempt to open dialogue between Black women and Black men by attacking Black feminists seems shortsighted and self-defeating. Yet this is what Robert Staples, Black sociologist, has done in *The Black Scholar*.

Despite our recent economic gains, Black women are still the lowest paid group in the nation by sex and race. This gives some idea of the inequity from which we started. In Staples' own words, Black women in 1979 only "*threaten* to overtake black men" [italics mine] by the "next century" in education, occupation, and income. In other words, the inequity is self-evident; but how is it justifiable?

Black feminists speak as women because we are women and do not need others to speak for us. It is for Black men to speak up and tell us why and how their manhood is so threatened that Black women should be the prime targets of their justifiable rage. What correct analysis of this capitalist dragon within which we live can legitimize the rape of Black women by Black men?

At least Black feminists and other Black women have begun this much-needed dialogue, however bitter our words. At least we are not

First published as "The Great American Disease," *Black Scholar* 10, no. 9 (May–June 1979), in response to Robert Staples, "The Myth of Black Macho: A Response to Angry Black Feminists," *Black Scholar* 10, no. 8 (March–April 1979).

mowing down our brothers in the street, or bludgeoning them to death with hammers. Yet. We recognize the fallacies of separatist solutions.

Staples pleads his cause by saying capitalism has left the Black man only his penis for fulfillment, and a "curious rage." Is this rage any more legitimate than the rage of Black women? And why are Black women supposed to absorb that male rage in silence? Why isn't that male rage turned upon those forces which limit his fulfillment, namely capitalism? Staples sees in Ntozake Shange's play *For Colored Girls* "a collective appetite for black male blood." Yet it is my female children and my Black sisters who lie bleeding all around me, victims of the appetites of our brothers.

Into what theoretical analysis would Staples fit Patricia Cowan? She answered an ad in Detroit for a Black actress to audition in a play called *Hammer*. As she acted out an argument scene, watched by the playwright's brother and her four-year-old son, the Black male playwright picked up a sledgehammer and bludgeoned her to death. Will Staples' "compassion for misguided black men" bring this young mother back, or make her senseless death more acceptable?

Black men's feelings of cancellation, their grievances, and their fear of vulnerability must be talked about, but not by Black women when it is at the expense of our own "curious rage."

If this society ascribes roles to Black men which they are not allowed to fulfill, is it Black women who must bend and alter our lives to compensate, or is it society that needs changing? And why should Black men accept these roles as correct ones, or anything other than a narcotic promise encouraging acceptance of other facets of their own oppression?

One tool of the Great-American-Double-Think is to blame the victim for victimization: Black people are said to invite lynching by not knowing our place; Black women are said to invite rape and murder and abuse by not being submissive enough, or by being too seductive, or too . . .

Staples' "fact" that Black women get their sense of fulfillment from having children is only a fact when stated out of the mouths of Black men, and any Black person in this country, even a "happily married" woman who has "no pent-up frustrations that need release" (!) is either a fool or insane. This smacks of the oldest sexist canard of all time, that all a woman needs to "keep her quiet" is a "good man." File that one alongside "Some of my best friends are . . ."

Instead of beginning the much-needed dialogue between Black men and Black women, Staples retreats to a defensive stance reminiscent of white liberals of the sixties, many of whom saw any statement of Black pride and self-assertion as an automatic threat to their own identity and an attempt to wipe them out. Here we have an intelligent Black man believing—or at least saying—that any call to Black women to love ourselves (and no one said only) is a denial of, or threat to, his Black male identity!

In this country, Black women traditionally have had compassion for everybody else except ourselves. We have cared for whites because we had to for pay or survival; we have cared for our children and our fathers and our brothers and our lovers. History and popular culture, as well as our personal lives, are full of tales of Black women who had "compassion for misguided black men." Our scarred, broken, battered, and dead daughters and sisters are a mute testament to that reality. We need to learn to have care and compassion for ourselves, also.

In the light of what Black women often willingly sacrifice for our children and our men, this is a much needed exhortation, no matter what illegitimate use the white media makes of it. This call for self-value and self-love is quite different from narcissism, as Staples must certainly realize. Narcissism comes not out of self-love but out of self-hatred.

The lack of a reasonable and articulate Black male viewpoint on these questions is not the responsibility of Black women. We have too often been expected to be all things to all people and speak everyone else's position but our very own. Black men are not so passive that they must have Black women speak for them. Even my fourteen-year-old son knows that. Black men themselves must examine and articulate their own desires and positions and stand by the conclusions thereof. No point is served by a Black male professional who merely whines at the absence of his viewpoint in Black women's work. Oppressors always expect the oppressed to extend to them the understanding so lacking in themselves.

For Staples to suggest, for instance, that Black men leave their families as a form of male protest against female decision making in the home is in direct contradiction to his own observations in "The Myth of the Black Matriarchy."[*]

Now I am sure there are still some Black men who marry white women because they feel a white woman can better fit the model of "femininity" set forth in this country. But for Staples to justify that act using the reason it occurs, and take Black women to task for it, is not only another error in reasoning; it is like justifying the actions of a lemming who follows its companions over the cliff to sure death. Because it happens does not mean it should happen, nor that it is functional for the well-being of the individual or the group.

It is not the destiny of Black america to repeat white america's mistakes. But we will, if we mistake the trappings of success in a sick society for the signs of a meaningful life. If Black men continue to define "femininity" instead of their own desires, and to do it in archaic european terms, they restrict our access to each other's energies. Freedom and future for Blacks does not mean absorbing the dominant white male disease of sexism.

As Black women and men, we cannot hope to begin dialogue by denying the oppressive nature of male privilege. And if Black males choose to assume that privilege for whatever reason—raping, brutalizing, and killing Black women—then ignoring these acts of Black male oppression within our communities can only serve our destroyers. One oppression does not justify another.

It has been said that Black men cannot be denied their personal choice of the woman who meets their need to dominate. In that case, Black women also cannot be denied our personal choices, and those choices are becomingly increasingly self-assertive and female-oriented.

As a people, we most certainly must work together. It would be shortsighted to believe that Black men alone are to blame for the above

---

[*] Robert Staples, "The Myth of the Black Matriarchy," *Black Scholar* 1, nos. 3–4 (January–February 1970).

situations in a society dominated by white male privilege. But the Black male consciousness must be raised to the realization that sexism and woman-hating are critically dysfunctional to his liberation as a Black man because they arise out of the same constellation that engenders racism and homophobia. Until that consciousness is developed, Black men will view sexism and the destruction of Black women as tangential to Black liberation rather than as central to that struggle. So long as this occurs, we will never be able to embark upon that dialogue between Black women and Black men that is so essential to our survival as a people. This continued blindness between us can only serve the oppressive system within which we live.

Men avoid women's observations by accusing us of being too "visceral." But no amount of understanding the roots of Black woman-hating will bring back Patricia Cowan, nor mute her family's loss. Pain is very visceral, particularly to the people who are hurting. As the poet Mary McAnally said, "Pain teaches us to take our fingers OUT the fucking fire."[**]

If the problems of Black women are only derivatives of a larger contradiction between capital and labor, then so is racism, and both must be fought by all of us. The capitalist structure is a many-headed monster. I might add here that in no socialist country that I have visited have I found an absence of racism or of sexism, so the eradication of both of these diseases seems to involve more than the abolition of capitalism as an institution.

No reasonable Black man can possibly condone the rape and slaughter of Black women by Black men as a fitting response to capitalist oppression. And destruction of Black women by Black men clearly cuts across all class lines.

Whatever the "structural underpinnings" (Staples) for sexism in the Black community may be, it is obviously Black women who are bearing the brunt of that sexism, and so it is in our best interest to abolish it. We

---

** From Mary McAnally, *We Will Make a River: Poems* (Cambridge, Mass.: West End, 1979), 27.

From *Sister Outsider* and *A Burst of Light*

invite our Black brothers to join us, since ultimately that abolition is in their best interests also. For Black men are also diminished by a sexism which robs them of meaningful connections to Black women and our struggles. Since it is Black women who are being abused, however, and since it is our female blood that is being shed, it is for Black women to decide whether or not sexism in the Black community is pathological. And we do not approach that discussion theoretically. Those "creative relationships" which Staples speaks about within the Black community are almost invariably those which operate to the benefit of Black males, given the Black male/female ratio and the implied power balance within a supply and demand situation. Polygamy is seen as "creative," but a lesbian relationship is not. This is much the same as how the "creative relationships" between master and slave were always those benefiting the master.

The results of woman-hating in the Black community are tragedies which diminish all Black people. These acts must be seen in the context of a systematic devaluation of Black women within this society. It is within this context that we become approved and acceptable targets for Black male rage, so acceptable that even a Black male social scientist condones and excuses this depersonalizing abuse.

This abuse is no longer acceptable to Black women in the name of solidarity, nor of Black liberation. Any dialogue between Black women and Black men must begin there, no matter where it ends.

Without a rigorous and consistent evaluation of what kind of a future we wish to create, and a scrupulous examination of the expressions of power we choose to incorporate into all our relationships including our most private ones, we are not progressing, but merely recasting our own characters in the same old weary drama. . . . S/M is not the sharing of power, it is merely a depressing replay of the old and destructive dominant/subordinate mode of human relating and one-sided power, which is even now grinding our earth and our human consciousness into dust.

—Audre Lorde, "Letter to the Editor,"
Gay Community News

3

SADOMASOCHISM: NOT ABOUT CONDEMNATION

An Interview with Audre Lorde

Susan Leigh Star

I spent June and July of 1980 in rural Vermont, an idyllic, green, vital world, alive in a short summer season. I teach there summers and winters. One afternoon, Sue (another teacher) and I lay sunbathing on a dock in the middle of a small pond. I suddenly imagined what it would be like to see someone dressed in black leather and chains, trotting through the meadow, as I am accustomed to seeing in my urban neighborhood in San Francisco. I started laughing as one of the parameters of the theater of sadomasochism became clear: it is about cities and a created culture, like punk rock, which is sustained by a particularly urban technology.

Later in the week, Sue and I drove over bumpy dirt roads far into the Northeast Kingdom, the most rural area of Vermont, to interview Audre Lorde. Again, I was struck by the incongruity of sitting in the radiant sunshine, with radiant Audre and Frances [Clayton] and Sue, listening to bobwhites and watching the haze lift far down in the valley, and the subject of our conversation seemed to belong to another world.

I include this description of our physical surroundings because it seems important to me to recognize that all conversations about sadomasochism take place in particular places and at particular historical times, which ought to be noted and compared.

LEIGH: How do you see the phenomenon of sadomasochism
    in the lesbian community?
AUDRE: Sadomasochism in the lesbian-feminist community
    cannot be seen as separate from the larger economic and
    social issues surrounding our communities. It is reflective of
    a whole social and economic trend of this country.

    Sadly, sadomasochism feels comfortable to some people in
    this period of development. What is the nature of this allure?
    Why an emphasis on sadomasochism in the straight media?
    Sadomasochism is congruent with other developments going on
    in this country that have to do with dominance and submission,
    with disparate power—politically, culturally, and economically.

    The attention that Samois˙ is getting is probably out of
    proportion to the representation of sadomasochism in the
    lesbian community. Because s/m is a theme in the dominant
    culture, an attempt to "reclaim" it rather than question
    it is an excuse not to look at the content of the behavior.
    For instance, "We are lesbians doing this extreme thing,
    and you're criticizing *us!*" Thus, sadomasochism is used to
    delegitimize lesbian feminism, lesbianism, and feminism.
LEIGH: So you're saying that the straight media both helps
    amplify the phenomenon within the lesbian community

---

* A San Francisco–based lesbian s/m organization.

and that they focus on lesbians in particular as a way of not dealing with the larger implications and the very existence of the phenomenon in the world?

AUDRE: Yes. And because this power perspective is so much a part of the larger world, it is difficult to critique in isolation. As Erich Fromm once said, "The fact that millions of people take part in a delusion doesn't make it sane."

LEIGH: What about the doctrine of "live and let live" and civil liberties issues?

AUDRE: I don't see that as the point. I'm not questioning anyone's right to live. I'm saying we must observe the implications of our lives. If what we are talking about is feminism, then the personal is political and we can subject everything in our lives to scrutiny. We have been nurtured in a sick, abnormal society, and we should be about the process of reclaiming ourselves as well as the terms of that society. This is complex. *I speak not about condemnation* but about recognizing what is happening and questioning what it means. I'm not willing to regiment anyone's life, but if we are to scrutinize our human relationships, we must be willing to scrutinize all aspects of those relationships. The subject of revolution is ourselves, is our lives.

Sadomasochism is an institutionalized celebration of dominant/subordinate relationships. And, it prepares us either to accept subordination or to enforce dominance. *Even in play*, to affirm that the exertion of power over powerlessness is erotic, is empowering, is to set the emotional and social stage for the continuation of that relationship, politically, socially, and economically.

Sadomasochism feeds the belief that domination is inevitable and legitimately enjoyable. It can be compared to the phenomenon of worshipping a godhead with two faces, and worshipping only the white part on the full moon and the black part on the dark of the moon, as if totally separate. But you cannot corral any aspect within your life, divorce its implications, whether it's what you eat for breakfast or how you say good-bye. This is what *integrity* means.

LEIGH: That relates to two central arguments put forth by the women of Samois: that liberal tolerance is necessary in the realm of sexuality and that the *power over* part of the relationship is confined to the bedroom. I feel, as you do, that it is dangerous to try to cordon off such a vital part of our lives in this way.

AUDRE: If it is confined to the bedroom, then why was the Samois booklet (*What Color Is Your Handkerchief? A Lesbian S/M Sexuality Reader*) printed? If it is not, then what does that mean? It is in the interest of a capitalist profit system for us to privatize much of our experience. In order to make integrated life choices, we must open the sluice gates in our lives, create emotional consistency. This is not to say that we act the same way, or do not change and grow, but that there is an underlying integrity that asserts itself in all of our actions. None of us is perfect, or born with that integrity, but we can work toward it as a goal.

The erotic weaves throughout our lives, and integrity is a basic condition that we aspire to. If we do not have the lessons of our journeys toward that condition, then we have nothing. From that life vision, one is free to examine varying paths of behavior. But integrity has to be a basis for the journey.

Certain things in every society are defined as totally destructive. For instance, the old example of crying "fire" in a crowded theater. Liberalism allows pornography and has allowed wife beating as First Amendment rights. But this doesn't fit them into my life vision, and they are both an immediate threat to my life.

The question I ask, over and over, is *who is profiting from this?* When sadomasochism gets presented on center stage as a conflict in the feminist movement, I ask, what conflicts are *not* being presented?

LEIGH: How do you think sadomasochism starts? What are its roots?

AUDRE: In the superior/inferior mold which is inculcated within us at the deepest levels. The learned intolerance of differences.

Those involved with sadomasochism are acting out the intolerance of differences which we all learn: superiority and thereby the right to dominate. The conflict is supposedly self-limiting because it happens behind bedroom doors. Can this be so, when the erotic empowers, nourishes, and permeates all of our lives?

I ask myself, under close scrutiny, whether I am puritanical about this—and I have asked myself this very carefully—and the answer is no. I feel that we work toward making integrated life decisions about the networks of our lives, and those decisions lead us to other decisions and commitments—certain ways of viewing the world, looking for change. If they don't lead us toward growth and change, we have nothing to build upon, no future.

LEIGH: Do you think sadomasochism is different for gay men than for lesbians?

AUDRE: Who profits from lesbians beating each other? White men have been raised to believe that they're God; most gay white men are marginal in only one respect. Much of the gay white movement seeks to be included in the american dream and is angered when they do not receive the standard white male privileges, misnamed as "american democracy."

Often, white gay men are working *not* to change the system. This is one of the reasons why the gay male movement is as white as it is. Black gay men recognize, again by the facts of survival, that being Black, they are not going to be included in the same way. The Black/white gay male division is being examined and explored by some. Recently, for instance, there was a meeting of Third World lesbians and gays in Washington. It was recognized that there are things we do not share with white lesbians and gay men, as well as things that we do, and that clarification of goals is necessary between white gays and lesbians, and Third World gays and lesbians.

I see no essential battle between many gay men and the white male establishment. To be sure, there are gay men who do not view their oppression as isolated, and who work for a future. But it is a matter of majority politics: many gay white males are being pulled by the same strings as other white men in this society. You do not get people to work against what they have identified as their basic self-interest.

LEIGH: So one of the things that you're saying is that the politics of s/m are connected with the politics of the larger movements?

AUDRE: I do not believe that sexuality is separate from living. As a minority woman, I know dominance and subordination are not bedroom issues. In the same way that rape is not about sex, s/m is not about sex but about how we use power. If it were only about personal sexual exchange or private taste, why would it be presented as a political issue?

LEIGH: I often feel that there's a kind of tyranny about the whole concept of *feelings*, as though, if you feel something then you must act on it.

AUDRE: You don't *feel* a tank or a war—you feel hate or love. Feelings are not wrong, but you are accountable for the behavior you use to satisfy those feelings.

LEIGH: What about how Samois and other lesbian sadomasochists use the concept of power?

AUDRE: The s/m concept of "vanilla" sex is sex devoid of passion. They are saying that there can be no passion without unequal power. That feels very sad and lonely to me, and destructive. The linkage of passion to dominance/subordination is the prototype of the heterosexual image of male-female relationships, one which justifies pornography. Women are supposed to love being brutalized. This is also the prototypical justification of all relationships of oppression—that the subordinate one who is "different" enjoys the inferior position.

The gay male movement, for example, is invested in distinguishing between gay s/m pornography and heterosexual pornography. Gay men can allow themselves the luxury of not seeing the consequences. We, as women and as feminists, must scrutinize our actions and see what they imply, and upon what they are based.

As women, we have been trained to follow. We must look at the s/m phenomenon and educate ourselves, at the same time being aware of intricate manipulations from outside and within.

LEIGH: How does this relate specifically to lesbian feminism?

AUDRE: First, we must ask ourselves, is this whole question of s/m sex in the lesbian community perhaps being used to draw attention and energies away from other more pressing and immediately life-threatening issues facing us as women in this racist, conservative, and repressive period? A red herring? A smoke screen for provocateurs? Second, lesbian s/m is not about what you do in bed, just as lesbianism is not simply a sexual preference. For example, Barbara Smith's work on women-identified women, on "lesbian" experiences in Zora Hurston or Toni Morrison.[1] It is not who I sleep with that defines the quality of these acts, not what we do together, but what life statements I am led to make as the nature and effect of my erotic relationships percolate throughout my life and my being. As a deep lode of our erotic lives and knowledge, how does our sexuality enrich us and empower our actions?

Note

1. Barbara Smith, "Toward a Black Feminist Criticism," *Conditions* 2 (October 1977): 25–44.

From *Sister Outsider* and *A Burst of Light*

4

I AM YOUR SISTER

Black Women Organizing Across Sexualities

Whenever I come to Medgar Evers College I always feel a thrill of anticipation and delight because it feels like coming home, like talking to family, having a chance to speak about things that are very important to me with people who matter the most. And this is particularly true whenever I talk at the Women's Center. But, as with all families, we sometimes find it difficult to deal constructively with the genuine differences between us and to recognize that unity does not require that we be identical to each other. Black women are not one great vat of homogenized chocolate milk. We have many different faces, and we do not have to become each other in order to work together.

It is not easy for me to speak here with you as a Black Lesbian feminist, recognizing that some of the ways in which I identify myself make it difficult for you to hear me. But meeting across difference always requires mutual stretching, and until you can hear me as a Black Lesbian feminist, our strengths will not be truly available to each other as Black women.

Because I feel it is urgent that we not waste each other's resources, that we recognize each sister on her own terms so that we may better work together toward our mutual survival, I speak here about heterosexism and homophobia, two grave barriers to organizing among Black women. And so that we have a common language between us, I would like to define some of the terms I use:

Heterosexism—a belief in the inherent superiority of one form of loving over all others and thereby the right to dominance.

Homophobia—a terror surrounding feelings of love for
members of the same sex and thereby a hatred of those feelings
in others.

In the 1960s, when liberal white people decided that they didn't
want to appear racist, they wore dashikis, and danced Black, and ate
Black, and even married Black, but they did not want to feel Black or
think Black, so they never even questioned the textures of their daily
living (why should "flesh-colored" Bandaids always be pink?) and then
they wondered, "Why are those Black folks always taking offense so easily at the least little thing? Some of our best friends are Black . . ."

Well, it is not necessary for some of your best friends to be Lesbian,
although some of them probably are, no doubt. But it is necessary for
you to stop oppressing me through false judgment. I do not want you
to ignore my identity, nor do I want you to make it an insurmountable
barrier between our sharing of strengths.

When I say I am a Black feminist, I mean I recognize that my power
as well as my primary oppressions come as a result of my Blackness as
well as my womanness, and therefore my struggles on both these fronts
are inseparable.

When I say I am a Black Lesbian, I mean I am a woman whose primary focus of loving, physical as well as emotional, is directed to women.
It does not mean I hate men. Far from it. The harshest attacks I have ever
heard against Black men come from those women who are intimately
bound to them and cannot free themselves from a subservient and silent
position. I would never presume to speak about Black men the way I
have heard some of my straight sisters talk about the men they are at-
tached to. And of course that concerns me, because it reflects a situation
of noncommunication in the heterosexual Black community that is far
more truly threatening than the existence of Black Lesbians.

What does this have to do with Black women organizing?

I have heard it said—usually behind my back—that Black Lesbians
are not normal. But what is normal in this deranged society by which we
are all trapped? I remember, and so do many of you, when being Black
was considered not normal, when they talked about us in whispers, tried

to paint us, lynch us, bleach us, ignore us, pretend we did not exist. We called that racism.

I have heard it said that Black Lesbians are a threat to the Black family. But when 50 percent of children born to Black women are born out of wedlock, and 30 percent of all Black families are headed by women without husbands, we need to broaden and redefine what we mean by *family*.

I have heard it said that Black Lesbians will mean the death of the race. Yet Black Lesbians bear children in exactly the same way other women bear children, and a Lesbian household is simply another kind of family. Ask my son and daughter.

The terror of Black Lesbians is buried in that deep inner place where we have been taught to fear all difference—to kill it or ignore it. Be assured: loving women is not a communicable disease. You don't catch it like the common cold. Yet the one accusation that seems to render even the most vocal straight Black woman totally silent and ineffective is the suggestion that she might be a Black Lesbian.

If someone says you're Russian and you know you're not, you don't collapse into stunned silence. Even if someone calls you a bigamist, or a childbeater, and you know you're not, you don't crumple into bits. You say it's not true and keep on printing the posters. But let anyone, particularly a Black man, accuse a straight Black woman of being a Black *Lesbian*, and right away that sister becomes immobilized, as if that is the most horrible thing she could be, and must at all costs be proven false. That is homophobia. It is a waste of woman energy, and it puts a terrible weapon into the hands of your enemies to be used against you to silence you, to keep you docile and in line. It also serves to keep us isolated and apart.

I have heard it said that Black Lesbians are not political, that we have not been and are not involved in the struggles of Black people. But when I taught Black and Puerto Rican students writing at City College in the SEEK program in the sixties I was a Black Lesbian. I was a Black Lesbian when I helped organize and fight for the Black Studies Department of John Jay College. And because I was fifteen years younger then and less sure of myself, at one crucial moment I yielded to pressures that said I should step back for a Black man even though I knew him to be a serious error of choice, and I did, and he was. But I was a Black Lesbian then.

When my girlfriends and I went out in the car one July 4 night after fireworks with cans of white spray paint and our kids asleep in the back seat, one of us staying behind to keep the motor running and watch the kids while the other two worked our way down the suburban New Jersey street, spraying white paint over the black jockey statues, and their little red jackets, too, we were Black Lesbians.

When I drove through the Mississippi delta to Jackson in 1968 with a group of Black students from Tougaloo, another car full of redneck kids trying to bump us off the road all the way back into town, I was a Black Lesbian.

When I weaned my daughter in 1963 to go to Washington in August to work in the coffee tents along with Lena Horne, making coffee for the marshals because that was what most Black women did in the 1963 March on Washington, I was a Black Lesbian.

When I taught a poetry workshop at Tougaloo, a small Black college in Mississippi, where white rowdies shot up the edge of campus every night, and I felt the joy of seeing young Black poets find their voices and power through words in our mutual growth, I was a Black Lesbian. And there are strong Black poets today who date their growth and awareness from those workshops.

When Yoli [Yolanda Rios] and I cooked curried chicken and beans and rice and took our extra blankets and pillows up the hill to the striking students occupying buildings at City College in 1969, demanding open admissions and the right to an education, I was a Black Lesbian. When I walked through the midnight hallways of Lehman College that same year, carrying Midol and Kotex pads for the young Black radical women taking part in the action, and we tried to persuade them that their place in the revolution was not ten paces behind Black men, that spreading their legs to the guys on the tables in the cafeteria was not a revolutionary act no matter what the brothers said, I was a Black Lesbian. When I picketed for welfare mothers' rights, and against the enforced sterilization of young Black girls, when I fought institutionalized racism in the New York City schools, I was a Black Lesbian.

But you did not know it because we did not identify ourselves, so now you can say that Black Lesbians and Gay men have nothing to do with the struggles of the Black Nation.

And I am not alone.

When you read the words of Langston Hughes you are reading the words of a Black Gay man. When you read the words of Alice Dunbar-Nelson and Angelina Weld Grimké, poets of the Harlem Renaissance, you are reading the words of Black Lesbians. When you listen to the life-affirming voices of Bessie Smith and Ma Rainey, you are hearing Black Lesbian women. When you see the plays and read the words of Lorraine Hansberry, you are reading the words of a woman who loved women deeply.

Today, Lesbians and Gay men are some of the most active and engaged members of Art Against Apartheid, a group which is making visible and immediate our cultural responsibilities against the tragedy of South Africa. We have organizations such as the National Coalition of Black Lesbians and Gays, Dykes Against Racism Everywhere, and Men of All Colors Together, all of which are committed to and engaged in antiracist activity.

Homophobia and heterosexism mean you allow yourselves to be robbed of the sisterhood and strength of Black Lesbian women because you are afraid of being called a Lesbian yourself. Yet we share so many concerns as Black women, so much work to be done. The urgency of the destruction of our Black children and the theft of young Black minds are joint urgencies. Black children shot down or doped up on the streets of our cities are priorities for all of us. The fact of Black women's blood flowing with grim regularity in the streets and living rooms of Black communities is not a Black Lesbian rumor. It is sad statistical truth. The fact that there is widening and dangerous lack of communication around our differences between Black women and men is not a Black Lesbian plot. It is a reality that is starkly clarified as we see our young people becoming more and more uncaring of each other. Young Black boys believing that they can define their manhood between a sixth-grade girl's legs, growing up believing that Black women and girls are the fitting target for their justifiable furies rather than the racist structures grinding us all into dust, these are not Black Lesbian myths. These are sad realities of Black communities today and of immediate concern to us all. We cannot afford to waste each other's energies in our common battles.

What does homophobia mean? It means that high-powered Black women are told it is not safe to attend a Conference on the Status of Women in Nairobi simply because we are Lesbians. It means that in a political action, you rob yourselves of the vital insight and energies of political women such as Betty Powell and Barbara Smith and Gwendolyn Rogers and Raymina Mays and Robin Christian and Yvonne Flowers. It means another instance of the divide-and-conquer routine.

How do we organize around our differences, neither denying them nor blowing them up out of proportion?

The first step is an effort of will on your part. Try to remember to keep certain facts in mind. Black Lesbians are not apolitical. We have been a part of every freedom struggle within this country. Black Lesbians are not a threat to the Black family. Many of us have families of our own. We are not white, and we are not a disease. We are women who love women. This does not mean we are going to assault your daughters in an alley on Nostrand Avenue. It does not mean we are about to attack you if we pay you a compliment on your dress. It does not mean we only think about sex, any more than you only think about sex.

Even if you *do* believe any of these stereotypes about Black Lesbians, begin to practice *acting* like you don't believe them. Just as racist stereotypes are the problem of the white people who believe them, so also are homophobic stereotypes the problem of the heterosexuals who believe them. In other words, those stereotypes are yours to solve, not mine, and they are a terrible and wasteful barrier to our working together. I am not your enemy. We do not have to become each other's unique experiences and insights in order to share what we have learned through our particular battles for survival as Black women. . . .

There was a poster in the 1960s that was very popular: HE'S NOT BLACK, HE'S MY BROTHER! It used to infuriate me because it implied that the two were mutually exclusive—*he* couldn't be both brother and Black. Well, I do not want to be tolerated, nor misnamed. I want to be recognized.

I am a Black Lesbian, and I *am* your sister.

5

APARTHEID U.S.A.

New York City, 1985. The high sign that rules this summer is increasing fragmentation. I am filled with a sense of urgency and dread: dread at the apparently random waves of assaults against people and institutions closest to me; urgency to unearth the connections between these assaults. Those connections lurk beneath the newspaper reports of teargassed funeral processions in Tembisa and the charred remains of Baldwin Hills, California, a flourishing Black neighborhood leveled by arson.

I sit before the typewriter for days and nothing comes. It feels as if underlining these assaults, lining them up one after the other and looking at them squarely might give them an unbearable power. Yet I know exactly the opposite is true—no matter how difficult it may be to look at the realities of our lives, it is there that we will find the strength to change them. And to suppress any truth is to give it power beyond endurance.

As I write these words I am listening to the United Nations' special session considering the "state of emergency" in South Africa, their euphemism for the suspension of human rights for Blacks, which is the response of the Pretoria regime to the increasingly spontaneous eruptions in Black townships across that country. These outbursts against apartheid have greatly increased in the last eleven months since a new South African constitution further solidified the exclusion of the twenty-two million Black majority from the South African political process. These outbreaks, however severely curtailed by the South African police and military, are beginning to accomplish what Oliver Tambo, head of the African National Congress, hoped for in his call to make South Africa under apartheid "ungovernable."

So much Black blood has been shed upon that land, I thought, and so much more will fall. But blood will tell, and now the blood is speaking.

Has it finally started? What some of us prayed and worked and believed would—must—happen, wondering when, because so few of us here in america even seemed to know what was going on in South Africa, nor cared to hear. The connections have not been made, and they must be if African-Americans are to articulate our power in the struggle against a worldwide escalation of forces aligned against people of Color the world over: institutionalized racism grown more and more aggressive in the service of shrinking profit-oriented economies.

And who would have thought we'd live to see the day when Black South Africa took center stage on the world platform? As Ellen Kuzwayo, Black South African writer, would say, this is where we are right now in the world's story. . . . Perhaps this is how europe felt in the fall of 1939, on the brink. I remember that Sunday of December 7, 1941, and the chill certainty that some threat which hovered on my six-year-old horizon had finally been made real and frontal. August 6, 1945. Hiroshima. My father's tears—I had never seen him cry before and at first I thought it was sweat—a forty-six-year-old Black man in his vigor, yet only seven years away from death by overwork. He said, "Humanity can now destroy itself," and he wept. That's how it feels, except this time we know we're on the winning side. South Africa will be free, I thought, beneath the clatter of my waiting typewriter and the sonorous tones of the United Nations broadcast, the U.S. delegate, along with the one from Great Britain, talking their rot about what "we" have done for Black South Africa.

South Africa. Eighty-seven percent of the people, Black, occupy 13 percent of the land. Thirteen percent of the people, white, own 85 percent of the land. White South Africa has the highest standard of living of any nation in the world including the United States yet half the Black children born in South Africa die before they reach the age of five. Every thirty minutes, six Black children starve to death in South Africa. In response to questions about apartheid from a white U.S. reporter, a white South African reporter retorts, "You have solved the problem of your indigenous people—we are solving ours. You called them Indians, didn't you?" Apartheid—South Africa's Final Solution patterned after Nazi Germany's genocidal plan for european Jews.

Every year over 500 million american dollars flow into the white South African death machine. How many of those dollars do you control as you sit reading this? Where do you bank? Buy your gas? What pressure can you bring to bear upon companies doing business in South Africa? Five hundred million dollars a year. Divestment. The withdrawal of american financial support from South Africa. Those who counter that divestment would mean additional suffering for Black South Africans are either cynical or misguided or unaware of the extent to which Black South Africans suffer every day of their lives. For any South African to even discuss divestment in South Africa is considered an act of treason against the state.

Do you even know which companies your money supports that do business in South Africa? You won't find that information in the *New York Times* or the *San Francisco Chronicle* or *GQ*. But you can obtain that information and more from the African National Congress Weekly News Briefings ($15 a year) from ANC, 801 Second Avenue, New York, NY 10017, or from the American Committee on Africa, 198 Broadway, New York, NY 10038.

We are Black Lesbians and Gays, fighting many battles for survival. We are also citizens of the most powerful country in the world, a country which stands upon the wrong side of every liberation struggle on earth. African-Americans control 200 billion dollars in buying power annually. As African-Americans we must learn to use our power, to establish the connections instantly between consistent patterns of slaughter of Black children and youth in the roads of Sebokeng and Soweto in the name of law and order in Johannesburg, and white america's not-so-silent applause for the smiling white vigilante who coolly guns down four Black youths in the New York City subway. Or the white policemen guarding the store of a Middle Eastern shopkeeper who had killed three Black children in Brooklyn in a dispute over one can of Coca-Cola. The multicorporate financial connections are a matter of record; it is the emotional ones which must become inescapable for each of us. We are members of an international community of people of Color, and must see our struggles as connected within that light.

Made more arrogant daily by the connivance of the U.S. dollar and the encouragement of the U.S. policy of constructive engagement, South African police jail and murder six-year-old children, kick twelve-year-old Johannes to death in front of his garden, leave nine-year-old Joyce bleeding to death on her granny's floor. Decades of these actions are finally escalating into the world's consciousness.

How long will it take to escalate into our consciousness as Black people that this is *us*, that it is only a matter of location and progression of time and intensity from the Molotov cocktails that were hurled into the brush in Los Angeles, starting the conflagration that burned out well-to-do Black Baldwin Hills—fifty-three homes gone, three lives lost—to government-sanctioned segregation and violence. In California, U.S.A., the Aryan Brotherhood, the Posse Comitatus, and other white racist and anti-Semitic survivalist groups flourish rampant and poisonous, fertilized by a secretly sympathetic law enforcement team.

Eleanor Bumpurs, sixty-six, Black grandmother, evicted from her Bronx Housing Authority apartment with two fatal shotgun blasts from New York City housing police.

Allene Richardson, sixty-four, gunned down in her Detroit apartment house hallway by a policewoman after she was locked out of her apartment and a neighbor called the police to help her get back in.

It is ten years since a policeman shot ten-year-old Clifford Glover early one Saturday morning in front of his father in Queens, New York; eight years Thanksgiving Day since another white cop walked up to Randy Evans while he sat on his stoop talking with friends and blew his fifteen-year-old brains out. Temporary insanity, said the jury that acquitted that policeman.

Countless others since then—Seattle, New Orleans, Dallas. Yvonne Smallwood, a young Black woman arguing her husband's traffic ticket, kicked to death by police in Manhattan. Our dead line our dreams, their deaths becoming more and more commonplace.

How does a system bent upon our ultimate destruction make the unacceptable gradually tolerable? Observe closely, look around, read the Black press. How do you get a population to accept the denial of the most rudimentary freedoms this country is supposed to be about to over 12 percent of its population? And we know that Black americans are only the beginning, just as the moves against Black Lesbians and Gays are only the beginning within our communities.

In 1947, within my memory, apartheid was not the state policy of South Africa, but the supposedly far-out dream of the Afrikaner Broederbond. Living conditions of Black South Africans, although bad, were not yet governed by policies of institutional genocide. Blacks owned land, attended schools.

With the 1948 election of the Afrikaner white-supremacy advocate Malik, and the implementation of apartheid, the step-by-step attack upon Black existence was accelerated with the dismantling of any human rights as they pertained to Black people. Now, white South Africans who protest are being jailed and brutalized and blown up, also. Once liberal English-speaking white South Africans had to be conned into accepting this dismantling, lulled long enough for the apparatus which was to ensure all white-privileged survival to be cemented into place by H. Verwoerd, its architect and later South African prime minister.

Now Johannesburg, city of gold, sits literally upon a mountain of gold and Black blood.

After a Sharpeville, why not a Soweto? After a Michael Stewart, young Black artist beaten to death by New York City transit police, why not a Bernard Goetz? After a New York Eight Plus, why not a Philadelphia, where the Black mayor allows a white police chief to bomb a houseful of Black people into submission, killing eleven people and burning down a whole Black neighborhood to do it. Firemen refused to douse the flames. Five of those killed were children. Police pinned them down with gunfire when the occupants sought to escape the flames, making sure these Black people died. Because they were dirty and Black and obnoxious and Black and arrogant and Black and poor and Black and Black and Black and Black. And the mayor who allowed this to happen says he accepts full responsibility, and he is Black, too. How are we persuaded to participate in our own destruction by maintaining our silences? How is the american public persuaded to accept as natural the fact that at a time when prolonged negotiations can effect the release of hostages in the

Middle East or terminate an armed confrontation with police outside a white survivalist encampment, a mayor of an american city can order an incendiary device dropped on a house with five children in it and police pin down the occupants until they perish? Yes, African-Americans can still walk the streets of america without passbooks—for the time being.

In October 1984, 500 agents of the Joint Terrorist Task Force (see what your taxes are paying for?) rounded up eight middle-income Black radicals whose only crime seems to be their insistence upon their right to dissent, to call themselves Marxist-Leninists, and to question the oppressive nature of this U.S. society. They are currently imprisoned, and being tried in a grand jury proceeding that reads like the Star Chamber reports or the Spanish Inquisition. Twenty-two months of round-the-clock surveillance has so far not provided any evidence at all that these Black men and women, some grandmothers, were terrorists. I am reminded of the Johannesburg courts filled with cases brought against Black clericals and salesgirls accused of reading a book or wearing a T-shirt or listening to music thought to be sympathetic to the African National Congress. Two years' hard labor for pamphlets discovered in an office desk drawer.

How is the systematic erosion of freedoms gradually accomplished? What kind of gradual erosion of our status as United States citizens will Black people be persuaded first to ignore and then to accept?

In Louisville, Kentucky, a workmen's compensation ruling awards $231 weekly disability payments to a thirty-nine-year-old sanitation supervisor, white, for a mental breakdown he says he suffered as a result of having to work with Black people.

A peaceful, licensed march to the Haitian embassy in New York to protest living conditions on that island, and the imprisonment of three priests, is set upon by New York City mounted police and trained attack dogs. Sixteen people are injured, including women and children, and one man, struck in the head by hooves, may lose his eye. The next day, no major newspaper or TV news station carries a report of the incident, except for Black media.

In New York, the self-confessed and convicted white ex-G.I. killer of at least six Black men in New York City and Buffalo is quietly released from jail after less than one year, on a technicality. He had been sentenced to life for three of the murders and never tried on the others. White men attack three Black transit workers in Brooklyn, stomping one to death. Of the three who are tried for murder, two are sentenced to less than one year in prison and one goes scot-free.

So the message is clear: stock in Black human life in the U.S.A., never high, is plunging rapidly in the sight of white american complacencies. But as African-Americans we cannot afford to play that market; it is our lives and the lives of our children that are at stake.

The political and social flavor of the African-American position in the 1980s feels in particular aspects to be analogous to occurrences in the Black South African communities of the 1950s, the period of the postwar construction of the apparat[us] of apartheid, reaction, and suppression. Reaction in a large, manipulated, and oppressed population, particularly one where minimal material possessions allow a spurious comparison for the better to one's neighbors, is always slow in coming, preceded as it so often is by the preoccupation of energies in having to cope daily with worsening symptoms of threatened physical survival.

There has recently been increased discussion among African-Americans concerning crime and social breakdown within our communities, signaled in urban areas by highly visible groups of unemployed Black youths, already hopeless and distrustful of their or their elders' abilities to connect with any meaningful future. Our young Black people are being sacrificed to a society's determination to destroy whomever it no longer needs for cheap labor or cannon fodder.

No one in the U.S. government will say openly now that apartheid in South Africa is good, or that the advancing technocracy in this country is making a large underprivileged pool of cheap labor increasingly unnecessary. No one actually says that Black people are more frequently seen as expendable in this economy, but nonetheless the nation that plans to finance Star Wars in space and run shuttle flights to the moon cannot seem to remedy Black teenage unemployment. Because it does not wish to remedy it. Better to wipe them out, blow them away. African-Americans are increasingly superfluous to a shrinking economy. A different stage

From *Sister Outsider* and *A Burst of Light*

exists in South Africa where a cheap labor pool of Blacks is still pivotal to the economy. But the maintenance of the two systems is closely related, and they are both guided primarily by the needs of a white marketplace. Of course no one in the United States government will openly defend apartheid—they don't have to. Just support it by empty rhetorical slaps on the wrist and solid financial investments, all the time honoring South African orders for arms, nuclear technology, and sophisticated computerized riot-control mechanisms. The bully boys stick together.

I remember stories in the 1960s about the roving bands of homeless and predatory *tsotsis*, disenchanted and furious Black youths roaming the evening streets of Sharpeville and Soweto and other Black townships.

The fact that African-Americans can still move about relatively freely, do not yet have to carry passbooks or battle an officially named policy of apartheid, should not delude us for a minute about the disturbing similarities of the Black situation in each one of these profit-oriented economies. We examine these similarities so that we can more effectively devise mutually supportive strategies for action, at the same time as we remain acutely aware of our differences. Like the volcano, which is one form of extreme earth-change, in any revolutionary process there is a period of intensification and a period of explosion. We must become familiar with the requirements and symptoms of each period, and use the differences between them to our mutual advantage, learning and supporting each other's battles. African-Americans can wield the relative power of our dollars—for better or worse. We have the ability to affect South Africa where it lives, financially, through our support of divestment for companies doing business in South Africa. Black South Africans have the base of their own land upon which they operate. We lack that as African-Americans, suffer the rootlessness of a "hyphenated" people. But within those differences, we can join together to effect a future the world has not yet conceived, let alone seen.

For no matter what liberal commitment to human rights is mouthed in international circles by the U.S. government, we know it will not move beyond its investments in South Africa unless we make it unprofitable to invest there. For it is economic divestment, not moral sanction, that

South Africa fears most. No one will free us but ourselves, here nor there. So our survivals are not separate, even though the terms under which we struggle differ. African-Americans are bound to the Black struggle in South Africa by politics as well as blood. As Malcolm X observed more than twenty years ago, a militant, free Africa is a necessity to the dignity of African-American identity.

The mendacity of the U.S. ambassador to the United Nations, as he recited all the "help" this country has given to Black South Africans, is matched only by the cynicism of the South African president who self-righteously condemns the spontaneous violence against Black collaborators in the Black townships, calling that the reason for the current state of emergency. Of course, it is the picture of Blacks killing a Black that is flashed over and over across the white world's TV screens, not the images of white South African police firing into groups of Black schoolchildren, imprisoning six-year-olds, driving over Black schoolgirls. And I think about my feelings concerning that Black mayor of Philadelphia, and about Clarence Pendleton, Black man, Reagan-appointed head of the federal Civil Rights Commission, and mouthpiece of corruption, saying to young students at Cornell University, "The economic pie is just too small for everyone to have a fair share, and that's not the function of civil rights." Eventually institutional racism becomes a question of power and privilege rather than merely color, which then serves as a subterfuge.

The connections between Africans and African-Americans, African-Europeans, African-Asians, is real, however dimly seen at times, and we all need to examine without sentimentality or stereotype what the injection of Africanness into the sociopolitical consciousness of the world could mean. We need to join our differences and articulate our particular strengths in the service of our mutual survivals, and against the desperate backlash which attempts to keep that Africanness from altering the very bases of current world power and privilege.

From *Sister Outsider* and *A Burst of Light*

6

TURNING THE BEAT AROUND

Lesbian Parenting 1986

These days it seems like everywhere I turn somebody is either having a baby or talking about having a baby, and on one level that feels quite benign because I love babies. At the same time, I can't help asking myself what it means in terms of where we are as a country, as well as where we are as people of Color within a white racist system. And when infants begin to appear with noticeable regularity within the Gay and Lesbian community, I find this occurrence even more worthy of close and un-sentimental scrutiny.

We are Lesbians and Gays of Color surviving in a country that defines human—when it concerns itself with the question at all—as straight and white. We are Gays and Lesbians of Color at a time in that country's history when its domestic and international policies, as well as its posture toward those developing nations with which we share herit-age, are so reactionary that self-preservation demands we involve our-selves actively in those policies and postures. And we must have some input and effect upon those policies if we are ever to take a responsible place within the international community of peoples of Color, a human community which includes two-thirds of the world's population. It is a time when the increase in conservatism upon every front affecting our lives as people of Color is oppressively obvious, from the recent appoint-ment of a Supreme Court chief justice in flagrant disregard of his history of racial intolerance, to the largely unprotested rise in racial stereotypes and demeaning images saturating our popular media—radio, television, videos, movies, music.

We are Gays and Lesbians of Color at a time when the advent of a new and uncontrolled disease has carved wrenching inroads into the ranks of our comrades, our lovers, our friends. And the connection between these two facts—the rise in social and political conservatism and the appearance of what has become known in the general public's mind as the *gay* disease, AIDS—has not been sufficiently scrutinized. But we certainly see their unholy wedding in the increase of sanctioned and self-righteous acts of heterosexism and homophobia, from queer-bashing in our streets to the legal invasion of our bedrooms. Should we miss these connections between racism and homophobia, we are also asked to believe that this monstrously convenient disease—and I use *convenient* here in the sense of *convenient for extermination*—originated spontaneously and mysteriously in Africa. Yet, for all the public hysteria surrounding AIDS, almost nothing is heard of the growing incidence of CAIDS—along the Mexican border, in the Near East, and in the other areas of industrial imperialism. Chemically Acquired Immune Deficiency Syndrome is an industrial disease caused by prolonged exposure to trichloroethylene. TCE is a chemical in wholesale use in the electronic sweatshops of the world, where workers are primarily people of Color, in Malaysia, Sri Lanka, the Philippines, and Mexico.

It is a time when we, Lesbians and Gays of Color, cannot ignore our position as citizens of a country that stands on the wrong side of every liberation struggle on this globe; a country that publicly condones and connives with the most vicious and systematic program for genocide since Nazi Germany—apartheid South Africa.

How do we raise children to deal with these realities? For if we do not, we only disarm them, send them out into the jaws of the dragon unprepared. If we raise our children in the absence of an accurate picture of the world as we know it, then we blunt their most effective weapons for survival and growth, as well as their motivation for social change.

We are Gays and Lesbians of Color in a time when race-war is being fought in a small Idaho town, Coeur D'Alene. It is a time when the lynching of two Black people in California within twenty miles of each other is called nonracial and coincidental by the local media. One of the two victims was a Black Gay man, Timothy Lee; the other was a Black woman reporter investigating his death, Jacqueline Peters.

It is a time when local and national funds for day care and other programs which offer help to poor and working-class families are being cut, a time when even the definition of family is growing more and more restrictive.

But we are having babies! And I say, thank the goddess. As members of ethnic and racial communities historically under siege, every Gay man and Lesbian of Color knows deep down inside that the question of children is not merely an academic one, nor do our children represent a theoretical hold upon some vague immortality. Our parents are examples of survival as a living pursuit, and no matter how different from them we may now find ourselves, we have built their example into our definitions of self—which is why we can be here, naming ourselves. We know that all our work upon this planet is not going to be done in our lifetimes, and maybe not even in our children's lifetimes. But if we do what we came to do, our children will carry it on through their own living. And if we can keep this earth spinning and remain upon it long enough, the future belongs to us and our children because we are fashioning it with a vision rooted in human possibility and growth, a vision that does not shrivel before adversity.

There are those who say the urge to have children is a reaction to encroaching despair, a last desperate outcry before the leap into the void. I disagree. I believe that raising children is one way of participating in the future, in social change. On the other hand, it would be dangerous as well as sentimental to think that childrearing alone is enough to bring about a livable future in the absence of any definition of that future. For unless we develop some cohesive vision of that world in which we hope these children will participate, and some sense of our own responsibilities in the shaping of that world, we will only raise new performers in the master's sorry drama.

So what does this all have to do with Lesbian parenting? Well, when I talk about mothering, I do so with an urgency born of my consciousness as a Lesbian and a Black African Caribbean american woman staked out in white racist sexist homophobic america.

I gave birth to two children. I have a daughter and a son. The memory of their childhood years, storms and all, remains a joy to me. Those years were the most chaotic as well as the most creative of my life. Raising two children together with my lover, Frances, balancing the intricacies of relationship within that four-person interracial family, taught me invaluable measurements for my self, my capacities, my real agendas. It gave me tangible and sometimes painful lessons about difference, about power, and about purpose.

We were a Black and a white Lesbian in our forties, raising two Black children. Making do was not going to be a safe way to live our lives, nor was pretense, nor euphemism. *Lesbian* is a name for women who love each other. *Black* means of African ancestry. Our lives would never be simple. We had to learn and to teach what works while we lived, always, with a cautionary awareness of the social forces aligned against us—at the same time there was laundry to be done, dental appointments to be kept, and no you can't watch cartoons because we think they rot your feelings and we pay the electricity.

I knew, for example, that the rage I felt and kept carefully under lock and key would one day be matched by a similar rage in my children: the rage of Black survival within the daily trivializations of white racism. I had to discover ways to own and use that rage if I was to teach them how to own and use theirs, so that we did not wind up torturing ourselves by turning our rage against each other. It was not restraint I had to learn, but ways to use my rage to fuel actions, actions that could alter the very circumstances of oppression feeding my rage.

Screaming at my daughter's childish banter instead of standing up to a racist bus driver was misplacing my anger, making her its innocent victim. Getting a migraine headache instead of injecting my Black woman's voice into the smug whiteness of a women's studies meeting was swallowing that anger, turning it against myself. Neither one of these actions offered solutions I wanted to give my children for dealing with relationships or racism. Learning to recognize and label my angers, and to put them where they belonged in some effective way, became crucial—not only for my own survival, but also for my children's. So that when I was justifiably angry with one of them—and no one short of sainthood can live around growing children and not get angry at one time or another—I could express the anger appropriate to the situation and not have that anger magnified and distorted by all my other unexpressed and unused furies. I was not always successful in achieving that distinction, but trying kept me conscious of the difference.

If I could not learn to handle my anger, how could I expect the children to learn to handle theirs in some constructive way—not deny it or hide it or self-destruct upon it? As a Black Lesbian mother I came to realize I could not afford the energy drains of denial and still be open to my own growth. And if we do not grow with our children, they cannot learn.

That was a long and sometimes arduous journey toward self-possession. And that journey was sweetened by an increasing ability to stretch far beyond what I had previously thought possible—in understanding, in seeing common events in a new perspective, in trusting my own perceptions. It was an exciting journey, sweetened also by the sounds of their laughter in the street and the endearing beauty of the bodies of children sleeping. My daughter and my son made issues of survival daily questions, the answers to which had to be scrutinized as well as practiced. And what our children learned about using their own power and difference within our family, I hope they will someday use to save the world. I can hope for no less. I know that I am constantly learning from them. Still.

Like getting used to looking up instead of down. How looking up all the time gives you a slight ache in the back of the neck. Jonathan, at seventeen, asking, "Hey, Ma, how come you never hit us until we were bigger'n you?" At that moment realizing I guess I never hit my kids when they were little for the same reason my father never hit me: because we were afraid that our rage at the world in which we lived might leak out to contaminate and destroy someone we loved. But my father never learned to express his anger beyond imaginary conversations behind closed doors. Instead, he stoppered it, denying me his image, and he died of inchoate rage at fifty-one. My mother, on the other hand, would beat me until she wept from weariness. But it was not me, the overly rambunctious child, who sold her rotting food and spat upon her and her children in the street.

Frances and I wanted the children to know who we were and who they were, and that we were proud of them and of ourselves, and we hoped they would be proud of themselves and of us, too. But I remember Beth's fifteen-year-old angry coolness: "You think just because you're lesbians you're so different from the rest of them, but you're not, you're just like all the other parents . . ." Then she launched into a fairly accurate record of our disciplines, our demands, our errors.

What I remember most of all now is that we were not just like all the other parents. Our family was not just like all the other families. That did not keep us from being a family any more than our being Lesbians kept Frances and me from being parents. But we did not have to be just like all the rest in order to be valid. We were an interracial Lesbian family with radical parents in the most conservative borough of New York City. Exploring the meaning of those differences kept us all stretching and learning, and we used that exploration to get us from Friday to Thursday, from toothache through homework to who was going to babysit when we both worked late, and did Frances go to PTA meetings.

There are certain basic requirements of any child—food, clothing, shelter, love. So what makes our children different? We do. Gays and Lesbians of Color are different because we are embattled by reason of our sexuality and our Color, and if there is any lesson we must teach our children, it is that difference is a creative force for change, that survival and struggle for the future is not a theoretical issue. It is the very texture of our lives, just as revolution is the texture of the lives of the children who stuff their pockets with stones in Soweto and quickstep all the way to Johannesburg to fall in the streets from tear gas and rubber bullets in front of Anglo-American Corporation. Those children did not choose to die little heroes. They did not ask their mothers and fathers for permission to run in the streets and die. They do it because somewhere their parents gave them an example of what can be paid for survival, and these children carry on the same work by redefining their roles in an inhuman environment.

From *Sister Outsider* and *A Burst of Light*

The children of Lesbians of Color did not choose their Color nor their mamas. But these are the facts of their lives, and the power as well as the peril of these realities must not be hidden from them as they seek self-definition.

And yes, sometimes our daughter and son did pay a price for our insisting upon the articulation of our differences—political, racial, sexual. That is difficult for me to say, because it hurts to raise your children knowing they may be sacrificed to your vision, your belief. But as children of Color, Lesbian parents or no, our children are programmed to be sacrifices to the vision of white racist profit-oriented sexist homophobic america, and that we cannot allow. So if we must raise our children to be warriors rather than cannon fodder, at least let us be very clear in what war we are fighting and what inevitable shape victory will wear. Then our children will choose their own battles.

Lesbians and Gays of Color and the children of Lesbians and Gays of Color are in the forefront of every struggle for human dignity in this country today, and that is not by accident. At the same time, we must remember when they are children that they are children, and need love, protection, and direction. From the beginning, Frances and I tried to teach the children that they each had a right to define herself and himself and to feel his own and her own feelings. They also had to take responsibility for the actions which arose out of those feelings. In order to do this teaching, we had to make sure that Beth and Jonathan had access to information from which to form those definitions—true information, no matter how uncomfortable it might be for us. We also had to provide them with sufficient space within which to feel anger, fear, rebellion, joy.

We were very lucky to have the love and support of other Lesbians, most of whom did not have children of their own, but who loved us and our son and daughter. That support was particularly important at those times when some apparently insurmountable breach left us feeling isolated and alone as Lesbian parents. Another source of support and connection came from other Black women who were raising children alone. Even so, there were times when it seemed to Frances and me that we would not survive neighborhood disapproval, a double case of chickenpox, or escalating teenage rebellion. It is really scary when your children take what they have learned about self-assertion and nonviolent power and decide to test it in confrontations with you. But that is a necessary part of learning themselves, and the primary question is, have they learned to use it well?

Our daughter and son are in their twenties now. They are both warriors, and the battlefields shift: the war is the same. It stretches from the brothels of Southeast Asia to the blood-ridden alleys of Capetown to the incinerated Lesbian in Berlin to Michael Stewart's purloined eyes and grandmother Eleanor Bumpurs shot dead in the projects of New York. It stretches from the classroom where our daughter teaches Black and Latino third graders to chant, "I am somebody beautiful," to the college campus where our son replaced the Stars and Stripes with the flag of South Africa to protest his school's refusal to divest. They are in the process of choosing their own weapons, and no doubt some of those weapons will feel completely alien to me. Yet I trust them, deeply, because they were raised to be their own woman, their own man, in struggle, and in the service of all of our futures.

From *Sister Outsider* and *A Burst of Light*

though we may land here there is no other landing to choose
our meaning we must make it new. —Muriel Rukeyser

A BURST OF LIGHT

Living with Cancer

INTRODUCTION

The year I became fifty felt like a great coming together for me. I was very proud of having made it for half a century, and in my own style. "Time for a change," I thought, "I wonder how I'm going to live the next half."

On February 1, two weeks before my fiftieth birthday, I was told by my doctor that I had liver cancer, metastasized from the breast cancer for which I had had a mastectomy six years before.

At first I did not believe it. I continued with my previously planned teaching trip to europe. As I grew steadily sicker in Berlin, I received medical information about homeopathic alternatives to surgery, which strengthened my decision to maintain some control over my life for as long as possible. I believe that decision has prolonged my life, together with the loving energies of women who supported me in that decision and in the work which gives that life shape.

The struggle with cancer now informs all my days, but it is only another face of that continuing battle for self-determination and survival that Black women fight daily, often in triumph. The following excerpts are from journals kept during my first three years of living with cancer.

January 15, 1984
New York City

I've just returned from three days in Washington, D.C. It was an extraordinary reading. The second evening spent with the Sapphire Sapphos was like *2001 Space Odyssey* time—the past dreaming the future blooming real and tasty into the present, now. During our evening together, I felt the love and admiration of other Black women in a way I had not before—a web woven between us of the uses to which my work has been put.

The Sapphire Sapphos are a group of Lesbians of Color who had invited me to a special dinner at their regular monthly meeting. It was held at the Clubhouse, a cozy wooden building at the back of a city lot.

Coming in out of the D.C. winter storm felt like walking into an embrace. The roaring fireplace, the low-beamed wooden room filled with beautiful Black and Brown women, a table laden with delicious foods so obviously cooked with love. There was sweet potato pie, rice and red beans, black beans and rice, pigeon peas and rice, beans and pimentos, spaghetti with Swedish meatballs, codfish and ackee, spinach noodles with clam sauce, five-bean salad, fish salad, and other salads of different combinations.

On gaily decorated trays and platters, a profusion of carefully prepared dishes waited proudly: steamed fish and fried fish and fish pâté, cornbread and succulent collard greens, stir-fry vegetables with ginger and tree ears, startling and deliciously sensual. There was roti and almond bread, Jamaican harddough bread and sweet rolls, johnnycake and sourdough biscuits. And the punch! A cut-glass punchbowl filled with cassis and mineral water with a blessing of rum, fresh fruit floating seductively on top.

The whole spread reflected a dreamlike fullness of women sharing color and food and warmth and light—*Zami* come true. It filled me with pleasure that such a space could finally come to pass on an icy Tuesday evening in Washington, D.C., and I said so. Majote from Haiti looked exactly like Ginger, and we danced the night down.

January 19, 1984
New York City

I watched the movie *King* on TV tonight, and it brought those days of 1968 vividly back to me—the hope and the pain and the fury and the horror coming so close upon the possibility of change, a bare month after I'd left the Black student poets and my first meeting with Frances, at Tougaloo College in Mississippi. That night at Carnegie Hall when the Tougaloo Choir sang with Duke Ellington. A wealth of promise, of the student singers with their beautiful young Black faces, believing.

I was there to cover the concert for the Jackson, Mississippi, *Clarion Star Ledger*. "What the world needs now is love," they sang. Halfway through the song, the master of ceremonies interrupted to say that Dr. Martin Luther King had just been shot. "What the world needs now is love," they sang, tears lining their faces on stage catching the light, tears rolling down Mr. Honeywell's cheeks. "What the world needs now is love," they sang, his dark rhythmic arms directing the voices through all their weeping. And Dr. King is dead dead dead.

While I watched this movie I was also thinking about the course of my own life, the paths I feel bound for inside myself, the way of life that feels most real to me. And I wonder what I may be risking as I become more and more committed to telling whatever truth comes across my eyes my tongue my pen—no matter how difficult—the world as I see it, people as I feel them. And I wonder what I will have to pay someday for that privilege, and in whose coin? Will those forces which serve non-life in the name of power and profit kill me too, or merely dismember me in the eyes of whoever can use what I do?

When I stand in the radiance of a place like the Sapphire Sapphos dinner, with the elegant food and abundance of love and beautiful dark women, when I stand in that moment of sweetness, I sometimes become almost afraid. Afraid of their warmth and loving, as if that same loving warmth might doom me. I know this is not so, but it can feel like it. As if so long as I remained too different from my own time and surroundings I was safe, if terribly lonely. But now that I am becoming less lonely and more loved, I am also becoming more visible, and therefore more vulnerable. Malcolm saying to Martin in the film, "I love you, Martin, and we are both dead men."

February 9, 1984
New York City

So. No doubt about where we are in the world's story. It has just cost $32,000 to complete a government-commissioned study that purports to show there is no rampant hunger in the U.S.A. I wonder if they realize *rampant* means *aggressive*.

So. The starving old women who used to sit in broken-down rooming houses waiting for a welfare check now lie under park benches and eat out of garbage bins. "I only eat fruit," she mumbled, rummaging through the refuse bin behind Gristede's supermarket, while her gnarled Black hands carefully cut away the rotted parts of a cantaloupe with a plastic Burger King knife.

February 18, 1984
Ohio

How does it *feel*, Ms. L., to be a fifty-year-old Black woman who is still bleeding! Cheers to the years! Doing what I like to do best.

Last night I gave a talk to the Black students at the university about coming to see ourselves as part of an international community of people of Color, how we must train ourselves to question what our Blackness— our Africanness—can mean on the world stage. And how as members of that international community, we must assume responsibility for our actions, or lack of action, as americans. Otherwise, no matter how relative that power might be, we are yielding it up to the opposition to be used against us, and against the forces for liberation around the world. For instance, what are our responsibilities as educated Black women toward the land-rights struggles of other people of Color here and abroad?

I want to write down everything I know about being afraid, but I'd probably never have enough time to write anything else. Afraid is a country where they issue us passports at birth and hope we never seek citizenship in any other country. The face of afraid keeps changing constantly,

From *Sister Outsider* and *A Burst of Light*

and I can count on that change. I need to travel light and fast, and there's a lot of baggage I'm going to have to leave behind me. Jettison cargo.

February 19, 1984
New York City

Last night at Blanche and Clare's house was a celebration of my first fifty years. Liz Maybank called—such a wonderful gift to hear her voice across all these years since she helped care for my children. Black Women's Survival 101. I've had many teachers.

Forever is too long to think about. But the future has always been so real to me. Still is. Chances are I don't have liver cancer. No matter what they say. Chances are. That's good. That's bad. Either way I'm a hostage. So what's new?

Coming to terms with the sadness and the fury. And the curiosity.

March 18, 1984
En route to St. Croix, Virgin Islands

I've written nothing of the intensity with which I've lived the last few weeks. The hepatologist who tried to frighten me into an immediate liver biopsy without even listening to my objections and questions. Seeing the growth in my liver on the CAT scan, doing a face-off with death, again. Not again, just escalated. This mass in my liver is not a primary liver tumor, so if it is malignant, it's most likely metastasized breast cancer. Not curable. Arrestable, not curable. This is a very bad dream, and I'm the only person who can wake myself up. I had a talk before I left with Peter, my breast surgeon. He says that if it is liver cancer, with the standard treatments—surgery, radiation, and chemotherapy—we're talking four or five years at best. Without treatment, he says, maybe three or four.

In other words, western medicine doesn't have a very impressive track record with cancer metastasized to the liver.

In the light of those facts, and from all the reading I've been doing these past weeks (thank the goddess for Barnes & Noble's medical section), I've made up my mind not to have a liver biopsy. It feels like the only reasonable decision for me. I'm asymptomatic now except for a vicious gallbladder. And I can placate her. There are too many things I'm determined to do that I haven't done yet. Finish the poem "Outlines." See what europe's all about. Make Deotha Chambers' story live.

If I have this biopsy and it is malignant, then a whole course of action will be established simply by their intrusion into the suspect site. Yet if this tumor is malignant, I want as much good time as possible, and their treatments aren't going to make a hell of a lot of difference in terms of extended time. But they'll make a hell of a lot of difference in terms of my general condition and how I live my life.

On the other hand, if this is benign, I believe surgical intervention into fatty tissue of any kind can start the malignant process in what otherwise might remain benign for a long time. I've been down that road before.

I've decided this is a chance I have to take. If this were another breast tumor, I'd go for surgery again, because the organ comes off. But with the tie-in between estrogens, fat cells, and malignancies I've been reading about, cutting into my liver seems to me to be too much of a risk for too little return in terms of time. And it might be benign, some little aberrant joke between my liver and the universe.

Twenty-two hours of most days I don't believe I have liver cancer. Most days. Those other two hours of the day are pure hell, and there's so much work I have to do in my head in those two hours, too, through all the terror and uncertainties.

I wish I knew a doctor I could really trust to talk it all over with. Am I making the right decision? I know I have to listen to my body. If there's one thing I've learned from all the work I've done since my mastectomy, it's that I must listen keenly to the messages my body sends. But sometimes they are contradictory.

Dear goddess! Face-up again against the renewal of vows. Do not let me die a coward, mother. Nor forget how to sing. Nor forget song is a part of mourning as light is a part of sun.

March 22, 1984
En route to New York City

This was a good trip. Good connections with the Sojourner Sisters and other women in St. Croix. And I finally taught myself to relax in water, swimming about under the sun in Gloria's pool to the sound of Donna Summers blowing across the bright water, "State of Independence," and the coconut tree singing along in the gentle trade winds.

There was a poetry reading last night at the library, with a wide range of age and ability among the poets, but the audience was very responsive. It reminded me again of how important poetry can be in the life of an ordinary Black community when that poetry is really the poetry of the lives of the people who make up that community.

I suspect I shall have to concentrate upon how painful it is to think about death all the time.

[*In the spring of 1984, I spent three months in Berlin conducting a course in Black american women poets and a poetry workshop in English for German students. One of my aims for this trip was to meet Black German women. I'd been told there were quite a few in Berlin, but I had been unable to obtain much information about them in New York.*]

May 23, 1984
Berlin, West Germany

Who are they, the German women of the diaspora? Where do our paths intersect as women of Color—beyond the details of our particular oppressions, although certainly not outside the reference of those details? And where do our paths diverge? Most important, what can we learn from our connected differences that will be useful to us both, Afro-German and Afro-American?

Afro-German. The women say they've never heard that term used before.

I asked one of my Black students how she'd thought about herself growing up. "The nicest thing they ever called us was 'warbaby,'" she said. But the existence of most Black Germans has nothing to do with the Second World War, and, in fact, predates it by many decades. I have Black German women in my class who trace their Afro-German heritage back to the 1890s.

For me, Afro-German means the shining faces of Katharina and May in animated conversation about their fathers' homelands, the comparisons, joys, disappointments. It means my pleasure at seeing another

Black woman walk into my classroom, her reticence slowly giving way as she explores a new self-awareness, gains a new way of thinking about herself in relation to other Black women.

"I've never thought of Afro-German as a positive concept before," she said, speaking out of the pain of having to live a difference that has no name, speaking out of the growing power self-scrutiny has forged from that difference.

I am excited by these women, by their blossoming sense of identity as they're beginning to say in one way or another, "Let us be ourselves now as we define us. We are not a figment of your imagination or an exotic answer to your desires. We are not some button on the pocket of your longing." I can see these women as a growing force for international change, in concert with other Afro-Europeans, Afro-Asians, Afro-Americans.

We are the hyphenated people of the diaspora whose self-defined identities are no longer shameful secrets in the countries of our origin, but rather declarations of strength and solidarity. We are an increasingly united front from which the world has not yet heard.

June 1, 1984
Berlin

My classes are exciting and exhausting. Black women are hearing about them and their number is increasing.

I can't eat cooked food and I am getting sicker. My liver is so swollen I can feel it under my ribs. I've lost almost fifty pounds. That's a switch, worrying about losing weight. My friend Dagmar, who teaches here, has given me the name of a homeopathic doctor specializing in the treatment of cancer, and I've made an appointment to see her when I come back from the feminist book fair in London next week. She's an anthroposophic doctor, and they believe in surgery only as a last resort.

In spite of all this, I'm doing good work here. I'm certainly enjoying life in Berlin, sick or not. The city itself is very different from what I'd expected. It is lively and beautiful, but its past is never very far away, at least not for me. The silence about Jews is absolutely deafening, chilling. There is only one memorial in the whole city and it is to the Resistance.

At the entrance is a huge grey urn with the sign, "This urn contains earth from German concentration camps." It is such a euphemistic evasion of responsibility and an invitation to amnesia for the children that it's no wonder my students act like Nazism was a bad dream not to be remembered.

There is a lot of networking going on here among women, collectives, and work enterprises as well as political initiatives, and a very active women's cultural scene. I may be too thin, but I can still dance!

June 7, 1984
Berlin

Dr. Rosenberg agrees with my decision not to have a biopsy, but she has said I must do something quickly to strengthen my bodily defenses. She's recommended I begin Iscador injections three times weekly.

Iscador is a biological made from mistletoe which strengthens the natural immune system, and works against the growth of malignant cells. I've started the injections, along with two other herbals that stimulate liver function. I feel less weak.

I am listening to what fear teaches. I will never be gone. I am a scar, a report from the front lines, a talisman, a resurrection. A rough place on the chin of complacency. "What are you getting so upset about, anyway?" a student asked in class. "You're not Jewish!"

So what if I am afraid? Of stepping out into the morning? Of dying? Of unleashing the damned gall where hatred swims like a tadpole waiting to swell into the arms of war? And what does that war teach when the bruised leavings jump an insurmountable wall where the glorious Berlin chestnuts and orange poppies hide detection wires that spray bullets which kill?

My poems are filled with blood these days because the future is so bloody. When the blood of four-year-old children runs unremarked through the alleys of Soweto, how can I pretend that sweetness is anything more than armor and ammunition in an ongoing war?

I am saving my life by using my life in the service of what must be done. Tonight as I listened to the ANC speakers from South Africa at the Third World People's Center here, I was filled with a sense of self answering necessity, of commitment as a survival weapon. Our battles are inseparable. Every person I have ever been must be actively enlisted in those battles, as well as in the battle to save my life.

June 9, 1984
Berlin

At the poetry reading in Zurich this weekend, I found it so much easier to discuss racism than to talk about *The Cancer Journals*. Chemical plants between Zurich and Basel have been implicated in a definite rise in breast cancer in this region, and women wanted to discuss this. I talked as honestly as I could, but it was really hard. Their questions presume a clarity I no longer have.

It was great to have Gloria there to help field all those questions about racism. For the first time in europe, I felt I was not alone but answering as one of a group of Black women—not just Audre Lorde!

I am cultivating every iota of my energies to do battle with the possibility of liver cancer. At the same time, I am discovering how furious and resistant some pieces of me are, as well as how terrified.

In this loneliest of places, I examine every decision I make within the light of what I've learned about myself and that self-destructiveness implanted inside of me by racism and sexism and the circumstances of my life as a Black woman.

Mother why were we armed to fight
with cloud wreathed swords and javelins of dust?

Survival isn't some theory operating in a vacuum. It's a matter of my everyday living and making decisions.

How do I hold faith with sun in a sunless place? It is so hard not to counter this despair with a refusal to see. But I have to stay open and filtering no matter what's coming at me, because that arms me in a particularly Black woman's way. When I'm open, I'm also less despairing. The more clearly I see what I'm up against, the more able I am to fight this process going on in my body that they're calling liver cancer. And I am determined to fight it even when I am not sure of the terms of the battle nor the face of victory. I just know I must not surrender my body

From *Sister Outsider* and *A Burst of Light*

to others unless I completely understand and agree with what they think should be done to it. I've got to look at all of my options carefully, even the ones I find distasteful. I know I can broaden the definition of winning to the point where I can't lose.

June 10, 1984
Berlin

Dr. Rosenberg is honest, straightforward, and pretty discouraging. I don't know what I'd do without Dagmar there to translate all her grim pronouncements for me. She thinks it's liver cancer, too, but she respects my decision against surgery. I mustn't let my unwillingness to accept this diagnosis interfere with getting help. Whatever it is, this seems to be working.

We all have to die at least once. Making that death useful would be winning for me. I wasn't supposed to exist anyway, not in any meaningful way in this fucked-up whiteboys' world. I want desperately to live, and I'm ready to fight for that living even if I die shortly. Just writing those words down snaps everything I want to do into a neon clarity. This european trip and the Afro-German women, the Sister Outsider collective in Holland, Gloria's great idea of starting an organization that can be a connection between us and South African women. For the first time I really feel that my writing has a substance and stature that will survive me.

I have done good work. I see it in the letters that come to me about *Sister Outsider*, I see it in the use the women here give the poetry and the prose. But first and last I am a poet. I've worked very hard for that approach to living inside myself, and everything I do, I hope, reflects that view of life, even the ways I must move now in order to save my life.

I have done good work. There is a hell of a lot more I have to do. And sitting here tonight in this lovely green park in Berlin, dusk approaching and the walking willows leaning over the edge of the pool caressing each other's fingers, birds birds birds singing under and over the frogs, and the smell of new-mown grass enveloping my sad pen, I feel I still have enough moxie to do it all, on whatever terms I'm dealt, timely or not. Enough moxie to chew the whole world up and spit it out in bite-sized pieces, useful and warm and wet and delectable because they came out of my mouth.

June 17, 1984
Berlin

I am feeling more like an Audre I recognize, thank the goddess for Dr. Rosenberg, and for Dagmar for introducing me to her.

I've been reading Christa Wolf's *The Search for Christa T.*, and finding it very difficult. At first I couldn't grapple with it because it was just too painful to read about a woman dying. Dagmar and a number of the women here in Berlin say the author and I should meet. But now that I'm finished I don't know if I want to meet the woman who wrote it. There is so much pain there that is so far from being felt in any way I recognize or can use, that it makes me very uncomfortable. I feel speechless.

But there is one part of the book that really spoke to me. In chapter 5, she talks about a mistaken urge to laugh at one's younger self's belief in paradise, in miracles. Each one of us who survives, she says, at least once in our lifetime, at some crucial and inescapable moment, has had to absolutely believe in the impossible. Of course, it occurs to me to ask myself if that's what I'm doing right now, believing in the impossible by refusing a biopsy.

It's been very reassuring to find a medical doctor who agrees with my view of the dangers involved. And I certainly don't reject nondamaging treatment, which is why I'm taking these shots, even though I hate giving myself injections. But that's a small price balanced against the possibility of cancer.

June 20, 1984
Berlin

I didn't go to London because I loved bookfairs, but because the idea of the First International Feminist Bookfair excited me, and in particular, I wanted to make contact with the Black feminists of England. Well, the fact remains: the First International Feminist Bookfair was a monstrosity of racism, and this racism coated and distorted much of what was good, creative, and visionary about such a fair. The white women organizers'

From *Sister Outsider* and *A Burst of Light*

defensiveness to any question of where the Black women were is rooted in that tiresome white guilt that serves neither us nor them. It reminded me of those old tacky battles of the seventies in the States: a Black woman would suggest that if white women wished to be truly feminist, they would have to examine and alter some of their actions vis-à-vis women of Color. And this discussion would immediately be perceived as an attack upon their very essence. So wasteful and destructive.

I think the organizers of the bookfair really believed that by inviting foreign Black women they were absolving themselves of any fault in ignoring input from local Black women. But we should be able to learn from our errors. They totally objectified *all* Black women by not dealing with the Black women of the London community. Now if anything is to be learned from that whole experience, it should be so that the *next* International Feminist Bookfair does not repeat those errors. And there must be another. But we don't get *there* from *here* by ignoring the mud in between those two positions. If the white women's movement does not learn from its errors, like any other movement, it will die by them. When I stood up for my first reading to a packed house with no Black women's faces, after I'd gotten letter after letter from Black British women asking when was I coming to England, that was the kiss-off. I knew immediately what was up, and the rest is history.

Of course, I was accused of "brutalizing" the organizers by simply asking why Black women were absent. And if my yelling and "jumping up and down" got dirty looks and made white women cry and say all kinds of outrageous nonsense about me, I know it also reinforced other Black women's perceptions about racism here in the women's movement, and contributed to further solidarity among Black women of different communities.

Feminism must be on the cutting edge of real social change if it is to survive as a movement in any particular country. Whatever the core problems are for the people of that country must also be the core problems addressed by women, for we do not exist in a vacuum. We are anchored in our own place and time, looking out and beyond to the future we are creating, and we are part of communities that interact. To pretend otherwise is ridiculous. While we fortify ourselves with visions of the future, we must arm ourselves with accurate perceptions of the barriers between us and that future.

June 21, 1984
Berlin

Rather than siphoning off energies in vain attempts to connect with women who refuse to deal with their own history or ours, Black women need to choose the areas where that energy can be most effective. Who are we? What are the ways in which we do not see each other? And how can we better operate together as a united front even while we explore our differences? Rather than keep yelling at white women's gates, we need to look at our own needs and start giving top priority to satisfying those needs in the service of our joint tasks. How do we deal across our differences of community, time, place, and history? In other words, how do we learn to love each other while we are embattled on so many fronts? I hope for an International Conference of Black Feminists, asking some of these questions of definition of women from Amsterdam, Melbourne, the South Pacific, Kentucky, New York, and London, all of whom call ourselves Black feminists and all of whom have different strengths.

To paraphrase June Jordan, we are the women we want to become.

August 1, 1984
New York City

Saints be praised! The new CAT scan is unchanged. The tumor has not grown, which means either Iscador is working or the tumor is not malignant! I feel relieved, vindicated, and hopeful. The pain in my middle is gone, as long as I don't eat very much and stick to fruits and veggies. That's livable. I feel like a second chance, for true! I'm making myself a new office upstairs in Jonathan's old room. It's going to be a good year.

October 10, 1984
New York City

I've been thinking about my time in Germany again, unencumbered by artificial shades of terror and self-concern. I don't want my involvement with health matters to obscure the revelation of differences I encountered.

The Afro-European women. What I learned about the differences when one teaches about feeling and poetry in a language that is not the original language of the people learning, even when they speak that language fluently. (Of course, all poets learn about feeling as children in our native tongue, and the psychosocial strictures and emotional biases of that language pass over into how we think about feeling for the rest of our lives.) I will never forget the emotional impact of Raja's poetry, and how what she is doing with the German language is so close to what Black poets here are doing with English. It was another example of how our Africanness impacts upon the world's consciousness in intersecting ways.

As an African-American woman, I feel the tragedy of being an oppressed hyphenated person in america, of having no land to be our primary teacher. And this distorts us in so many ways. Yet there is a vital part that we play as Black people in the liberation consciousness of every freedom-seeking people upon this globe, no matter what they say they think about us as Black americans. And whatever our differences are that make for difficulty in communication between us and other oppressed peoples, as Afro-Americans we must recognize the promise we represent for some new social synthesis that the world has not yet experienced. I think of the Afro-Dutch, Afro-German, Afro-French women I met this spring in europe, and how they are beginning to recognize each other and come together openly in terms of their identities, and I see that they are also beginning to cut a distinct shape across the cultural face of every country where they are at home.

I am thinking about issues of color as color, Black as a chromatic fact, gradations and all. There is the reality of defining Black as a geographical fact of culture and heritage emanating from the continent of Africa—Black meaning Africans and other members of a diaspora, with or without color.

Then there is a quite different reality of defining Black as a political position, acknowledging that color is the bottom line the world over, no matter how many other issues exist alongside it. Within this definition, Black becomes a codeword, a rallying identity for all oppressed people of Color. And this position reflects the empowerment and the worldwide militant legacy of our Black Revolution of the 1960s, the effects of which are sometimes more obvious in other countries than in our own.

I see certain pitfalls in defining Black as a political position. It takes the cultural identity of a widespread but definite group and makes it a generic identity for many culturally diverse peoples, all on the basis of a shared oppression. This runs the risk of providing a convenient blanket of apparent similarity under which our actual and unaccepted differences can be distorted or misused. This blanket would diminish our chances of forming genuine working coalitions built upon the recognition and creative use of acknowledged difference, rather than upon the shaky foundations of a false sense of similarity. When a Javanese Dutch woman says she is Black, she also knows she goes home to another cultural reality that is particular to her people and precious to her—it is Asian, and Javanese. When an African-American woman says she is Black, she is speaking of her cultural reality, no matter how modified it may be by time, place, or circumstances of removal. Yet even the Maori women of New Zealand and the Aboriginal women of Australia call themselves Black. There must be a way for us to deal with this, if only on the level of language. For example, those of us for whom Black is our cultural reality relinquishing the word in favor of some other designation of the African diaspora, perhaps simply *African.*

[*The first half of 1985 spins past: a trip to Cuba with a group of Black women writers, a reading tour through the Midwest, the great workspace I created from my son's old room, the beginning of a new collection of poems, my daughter's graduation from college. My general health seemed stable, if somewhat delicate. I removed the question of cancer from my consciousness beyond my regular Iscador treatments, my meager diet, and my lessened energies. In August and September I spent six weeks traveling and giving poetry readings in Australia and New Zealand, a guest of women's groups at various community organizations and universities. It was an exciting and exhausting time, one where thoughts about cancer were constant but never central.*]

May 28, 1985
Cambridge, Massachusetts

My daughter Beth's graduation from Harvard this weekend was a rite of passage for both of us. This institution takes itself very seriously, and there was enormous pomp and circumstance for three days. I couldn't help but think of all the racist, sexist ways they've tried through the last four years to diminish and destroy the essence of all the young Black women enrolled here. But it was a very important moment for Beth, a triumph that she'd survived Harvard, that she'd made it out, intact, and in a self she can continue living with. Of course, the point of so much of what goes on at places like Harvard—supposed to be about learning—is actually geared to either destroying these young people, or altering their substance into effigies that will be pliant, acceptable, and nonproblematic to the system. So I was proud of Beth standing there in the manicured garden of Adams House, wearing her broad white Disinvestment banner across her black commencement gown, but I was also very scared for her. Out there can be even more difficult, although now she knows at least that she can and did survive Harvard. And with her own style unimpaired.

I embarrassed myself because I kept trying to find secret places to cry in, but it was still a very emotionally fulfilling occasion. I feel she's on her way now in a specific sense that must leave me behind, and that is both sad and very reassuring to me. I am convinced that Beth has the stuff—the emotional and psychic wherewithal to do whatever she needs to do for her living, and I have given her the best I have to offer. I remember writing "What My Child Learns of the Sea" when she was three months old, and it's both terrifying and wonderful to see it all coming true. I bless the goddess that I am still here to see it.

I tremble for her, for them all, because of the world we are giving them and all the work still to be done, and the gnawing question of will there be enough time? But I celebrate her, too, another one of those fine, strong, young Black women moving out to war, outrageous and resilient, plucky and beautiful.

I'm proud of her, and I'm proud of having seen her this far. It's a relief for me to know that whatever happens with my health now, and no matter how short my life may be, she is essentially on her way in the world, and next year Jonathan will be stepping out with his fine self, too. I look at them and they make my heart sing. Frances and I have done good work.

August 10, 1985
Melbourne, Australia

A group of white Australian women writers invited me to give the keynote address on "The Language of Difference" at a women's writing conference held in Melbourne as part of the 150-year celebration of the founding of the state of Victoria. These are my remarks:

> I am here upon your invitation, a Black African-American woman speaking of the language of difference. We come together in this place on the 150th anniversary of the state of Victoria, an Australian state built upon racism, destruction, and a borrowed sameness. We were never meant to speak together at all. I have struggled for many weeks to find your part in me, to see what we could share that would have meaning for us all. When language becomes most similar, it becomes most dangerous, for then differences may pass unremarked. As women of good faith we can only become familiar with the language of difference within a determined commitment to its use within our lives, without romanticism and without guilt. Because we share a common language which is not of our own making and which does not reflect our deeper knowledge as women, our words frequently sound the same. But it is an error to believe that we mean the same experience, the same commitment, the same future, unless we agree to examine the history and particular passions that lie beneath each other's words.
>
> When I say I am Black, I mean I am of African descent. When I say I am a woman of Color, I mean I recognize common cause with American Indian, Chicana, Latina, and Asian-American sisters of North America. I also mean I share common cause with women of Eritrea who spend most of each day searching for enough water for their children, as well as with Black South African women who bury 50 percent of their children before they reach the age of five. And I also share cause with my Black sisters of Australia, the Aboriginal women of this land who were raped of their history and their children and their culture by a genocidal conquest in whose recognition we are gathered here today.

From *Sister Outsider* and *A Burst of Light*

I have reached down deep inside of me to find what it was we could share, and it has been very difficult, because I find my tongue weighted down by the blood of my Aboriginal sisters that has been shed upon this earth. For the true language of difference is yet to be spoken in this place. Here that language must be spoken by my Aboriginal sisters, the daughters of those indigenous peoples of Australia with whom each one of you shares a destiny, but whose voices and language most of you here have never heard.

One hundred and fifty years ago, when the state of Victoria was declared a reality for european settlers, there were still 15,000 Black Aboriginal people living on this land that is now called Victoria. Where we sit now today, Wurundjeri women once dreamed and laughed and sang. They nurtured this earth, gum tree and wattle, and they were nurtured by it. I do not see their daughters sitting here among you today. Where are these women?

Their mothers' blood cries out to me. Their daughters come to my dreams nightly in the Windsor Hotel across the street from your Parliament. And their voices are haunting and brave and sad. Do you hear them? Listen very carefully, with your hearts open. They are speaking. Out of their mouths come what you have said you most want to hear.

Their history is my history. While white immigrant settlers in Australia were feeding Wurundjeri women and children bread made from arsenic and flour, white immigrant settlers in North America were selling seven-year-old African girls for $35 a head. And these same white immigrant settlers were giving blankets lethal with smallpox germs to the indigenous peoples of North America, the American Indians.

Each of you has come here today to touch some piece of your own power, for a purpose. I urge you to approach that work with a particular focus and urgency, for a terrible amount of Wurundjeri women's blood has already been shed in order for you to sit and write here.

I do not say these things to instigate an orgy of guilt, but rather to encourage an examination of what the excavation and use of the true language of difference can mean within your living. You and I can talk about the language of difference, but that will always remain essentially a safe discussion, because this is not my place. I will move on. But it is the language of the Black Aboriginal women of this country that you must learn to hear and to feel. And as your writing and your lives intersect within that language, you will come to decide what mistress your art must serve.

October 24, 1985
East Lansing, Michigan

Tomorrow is the second anniversary of the invasion of Grenada. The smallest nation in the western hemisphere occupied by the largest. I spoke about it to a group of Black women here tonight. It's depressing to see how few of us remember, how few of us still seem to care.

The conference on "The Black Woman Writer and the Diaspora" being held here is problematic in some ways, particularly in the unclear position of Ellen Kuzwayo, who had come all the way from South Africa to give the keynote address and arrived here to find the schedule shifted. But it was so good to see Ellen again. I'm sorry to hear her sister in Botswana has had another mastectomy.

It's been very exciting to sit down with African and Caribbean women writers whom I've always wanted to meet. Octavia Butler is here also, and Andrea Canaan from New Orleans. I haven't seen her in over a year, and the look in her eyes when she saw me made me really angry, but it also made me realize how much weight I've lost in the past year and how bad my color's been since I came home from Australia. I've got to go see Dr. C. for a checkup when I get home.

October 25, 1985
East Lansing

I gave a brief talk tonight on "Sisterhood and Survival," what it means to me. And first off I identified myself as a Black Feminist Lesbian poet, although it felt unsafe, which is probably why I had to do it. I explained that I identified myself as such because if there was one other Black

Feminist Lesbian poet in isolation somewhere within the reach of my voice, I wanted her to know she was not alone. I think a lot about Angelina Weld Grimké, a Black Lesbian poet of the Harlem Renaissance who is never identified as such, when she is mentioned at all, although the work of Gloria Hull and Erlene Stetson recently has focused renewed attention upon her. But I never even knew her name when I was going to school, and later, she was the briefest of mentions in a list of "other" Harlem Renaissance writers.

I often think of Angelina Weld Grimké dying alone in an apartment in New York City in 1958 while I was a young Black Lesbian struggling in isolation at Hunter College, and I think of what it could have meant in terms of sisterhood and survival for each one of us to have known of the other's existence: for me to have had her words and her wisdom, and for her to have known I needed them! It is so crucial for each one of us to know she is not alone. I've been traveling a lot in the last two years since my children are grown, and I've been learning what an enormous amount I don't know as a Black american woman. And wherever I go, it's been so heartening to see women of Color reclaiming our lands, our heritages, our cultures, our selves—usually in the face of enormous odds.

For me as an African-American woman writer, sisterhood and survival means it's not enough to say I believe in peace when my sisters' children are dying in the streets of Soweto and New Caledonia in the South Pacific. Closer to home, what are we as Black women saying to our sons and our nephews and our students as they are, even now, being herded into the military by unemployment and despair, someday to become meat in the battles to occupy the lands of other people of Color?

How can we ever, ever forget the faces of those young Black american soldiers, their gleaming bayonets drawn, staking out a wooden shack in the hills of Grenada? What is our real work as Black women writers of the diaspora? Our responsibilities to other Black women and their children across this globe we share, struggling for our joint future? And what if our sons are someday ordered into Namibia, or Southwest Africa, or Zimbabwe, or Angola?

Where does our power lie and how do we school ourselves to use it in the service of what we believe?

Sitting with Black women from all over the earth has made me think a great deal about what it means to be indigenous, and what my relationship as a Black woman in North America is to the land-rights struggles of the indigenous peoples of this land, to Native American Indian women, and how we can translate that consciousness into a new level of working together. In other words, how can we use each other's differences in our common battles for a livable future?

All of our children are prey. How do we raise them not to prey upon themselves and each other? And this is why we cannot be silent, because our silences will come to testify against us out of the mouths of our children.

November 21, 1985
New York City

It feels like the axe is falling. There it is on the new CAT scan—another mass growing in my liver, and the first one is spreading. I've found an anthroposophic doctor in Spring Valley who suggests I go to the Lukas Klinik, a hospital in Switzerland where they are conducting the primary research on Iscador, as well as diagnosing and treating cancers.

I've known something is wrong from the returning pains and the dimming energies of my body. My classes have been difficult, and most days I feel like I'm going on sheer will power alone which can be very freeing and seductive but also very dangerous. Limited. I'm running down. But I'd do exactly what I'm doing anyway, cancer or no cancer.

A. will lend us the money to go to Switzerland, and Frances will come with me. I think they will be able to find out what is really wrong with me at the Lukas Klinik, and if they say these growths in my liver are malignant, then I will accept that I have cancer of the liver. At least there they will be able to adjust my Iscador dosage upward to the maximum effect, because that is the way I have decided to go and I'm not going to change now. Obviously, I still don't accept these tumors in my liver as cancer, although I know that could just be denial on my part, which is certainly one mechanism for coping with cancer. I have to consider denial as a possibility in all of my planning, but I also feel that there is absolutely nothing they can do for me at Sloane [sic] Kettering except cut me open and then sew me back up with their condemnations inside me.

From *Sister Outsider* and *A Burst of Light*

December 7, 1985
New York City

My stomach x-rays are clear, and the problems in my GI series are all circumstantial. Now that the doctors here have decided I have liver cancer, they insist on reading all their findings as if that were a fait accompli. They refuse to look for any other reason for the irregularities in the x-rays, and they're treating my resistance to their diagnosis as a personal affront. But it's my body and my life and the goddess knows I'm paying enough for all this, I ought to have a say.

The flame is very dim these days. It's all I can do to teach my classes at Hunter and crawl home. Frances and I will leave for Switzerland as soon as school is over next week. The Women's Poetry Center will be dedicated at Hunter the night before I leave. No matter how sick I feel, I'm still afire with a need to do something for my living. How will I be allowed to live my own life, the rest of my life?

December 9, 1985
New York City

A better question is—how do I want to live the rest of my life and what am I going to do to insure that I get to do it exactly or as close as possible to how I want that living to be?

I want to live the rest of my life, however long or short, with as much sweetness as I can decently manage, loving all the people I love, and doing as much as I can of the work I still have to do. I am going to write fire until it comes out my ears, my eyes, my noseholes—everywhere. Until it's every breath I breathe. I'm going to go out like a fucking meteor!

December 13, 1985
New York City

There are some occasions in life too special to dissect, not only because they are everything they are supposed to be, but because they are also a sum of unexpected fantasies and deep satisfactions all come together at one point in time. Tonight the students of the Hunter College Women's Poetry Center Club and the *Returning Woman Newsletter* dedicated the Audre Lorde Women's Poetry Center. Walking into that hall, even thirty minutes late, was the beginning of exactly that kind of evening, and nothing I nor anyone else will ever do can lessen its meaning for me. Whatever happens to me, there has been a coming together in time and space of some of my best efforts, hopes, and desires. There is a tangible possibility to be built upon and strong young women committed to doing it. I wish them the power of their vision for what this center can be in their lives and in the life of a community of women's culture in this city, the vision of a living women's poetry as a force for social change. This evening brought together four of my deepest and longest-lasting interests—poetry, beautiful women, revolution, and me!

No matter what I find out in Switzerland, no matter what's going on in my body, this is my work. The recognition of it, the sweet strength and love in the faces tonight make me know how much what I do has meant to these women who are arming themselves to walk in places I've only dreamed of, and in their own step and as their own mistresses.

I listened tonight to these young poets, particularly the women of Color, reading their work, and it was wonderful for me to know that the real power of my words is not the pieces of me that reside within those words, but the life force—the energy and aspirations and desires at the complex core of each one of these women—which has been aroused to use and to answer my words. Gloria, Johnnetta, and I—three of the founding mothers of the Sisterhood in Support of Sisters in South Africa—within that precious space where we sit down together in my intricate life. The young poets shining like goldfire in the sun, their many-colored faces awash with pride and determination and love. Beth and Yolanda, daughter and old friend, my words coming out of their mouths illuminated exactly by who they are themselves, so different from each other and from me. The revelation of hearing my work translated through the beings of these women I love so dearly. Frances, smiling like a sunflower and really there; my sister Helen looking pleased and a part of it all; and Mabel Hampton, tough and snappy and hanging in, all eighty-three years of her! Charlotte's' generous perfume, and

* Ex-slave who led a workers' revolt in St. Croix in 1848.

I remember the sureness in her voice once, saying, "Well, we did what we had to do, and I think we changed the world!" Alexis[**] and her twinkling eyes, Clare's[†] warm graciousness. And Blanchie,[††] resplendent and cheeky in her tuxedo, orchestrating it all with her particular special flair, mistress of ceremonies to quite a party!

December 15, 1985
Arlesheim, Switzerland

So here I am at the Lukas Klinik while my body decides if it will live or die. I'm going to fight like hell to make it live, and this looks like the most promising possibility. At least it's something different from narcotics and other terminal aids, which is all Dr. C. had to offer me in New York City in lieu of surgery when I told her how badly I hurt in my middle. "Almost everything I eat now makes me sick," I told her. "Yes, I know," she said sorrowfully, writing me a prescription for codeine and looking at me as if there was nothing left she could do for me besides commiserate. Even though I like her very much, I wanted to punch her in her mouth.

I have found something interesting in a book here on active meditation as a form of self-control. There are six steps:

1. Control of Thought
   Think of a small object (i.e., a paper clip) for five minutes, exclusively. Practice for a month.
2. Control of Action
   Perform a small act every day at the same time. Practice, and be patient.
3. Control of Feeling (equanimity)
   Become aware of feelings and introduce equanimity into experiencing them—i.e., be afraid, not panic-stricken.
   (They're big on this one around here.)

[**] Alexis De Veaux, poet and biographer.
[†] Clare Cross, playwright, psychotherapist, and partner of Blanche Cook.
[††] Blanche Cook, classmate of Lorde at Hunter College, historian, and partner of Clare Cross.

4. Positivity (tolerance)
   Refrain from critical downgrading thoughts that sap energy
   from good work.
5. Openness (receptivity)
   Perceive even what is unpleasant in an unfettered, non-
   prejudiced way.
6. Harmony (perseverance)
   Work toward balancing the other five.

As a living creature I am part of two kinds of forces—growth and decay,
sprouting and withering, living and dying—and at any given moment
of our lives, each one of us is actively located somewhere along a con-
tinuum between these two forces.

December 16, 1985
Arlesheim

I brought some of my books with me, and reading *The Cancer Journals*
in this place is like excavating words out of the earth, like turning up
a crystal that has been buried at the bottom of a mine for a thousand
years, waiting. Even *Our Dead Behind Us*—now that it has gone to the
printer—seems prophetic. Like always, it feels like I plant what I will
need to harvest, without consciousness.

This is why the work is so important. Its power doesn't lie in the me
that lives in the words so much as in the heart's blood pumping behind
the eye that is reading, the muscle behind the desire that is sparked
by the word—hope as a living state that propels us, open-eyed and fear-
ful, into all [of] the battles of our lives. And some of those battles we do
not win.

But some of them we do.

December 17, 1985
Arlesheim

When I read in Basel last June, I never imagined I would be here again,
four miles away, in a hospital. I remember the women in the bookstore
that night, and their questions about survival rates that I could not answer then. And certainly not now.

Even in the bleak Swiss winter, the grounds of the Lukas Klinik are very beautiful. Much care has been given by the builders to the different shades of winter scenery, so there is a play of light and dark that hits the eye from the room's windows as well as from the beds. My private room is good-sized, spacious by american hospital standards. It is one of the few single rooms with a private bath, and they are usually for very sick or very rich people. I think the administration was not sure which category I fit into when I called from New York.

Even when it is not sunny, the room is light because everything in it is light. Not white, except for the bedsheets, but very light. Even the furniture is solid hand-hewn blond wood, made in one of the sheltered workshops run in conjunction with an anthroposophic school for developmentally handicapped people. The Rudolf Steiner schools have had great success in the area of special education.

There is a deep serenity here, relaxing and sometimes uncomfortable. The adjustable hospital bed is covered with a voluptuous down comforter under which a hot-water bottle had been slipped the first night I arrived. And six red rosebuds in a cut-glass vase. On the other side of the bedside table is an easy chair, and then a wide window and a glass door opening onto terraces that run the length of each of the tiered three stories of the building. The tiers provide plenty of sunlight on each floor. There are opaque dividers for privacy between the doors leading onto the terrace, and then a common strollway open to the sky.

Beneath the terraces is a carefully tended european garden, sculptured stone steps cut into one side winding back and forth through the low bushes and plantings throughout the grounds. In the grassy clearing in front of the terraces stands a red granite statue of a robed person with what I have come to think of as the Steiner look, blunt and massive, one arm upraised in the eurhythmic position for the vowel *i* which is considered in all languages to be the sound representing the affirmation of self in living. On a slight knoll, the statue is silhouetted against the green trees or the leaden sky.

At the foot of the statue and to one side is a large oval whirlpool fountain of red granite also, its perennial gurgle of softly flowing water a soothing counterpoint whenever the terrace door is opened, or when walking through the grounds.

A quite lovely pastel painting of a sunrise hangs on one wall of the room, executed according to the Rudolf Steiner theory of color and healing. It is the only wall decoration in the room, whose walls are painted a sunny yellow and peach.

Most of the patients are middle-aged Swiss and Germans, with two French women and myself. We all wear our own clothes. There is a large sitting room that contains a library, and a chapel, of course, and appropriate Steiner reading materials [are] always available.

Everyone who works with patients gives off a similar affect: it is calm, kind, and helpful, but also completely dogmatic. Staff, patients, and visitors eat lunch and dinner together in a spacious, well-draped but sunny dining room with real linens and individualized embroidered napkins. We are seated at tables holding six to ten diners, amid signs of the zodiac and planets sculpted from various kinds of european bedrock, also done in the Steiner artistic tradition of massive, solid lines.

Meals are a real chore for me, since it is difficult for me to eat anyway and I loathe eating around strangers. The feeling in the dining room is genteel, cultivated, and totally formal.

I take a one-and-a-half-hour class daily in curative eurhythmy with a tiny East Indian woman named Dilnawaz who was raised in Rudolf Steiner schools in India, trained in Germany, and speaks fluent English and German as well as her native tongue.

Eurhythmy is a combination of sustained rhythmical body movements and controlled breathing, based upon vowel and consonant sounds. As I learn and practice the stylized movements, they remind me of tai chi and feel like a complement to the Simonton visualization work I've been doing for a while. My body feels relaxed and good after eurhythmy, and my mind, too.

There is a part of me that wants to dismiss everything here other than Iscador as irrelevant or at least not useful to me, even before I try it, but I think that is very narrow and counterproductive and I don't want to do it. At least not without first giving myself fully to it, because that is why I came all this way and what do I have to lose at this point? Dilnawaz stresses that the treatment of any disease, and of cancer in particular, must be all of a piece, body and mind, and I am ready to try anything so long as they don't come at me with a knife.

Dilnawaz is the most human, the most friendly, and the most real person I've met here, as well as the most spiritual. She is also the most lonely. She is very friendly and helpful toward everyone, and people respond to her with considerable respect, but there is still an air of isolation about her that says to me she is not quite a part. She lives alone in Arlesheim town, and her sister is coming from Germany to spend Christmas with her.

I wonder how she feels as a woman of Color among all these white ethnocentric Swiss. She is very cautious about what she says, but she does talk of how reluctant most northern europeans are to give themselves to eurhythmy. I find her a touch of emotional color within a scene of extraordinary blandness.

Dilnawaz seems to be relieved to see me, too. I think she knows I have a deep respect for the spiritual aspect of our lives and its power over us. That is something most of the rationalists here do not have, despite their adherence to Steiner's anthroposophy. It seems they can only deal with spirituality if it comes with rigid rules imposed from the outside, i.e., Steiner, with his insistence upon the basic rule of a Christian god. It is limiting.

I take a class in painting and color theory according to Steiner. Afterward, an oil dispersion bath which alternates with a massage (also according to Steiner), then lunch, a hot yarrow liver poultice, and a two-hour rest period. Then I am free until dinner, unless there are medical consultations or tests. This is when Frances and I get to see each other privately for a while.

There are about fifty patients here right now, and about fifteen doctors, as well as some visiting doctors and medical trainees from different countries. The calm directness with which everyone seems to deal with the idea and reality of disease is quite unlike anything I've experienced in hospitals in the U.S., given that all the patients here either have cancer or are suspected of having cancer. At its best, the effect of this directness is very calming and reassuring, very centering. At its worst, it feels like

Mann's *Magic Mountain*. Because at the same time, nobody believes in talking about feelings, even the strong expression of which is considered to be harmful, or at least too stressful to be beneficial.

In the private room next door to me, there is a pretty young Swiss woman of no more than twenty, with a gold wedding band on and very expensive clothes and too much make-up. She appears terribly depressed all the time. Evidently she goes to church in town every morning, because I see her passing through the grounds early each day wearing a church cap. Her family seems very rich or very influential. They came to visit yesterday, and I saw them in the dining room—mother, father, and a young man who was either brother or husband. They sure looked rich, and everyone here bowed and scraped to them. (The social hierarchy is quite strongly observed.) It seems to me that anyone that young who has cancer must be filled with rage and should at least be able to talk about her feelings with someone. But that's not considered necessary or beneficial here.

There is an elderly woman schoolteacher from Hamburg who wears a beautifully carved rhodonite necklace to lunch every day. We have had an interesting conversation about rocks and minerals, which are considered to be very important and powerful in anthroposophy. She speaks English quite well and tries to be friendly. She has been an anthroposoph for many years, she says, and this is her second stay at the Klinik.

The most frequent question from English-speaking patients and medical trainees, couched in different ways, is: how does an american—and a Black one at that, although the latter is only inferred because everyone here is much too well-bred and polite to ever let on they notice, although Sister Maria did tell me yesterday that her brother is a missionary in South Africa so she understands why I like to eat raw vegetables—how does an american come to be at the Lukas Klinik in Switzerland? americans are known for being quite provincial.

One of the cardinal rules here is that we do not talk about our illness at mealtimes or at any social gathering, so everyone is very polite and small-talky and banal, because of course we are all preoccupied with our bodies and the processes going on within them or else we wouldn't be here. I don't know what makes the anthroposophs think this sort of false socializing is not more stressful than expressing real feelings, but I find it terribly wearing. Mercifully, I can usually retreat behind the language barrier.

December 19, 1985
Arlesheim

I sit lie paint walk dance weep in a Swiss hospital trying to find out what my body wants to do, waiting for doctors to come talk with me. Last night my stomach and liver cried all night. "So this is the way of dying," I thought, my body feeling almost transparent. In the sunlight now I think someone was dying next door, and I felt the sadness through the walls coupled with my own. When the sun came up I felt a lot better, until I saw the bed stripped down in the hallway, and the next-door buzzer silent at last.

The village of Arlesheim is very lovely and picturesque. Frances and I go for long walks in the park holding hands in our coat pockets, giving each other courage, and wondering about the future. I have written no letters, no poems, no journals except these notes, trying to make sense out of it all.

I am often in pain and I fear that it will get worse. I need to sharpen every possible weapon against it, but even more so against the fear, or the fear of fear, which is what is so debilitating. And I want to learn how to do that while there is still time for learning in some state before desperation. Desperation. Reckless through despair.

There is no more time left to decide upon strange afflictions.

December 20, 1985
Arlesheim

A men's choir from the village sang Christmas carols tonight in the hospital stairwells, their voices echoing through the halls, sweet and poignant, and I cried for Christmases I have had that are past. But I simply cannot allow myself to believe that there will never be any more of them, so there surely must be. How different this season is from any holiday season I could possibly have foreseen. Dear goddess! How many more?

Frances' being here makes it complete in an essential way no matter what, and at least we can wander about the village in the afternoons together looking at the shops, or walk the hills enjoying the countryside and the manicured little winter gardens. I stretch to be able to appreciate the loveliness in its own—european—right, before it is gone, too, and I no longer have a chance to explore it for whatever it can mean for me.

December 21, 1985
Arlesheim

I sleep well here when I sleep. Yesterday was another horrendous communal dinner. Difficult as it is for me to get anything down, I find the genteel smugness, the sameness, infuriating. It's better now that Frances has started taking her meals here with me. At least we can talk to each other.

I had to do battle between the soup and the salad with an Australian pig who proved that racism is as alive and well in Arlesheim as it was on that wretched bus in Melbourne when that drunken Aussie accosted me thinking I was *Koori* (Aborigine).

The choir really got to me tonight, mellow and measured and very civilized, so long as you accept their terms of living and their way of life and values. The sweet voices, the smell of pine, and the lovely candle arrangements with red and green holly in every hallway, the Christmas decorations in all the corridors, the determined cheerfulness. Nurses go around and open every door a bit so that everyone can hear the music. Soft lights shining in the twilight windows. Very lovely. Just don't be different. Don't even think about being different. It's bad for you.

Today is the day the sun returns. Sweet Solstice. Mother, arm me for whatever is ahead of me. Let me at the very least be equal to it, if not totally in charge of changing it. Last night Gloria called. As she said, take whatever you can use there and let the rest go.

Another choir is singing now in the halls. If I had the strength, I would get up from this bed and run out into the starlit freezing night and keep running until I collapsed into a heap of huffs and puffs of effort and strained muscles. But I can't quite manage that, and Frances has gone back to her hotel, and my heart aches from strangeness. The sound of these voices singing familiar melodies in a foreign tongue only reminds me of the distance between me and my familiar places.

Yet this is the only place I know right now that offers me any hope, and that will treat me and my liver seriously.

December 22, 1985
Arlesheim

I have brought some of my stones and macramé threads with me. I've laid out the stones on my windowsill, and they are beautiful in the light. I'm going to make a new healing necklace for myself from them while I'm here, and I'm going to make the heart-piece from carnelian, which is a specific against melancholy. And that's my answer to Sister Marie's cautioning me against the dangers of an excess of joy!

It's the nights after Frances goes back to the hotel that are the hardest. I spend my day racing around between those dreadful public meals and the eurhythmics and painting and baths and tests and running over to Frances' hotel for a quick cuddle then back here for a liver compress or to take my temperature or something else equally vital in this half-seen scheme of things that feels like a pact I've made with myself to do as they believe is best for a stated period of time—three weeks. In other words, to give the Lukas Klinik my best shot because it is the only thing I have going for me right now, and tomorrow the results from all my liver tests and other diagnostic analyses will be back. I haven't really thought about what they will be because I just can't spend any more energy in being scared.

What I have to fight the hardest against here is feeling that it is just not worth it—too much fight for too little return, and I hurt all the damn time. Something is going on inside me, and it's interfering with my life. There is a persistent and pernicious despair hovering over me constantly that feels physiological, even when my basic mood is quite happy. I don't understand it, but I do not want to slip or fall into any kind of resignation. I am not going to go gently into anybody's damn good night!

December 23, 1985, 10:30 a.m.
Arlesheim

I have cancer of the liver.

Dr. Lorenz just came in and told me. The crystallization test and the liver sonogram are all positive. The two masses in my liver are malignant. He says I should begin an increased Iscador program and antihormone therapy right away, if I decide that is the way I want to go. Well. The last possibility of doubt based on belief is gone. I said I'd come to Lukas because I trusted the anthroposophic doctors, and if they said it was malignant then I would accept their diagnosis. So here it is, and all the yelling and head-banging isn't going to change it. I guess it helps to finally know. I wish Frances were here.

I cannot afford to waste any more time in doubting, or in fury. The question is, what do I do now? Listen to my body, of course, but the messages get dimmer and dimmer. In two weeks I go back home. Iscador or chemotherapy or both?

How did I ever come to be in this place? What can I use it for?

December 24, 1985
Arlesheim

I feel trapped on a lonely star. Someone else is very sick next door, and the vibes are almost too painful to bear. But I must stop saying that now so glibly. Someday something will, in fact, be too painful to bear and then I will have to act. Does one simply get tired of living? I can't imagine right now what that would be like, but that is because I feel filled with a fury to live—because I believe life can be good even when it is painful—a fury that my energies just don't match my desires anymore.

December 25, 1985
Arlesheim

Good morning, Christmas. A Swiss bubble is keeping me from talking to my children and the women I love. The front desk won't put my calls through. Nobody here wants to pierce this fragile, delicate bubble that is the best of all possible worlds, they believe. So frighteningly insular. Don't they know good things get better by opening them up to others, giving and taking and changing? Most people here seem to feel that rigidity is a bona fide pathway to peace, and every fiber of me rebels against that.

December 26, 1985
Arlesheim

Adrienne [Rich] and Michelle [Cliff] and Gloria [Joseph] just called from California. I feel so physically cut off from the people I love. I need them, the sharing of grief and energy.

I am avoiding plunging directly into the nightmare of liver cancer as a fact of my life by edging into it like an icy bath. I am trying to edge my friends into it, too, without having to deal with more of their fury and grief than I can handle. There is some we share, and that mutual support makes us closer and more resolved. But there is some that they will have to deal with on their own, just as there is some fury and grief that I can only meet in a private place. Frances has been so true and staunch here. It is more difficult for her sometimes because she does not have the fount of desperate determination that survival is generating inside me.

There is so much to keep track of. I think it's crucial that I not only suffer this but record, in the fullness and the lean, some of the raw as well as digested qualities of now.

Last night there was a Christmas full moon, and it felt like a hopeful sign. I stood out in the road in front of the hospital under the full moon on Christmas night and thought about all of my beloved people, the women I love, my children, my family, all the dear faces before my eyes. The moon was so clear and bright, I could feel her upon my skin through Helen's fur coat.

After I had gone to bed she called me back to her twice. The first time I could not pierce through the veil of sleep, but I saw her light and heard her in my dreams. Then at 4:30 in the morning, her little fingers of light reached under the lined window curtains, and I got up as if bidden and went out onto the terrace to greet her. The night was very very still; she was low and bright and brilliantly clear. I stood on the terrace in my robe bathed in her strong quiet light. I raised my arms then and prayed for us all, prayed for the strength for all of us who must weather this time ahead with me. My mother moon had awakened me, calling me out into her brightness, and she shone down upon me as a sign, a blessing on that terrace with the soft gurgle of flowing water in my ears, a promise of answering strength to be whoever I need to be. I felt her in my heart, in my bones, in my thin blood, and I heard Margareta's voice again: "It's going to be a hard lonely road, but remember, help is on the way." That was her farewell Tarot reading for me, seventeen years ago.

December 27, 1985
Arlesheim

Last night I dreamed I was asleep here in my bed at the Klinik and there was a strange physical presence lying beside me on the left side. I couldn't see it because it was dark, but I felt this body start to touch me on my left thigh, and I knew that this meant great danger. "It must think I'm dead so it can have (claim) me," I thought, "but if I moan it will know I'm awake and alive and it'll leave me alone." So I began to moan softly, but the creature didn't stop. I could feel its cold fingers beginning to creep over my left hip, and I thought to myself, "Oh, oh, nightmare time! I've got to scream louder. Maybe that noise will make it go away, because there is nobody else here to wake me up!" So I screamed and roared in my sleep, and finally after what seemed like a very long time, I woke myself up calling out, and of course there was nothing in my bed at all, but it still felt as if death had really been trying.

December 30, 1985
Arlesheim

Frances and I went to the Konditorei [pastry shop] in town this afternoon to have a cup of tea and be together away from the hospital, when the elderly schoolteacher with the rhodonite necklace came in and wanted to sit down with us. It was so apparent how badly she wanted to talk that we couldn't say no, even though we never have enough time alone together.

It was actually quite sad. Dr. Lorenz had just told her that her breast cancer has spread to her bones, and she doesn't know what she is going to do. She has to make plans for her elderly mother for whom she now cares at home but will no longer be able to. There is no one she knows to whom she can turn for help because her sister died last year. I felt very sorry for her. Here it is, almost New Year's Eve, and there isn't even anyone she can talk to about her worries except two strange americans in a tea shop.

Then she went on to explain that she and her sister had had to live with foreign workers (she meant Italians) in the factory where they worked during World War II, and that the foreigners were very dirty, with lice and fleas, so she and her sister would sprinkle DDT in their hair and their beds every night so as not to catch diseases! And she is sure that is why the cancer has spread to her bones now. There was something so grotesque about this sad lonely old woman dying of bone cancer still holding on to her ethnic prejudices, even when she was realizing that they were going to cost her her life. The image of her as a young healthy aryan bigot was at war inside me with the pathetic old woman at our table, and I had to get out of there immediately.

December 31, 1985
Arlesheim

Old Year's Day, the last day of this troubled year. And yes, all the stories we tell are about healing in some form or the other.

In this place that makes such a point of togetherness and community, Frances and I sat through an ornate New Year's Eve dinner tonight surrounded by empty chairs on each side of us, an island unto ourselves in the festive hall. It's good that we have each other, but why should I have to suffer through this ostracism and pay for it as well? I guess because the point is not that I enjoy it but that I gain from it, and that's up to me. As Gloria said on the phone, "Take what you can use and let the rest GO!" They don't have to love me, just help me.

My Maori jade tiki is gone forever, either lost or stolen from my room. How much more do I have to lose before it is enough?

I cannot bear to think that this might be my last New Year's Eve. But it might be. What a bummer! But if that's true at least I have had others which were sweet and full past comparing, and filled with enough love and promise to last forever and beyond me. Frances, Beth and Jonathan, Helen, Blanche and Clare, our loving circle. I hold now to what I know and have always known in my heart ever since I first knew what loving was—that when it truly exists it is the most potent and lasting force in life, even if certainly not the fastest. But without it nothing else is worth a damn.

After Frances went back to the hotel I washed my hair (wishing I had some white flowers to put in the water for a blessing), listened to Bob Marley, and went to bed.

> . . . this is my message to you-u-u-u-u,
> every lil thing——is gon be allright-t-t-t . . .

January 1, 1986
Arlesheim

Today Frances and I hiked to the top of a mountain to see the Dornach ruins, and the whole Rhine valley spread out beneath us. It felt so good to be moving my body again. My mother always used to say that whatever you do on New Year's Day you will do all year round, and I'd certainly like to believe that's true.

It was very cold and sunny and bright, three miles up and back. The ruins rang with that historical echo and the presence of trials labored and past, although not as profoundly as the stones of El Morro in Cuba, and certainly not as desperately as the walls of Elmina Castle in Ghana, from whence so many Black women and children and men were sent to hell—slavery.

February 20, 1986
Anguilla, British West Indies

I am here seeking sun on my bones. A dry little island with outlandishly beautiful beaches, and soft-voiced West Indian people living their lives by the sea. Anguilla's primary source of income is from import duties, second comes fishing. I go out at dawn to see the fishermen put out from Crocus Bay, and when they return they sometimes give Gloria and me fish. An intricate network of ownership and shares governs the dividing up of each catch.

Fossilized sand dollars wash out of the sand banks onto the beaches of Anguilla and out of the claystone bluffs that grade downward toward the beach. I spend hours wandering the beaches and searching for them, or collecting shells that I rinse at the water's green edge. I would never have known about this island except for Gloria. Anguilla feels like a piece of home, a very healing, restful place, but with the rich essences of life.

The sun and the sea here are helping me save my life. They are a far softer cry from the East River, Spuyten Duyvil, and the lower New York Bay. But always, the sea speaks to me no matter where I get to her. I suppose that is a legacy of my mother's, from when we used to stand, all those years ago, staring out over the sooty pebbles at the foot of 142nd Street and the Harlem River. Anguilla reminds me of Carriacou, the tiny island off the coast of Grenada where my mother was born.

When I am next to the sea, the wide spread of water laps over me with an enduring peace and excitement that feels like finding some precious rock in the earth, a sense of touching something that is most essentially me in a place where my past and my future intersect along the present. The present, that line of stress and connection and performance, the intense crashing now. Yet only earth and sky last forever, and the ocean joins them.

I hear the waters' song, feel the tides within the fluids of my body, hear the sea echoing my mothers' voices of survival from Elmina to Grenville to Harlem. I hear them resounding inside me from swish to boom—from the dark of the moon to fullness.

April 2, 1986
St. Croix, Virgin Islands

This is the year I spent spring beachcombing in St. Croix, awash with the trade winds and coconuts, sand and the sea. West Indian voices in the supermarket and Chase Bank, and the Caribbean flavors that have always meant home. Healing within a network of Black women who supplied everything from a steady stream of tender coconuts to spicy gossip to sunshine to fresh parrot fish to advice on how to cool out from academic burnout to a place where I can remember how the earth feels at 6:30 in the morning under a tropical crescent moon working in the still-cool garden—a loving context within which I fit and thrive.

I have been invited to take part in a conference on Caribbean women, "The Ties That Bind." At first I didn't think I'd have the energy to do it, but the whole experience has been a powerful and nourishing reminder of how good it feels to be doing my work where I'm convinced it matters the most, among the women—my sisters—who I most want to reach. It feels like I'm talking to Helen, my sister, and Carmen, my cousin, with all the attendant frustrations and joys rolled up together. It's always like this when you're trying to get people you love mightily to hear and use the ways in which you all are totally different, knowing they are the most difficult to reach. But it is the ways in which you are the same that make it possible to communicate at all.

The conference was organized by Gloria and the other three Sojourner Sisters, and it's an incredible accomplishment for four Black women with full-time jobs elsewhere to have pulled together such an ambitious enterprise. They orchestrated the entire event, bringing together presenters from ten different countries, feeding and housing us royally, as well as organizing four days of historical, cultural, and political presentations and workshops that were enjoyable and provocative for the more than 200 women who attended.

Johnnetta Cole's moving presentation of the Cuban revolution and its meaning in the lives of Caribbean women; Merle Hodge's incisive analysis of the sexism in calypsos; Dessima Williams, former ambassador from Grenada to the Organization of American States, proud and beautiful, recalling Maurice Bishop and Grenadian liberation with tears in her eyes.

In addition to being a tremendous high, these days are such a thrilling example to me of the real power of a small group of Black women of the diaspora in action. Four community women, meeting after work for almost a year, dreamed, planned, financed, and executed this conference without institutional assistance. It has been an outstanding success, so much information and affirmation for those of us who participated as well as for those of us who attended.

From *Sister Outsider* and *A Burst of Light*

It was a very centering experience for me, an ideal place for me to step out again, and I was so proud to be a part of it, and to speak and read my work as a Caribbean woman.

April 5, 1986
St. Croix

Yesterday was the eighteenth anniversary of Martin Luther King's murder. Carnegie Hall, Duke Ellington, the Tougaloo Choir. Their young Black voices tear in my blood to this day. *What the world needs now is love . . .* There was still a space left for hope then, but the shore was fading fast. I wonder where all those kids from Tougaloo are now who stood so brave and tearful and together in their aloneness. I wonder how each of their lives is being influenced/formed/informed by the emotions and events upon that stage of Carnegie Hall that night King died. I wonder if I will ever hear from any one of them again.

April 20, 1986
St. Croix

Blanchie's birthday. When Blanche had her mastectomy last year, it was the first time that I had to face, in a woman I loved, feelings and fears I had faced within my own self, but never dealt with externally. Now I had to speak to these feelings in some way that was meaningful and urgent in the name of my love. Somehow I had known for the past eight years that someday it would be this way, that personal salvation of whatever kind is never *just* personal.

I talked with Blanchie today over the phone about this feeling I have that I must rally everything I know, made alive and immediate with the fire of what is.

I have always been haunted by the fear of not being able to reach the women I am closest to, of not being able to make available to the women I love most dearly what I can make available to so many others. The women in my family, my closest friends. If what I know to be true cannot be of use to them, can it ever have been said to be true at all? On the other hand, that lays a terrible burden on all of us concerned, doesn't it?

It is a matter of learning languages, or of learning to use them with precision to do what needs to be done with them, and it is the Blanchie in myself to whom I need to speak with such urgency. It's one of the great things friends are for each other when you've been very close for a long time.

And of course cancer is political—look at how many of our comrades have died of it during the last ten years! As warriors, our job is to actively and consciously survive it for as long as possible, remembering that in order to win, the aggressor must conquer, but the resisters need only survive. Our battle is to define survival in ways that are acceptable and nourishing to us, meaning with substance and style. Substance. Our work. Style. True to our selves.

What would it be like to be living in a place where the pursuit of definition within this crucial part of our lives was not circumscribed and fractionalized by the economics of disease in america? Here the first consideration concerning cancer is not what does this mean in my living, but how much is this going to cost?

April 22, 1986
St. Croix

I got a letter from Ellen Kuzwayo this morning. Her sister in Botswana has died. I wish I were in Soweto to put my arms around her and rest her head on my shoulder. She sounds so strong and sanguine in her unshakable faith, yet so much alone. In the fabric of horrors that she and the other women live through daily in South Africa, this loss takes its place among so many others, at the same time particular and poignant.

May 8, 1986
New York City

Tomorrow belongs to those of us who conceive of it as belonging to everyone, who lend the best of ourselves to it, and with joy.

It takes all of my selves, working together, to integrate what I learn of women of Color around the world into my consciousness and work. It takes all of my selves working together to effectively focus attention and action against the holocaust progressing in South Africa and the South

From *Sister Outsider* and *A Burst of Light*

Bronx and Black schools across this nation, not to speak of the streets. Laying myself on the line. It takes all of my selves working together to fight this death inside me. Every one of these battles generates energies useful in the others.

I am on the cusp of change, and the curve is shifting fast.

In the bleakest days I am kept afloat, maintained, empowered, by the positive energies of so many women who carry the breath of my loving like firelight in their strong hair.

May 23, 1986
New York City

I spoke with Andrea in New Orleans this morning. She and Diana are helping to organize a Black Women's Book Fair. Despite its size, there is not one feminist bookstore in the whole city. She's very excited about the project, and it was a real charge talking to her about it. There are so many young Black women across this country stepping out wherever they may be and making themselves felt within their communities in very real ways. These women make the early silence and the doubts and the wear and tear of it all worth it. I feel like they are my inheritors, and sometimes I breathe a sigh of relief that they exist, that I don't have to do it all.

It's a two-way street, and even I don't always realize it. Like the little sister from AA who stood up at my poetry reading last week and talked about how much courage I'd given her, and I was quaking in my boots because when she began I'd thought she was about to lay a heavy cancer rap on me in public, and I just wasn't quite ready for that yet. I feel very humbled behind that little episode. I want to acknowledge all those intricate connections between us by which we sustain and empower each other.

June 20, 1986
Bonnieux, France

How incredibly rich to be here in the south of France with the Zamani Soweto Sisters from South Africa. Gloria and I became acquainted with them through Ellen Kuzwayo and our fundraising work with the Sisters in Support of Sisters in South Africa. They are one of the groups we help support through contributions. I'm only sorry that Ellen couldn't be here also, but at least I had a chance to share time and space with her in London on June 16, the anniversary of the Soweto uprising.

I learn tremendous courage from these women, from their laughter and their tears, from their grace under constant adversity, from their joy in living which is one of their most potent weapons, from the deft power of their large, overworked bodies and their dancing, swollen feet. In this brief respite for us all made possible by Betty Wolpert's kindness, these women have taught me so much courage and perspective.

June 21, 1986
Bonnieux

Sweet Solstice, and again the goddess smiles upon me. I am sitting in the stone-ringed yard of Les Quelles, a beautiful old reclaimed silk factory, now a villa. Gloria and the women of the Zamani Soweto Sisters surround me, all of us brilliant and subtle under the spreading flowers of a lime-tea tree. It looks and feels like what I've always imagined the women's compound in some African village to have been, once. Some of us drink tea, some are sewing, sweeping the dirt ground of the yard, hanging out clothes in the sunlight at the edge of the enclosure, washing, combing each other's hair. Acacia blossoms perfume the noon air as Vivian tells the stories behind the tears in her glowing amber eyes.

The young students who do not ask their parents' permission to run in the streets and die. The wealthy Black undertaker who lends his funeral hearses to the police to transport the bodies of the slain children.

The three little children who saw a heavy-armored Casspir barreling down the road in Dube and ran to hide behind the silk-cotton tree at the edge of the yard, too young to know that they could be seen as the tank rolled down the road. The blond policeman leaning out from the side of the tank to fire behind the tree at the little ones as they hid, reaching back over his shoulder to fire again as the vehicle rolled along, just to make sure the babies were all dead.

She tells of the mothers in her street who stay home from work risking deportation to the barrenness of an alien "homeland," trudging from

From *Sister Outsider* and *A Burst of Light*

police station to police station all over Soweto asking, "Are my children here? Please sirs, this is her picture this is his school name he is nine years of age are my children here?" Her son leaving detention dragging his heels forever, achilles tendons torn and festering from untreated police dog bites.

Ruth, majestic and proud as Mujaji, ancient rain queen of the Lovedu. "I write my thoughts down on little scraps of paper," she says, talking about where the ideas come from for her intricate quilts. "And sometimes I pull them all out and read them and then I say no, that's not it at all and I throw them right away. But other times I smooth them out and save them for the quilts. I would like to keep a whole book of these stories from my life, but then a quilt is like a book of many stories done up together, and many people can read it all at the same time."

Gentle, strong, beautiful—the women of Soweto imprint their faces and their courage upon me. They enhance this French air, a cloud of soap and cosmetics and the lightest hint of hair cream. The knowledge of struggle never distant. Womanliness pervades this space.

Thembi, called Alice, flames under her taut sweetness, walking a dangerously narrow path too close to the swamp where there are bright lights flashing like stars just below the murky surface in harmony with the voices of astonished frogs in the green night. She begs me to release her from the pain of not doing enough for our own, of not making our daughters into ourselves. She tells me to dream upon all of their stories and write them a poem.

Petal, whose eyes are often too quiet as she moves about, short, solid, and graceful. We discuss love, comparing tales, and her eyes flash, amused and aglow. Other times they are wary, filled with distrust and grieving. Petal, who bore seven children and only two live. Who was tortured for weeks by the South African police. Who was helped by the International Hospital for Torture Victims in Switzerland.

Sula, wry and generous, knows how to get any question answered with a gentle inescapable persistence. Sometimes she drinks a lot. Her first husband broke her heart, but she quickly married again. "The missionaries lied to us so much about our bodies," she said, indignantly, "telling us they were dirty and we had to cover them up, and look now who is running about in bikinis on the Riviera, or naked and topless! I had a friend . . ." and she starts another story, like one most of these women tell, of a special woman friend who loved her past explaining.

Sweet-faced Emily tells of the militant young comrades in Soweto, their defiance of the old ways, carrying their determination for change into the streets. She demonstrates for us a spirited and high-stepping rendition of their rousing machine-gun dance.

She does not like to listen to the other women singing hymns. Emily, who loved her best friend so much she still cannot listen to the records they once enjoyed together, and it is five years already since her friend died.

Linda of the hypnotic eyes who was questioned once by the South African police every single day for an entire month. About Zamani Soweto Sisters and subversive activities, such as a tiny ANC flag stitched on the little dead boy's pocket in the corner of a funeral procession quilt. "The quilts tell stories from our own lives. We did not know it was forbidden to sew the truth, but we will caution the women never to stitch such a thing again. No, thank you, I do not wish to take a cup of tea with you." I can hear her grave dignity speaking. She finishes the tale with a satisfied laugh.

Linda has a nineteen-year-old daughter. The women joke and offer us their daughters to introduce to our sons and nephews in america. No one offers us their sons for our daughters.

Mariah lives next door to a famous woman writer in Soweto and offers to carry a letter to her from Kitchen Table: Women of Color Press. Posted mail from abroad so often does not reach its destination in Soweto. Round, quick, and with a brilliant smile, Mariah sits near the top of the executive board of Zamani. There is a presence about her of a successful African market woman, sharp, pleasant, outgoing, and awake to every opportunity.

Sofia keeps the books. She is quietly watchful and speaks with that soft humor that is shared by many of the women. She lives and sews alone now that her children are grown and gone away. She likes the way Gloria does her hair, and they discuss different hair preparations.

Her eyes are encouraging and attentive as she sits and sews with tiny, rhythmical stitches.

Vibrant young Etta of the beautiful body dances excitement in our frequent spontaneous dancing. She is also learning to run the film cameras. Etta is always laughing and full of frolic, and some of the older women watch her and shake their heads with that particular Black women's look. But mostly they laugh back, because Etta's gaiety is so infectious. Her face turns serious as she discusses what she wants to do with her life back home.

Helen is another one of the young ones, as they are called by everyone else. Their relationship to the other women is clearly one of respect, almost like daughters-in-law. And this is in addition to the warmth and mutual esteem evident between all the women. Helen already moves in a dignified and considered way, but she has twinkling and mischievous eyes and tells me confidentially that she is the naughtiest one of all.

Rita, the last of the young ones, is quiet and small and rather proper. All the "mas" like her a lot, and smile approvingly at her. She is always helpful and soft-voiced, and really enjoys singing religious songs.

Bembe, light-skinned and small-boned, cleans and irons all day and sometimes at night when she is disturbed about something, like their imminent trip home. She is Zulu, like Etta, and loves to dance. Butterfly marks across her cheeks suggest she has lacked vitamins for a long time.

Hannah sings a spirited and humorous song about marriage being a stamping out of a woman's freedom, just like her signature in the marriage register is a stamping out of her own name as written in the book of life. All the other women join in the high-spirited chorus with much laughter. This is one of their favorite songs. Hannah talks about mothers-in-law, and how sometimes when they finally get to have their own way, they take it out on their sons' wives. And by tradition, the daughters-in-law must remain meek and helpful, blowing their lungs out firing the wood braziers and coal stoves for the rest of the family every morning. She tells of her own young self rising at 4:00 a.m., even on the morning after her wedding night, lighting the fire to fix her father-in-law his coffee. But she not only eventually stopped this, she even joined her daughter once in punching out her daughter's philandering husband, caught in the act in his wife's bed.

Mary, the oldest woman in the group, is called Number One. Witty, wise, and soft-spoken, she says love and concern came to her very late in life, once she started to work with Zamani. She is very grateful for the existence of the group, a sentiment that is often expressed by many of the other women in various ways. When we part she kisses me on my lips. "I love you, my sister," she says.

Wassa, round-cheeked and matter-of-fact, talks of her fear of reentry into Johannesburg. "But at least we will be all together," she says, "so if something happens to one of us the others can tell her people." I remember Ellen talking of the horror of hitting Jo'burg alone, and how you never know what the South African police might be planning for you at the airport, nor why.

The night before we part we swim in the pool beneath the sweet evening of the grapevines. "We are naked here in this pool now," Wassa says softly, "and we will be naked when we go back home." We told the women we would carry them in our hearts until we were together again. Everyone is anxious to go back home, despite the fear, despite the uncertainty, despite the dangers.

There is work to be done.

August 12, 1986
New York City

Wonderful news! My liver scan shows both tumors slightly diminished. It feels good to be getting on with my life. I feel vindicated without ever becoming complacent—this is only one victory of a long battle in which I've got to expect to win some and lose some. But it does put a different perspective upon things to know that pain can be a sign of a disintegrating tumor. Of course, my oncologist is surprised and puzzled. He admits he doesn't understand what is happening, but it is a mark of his good spirit that he is genuinely pleased for me, nonetheless. I'm very pleased for me, too.

A good autumn coming, if I remember to take it easily. I have interesting classes, and SISSA is planning a benefit this fall around the quilt Gloria and I brought back from the Zamani Soweto Sisters in europe.

I'll be doing another benefit for Kitchen Table in Boston. That feels real good. It will be six years next month since the vision of KTP became a reality through the hard work of Barbara [Smith] and Cherrie [Moraga] and Myrna and the others.

August 15, 1986
New York City

Women of Color in struggle all over the world, our separateness, our connectedness, so many more options for survival. Whatever I call them, I know them for sister, mother, daughter, voice and teacher, inheritor of fire. Alice of Soweto cursing the mission songs: "We have our own political songs now for the young people to sing—no more damn forgiveness!" Her voice is almost hysterically alone in the shocked silence of the other hymn-singing women.

Katerina stands in the Berlin hall, two hours into the discussion that follows the poetry reading by her and other Afro-German women. "I have had enough," she says, "and yes, you may need to continue to air your feelings of racism because for you they are a new discovery here tonight. But I have known them and lived with them all of my life and tonight it is now time for me to go home." And she walks down the aisle and out, straight and beautiful, with that fine and familiar Black woman's audacity in the face of a totally unsupported situation.

Rangitunoa, Maori tribal woman, standing to speak in her people's sacred place, the *marae*. Women have not spoken here before because they have not known the ancient language. In the old days, women did not speak in the *marae* at all. Now this young woman who loves women stands to speak in the tongue of her people, eloquently alone and suspect in her elders' eyes.

Dinah, Aboriginal woman come down from the hot north hills of the outback, traveling by bus three days from mission to mission to meet with the writing women of Melbourne, because she had heard of this conference and she wishes to bring her stories to them.

The stern, shy Samoan women in Auckland, plush and mighty, organizing study groups for their teenaged kin, holding evening classes for them in how to understand the *Pakahas* (whites).

The Aboriginal women reclaiming the famous Ayers Rock as *Ulluru*, a place of women's Dreaming.

The women of the South Pacific islands demanding their peoples' land rights, rejecting the european and american nuclear madness that is devastating their islands.

Brown people filling the streets of downtown Auckland, marching in support of a Nuclear Free and Independent Pacific. It could almost be Washington, D.C.!

Black children sitting down in the middle of metropolitan Melbourne to celebrate Koori Day, the black, red, and yellow flag of Pacific liberation and revolution snapping in the sun. "What do we want? LAND RIGHTS! When do we want them? NOW!!" Banners ringing the shopping mall in black, red, and yellow: PAY THE RENT!

Merle, fierce and shining, a Caribbean woman writer calmly analyzing the sexism behind the lyrics of beloved calypsos.

The Black South African seamstresses telling their multifaceted stories of survival, their soft voices filled with what Gloria calls a revolutionary patience.

Black women taking care of business all over the world.

September 21, 1986
New York City

The Autumn Equinox, a time of balancing. Nudie died of lung cancer today in Puerto Rico. Frances and I had just come back from a beautiful weekend in Shelter Island, and as we walked in the phone was ringing and it was Yoli. I feel that same sadness and fury as when I heard Hyllus Maris had died in Melbourne last month. Some of us refuse to have anything to do with other people who have cancer, reluctant to invite another sorrow, as if any reflection of our own battle either lessens our power or makes it too realistic to be borne. Others of us fashion a connection of support, but sometimes that connection is not solid enough and invites another grief. I felt I had a special pact with Hyllus and with Nudie. As if we had promised each other we would make it, but nobody does, and they didn't, and I won't either.

But magical thinking doesn't work. I'm so glad Nudie had a chance to go back to Puerto Rico, which is where she always wanted to end up her time.

Making it really means doing it our way for as long as possible, same as crossing a busy avenue or telling unpleasant truths. But even though it's childish and useless, I'm still angry with both of them for dying.

That's probably how some of my friends feel about me right now, the ones who can't look me in the eye when they ask how I'm doing, even though I'm very much alive and kicking.

It's nine years ago today I had my first breast biopsy. Which was outstandingly and conclusively negative. So much for biopsies. Bob Marley weaving through my visualizations:

> won't you help me sing
> these songs of freedom
> was all I ever had
> redemption songs

September 27, 1986
New York City

I hope when I reread this journal later there will be more here than simply a record of who died in what month and how their passing touched me. Maybe at least how I can use that knowledge to move beyond the moments of terror. I much prefer to think about how I'd want to die—given that I don't want to die at all but will certainly have to—rather than just fall into death any old way, by default, according to somebody else's rules. It's not like you get a second chance to die the way you want to die.

Sometimes I have the eeriest feeling that I'm living some macabre soap opera. And *too besides*, it's being recorded in vivid living color. If so, I hope it'll be useful someday for something, if only for some other Black sister's afternoon entertainment when her real life gets to be too much. It'll sure beat *As the World Turns*. At least there will be real Black people in this one, and maybe if I'm lucky, I'll get to drag the story on interminably for twenty or thirty years like the TV soaps, until the writer dies of old age or the audience loses interest—which is another way of saying they no longer need to discharge the tensions in their lives that lie behind that particular story.

November 6, 1986
New York City

Black mother goddess, salt dragon of chaos, Seboulisa, Mawu. Attend me, hold me in your muscular flowering arms, protect me from throwing any part of myself away.

Women who have asked me to set these stories down are asking me for my air to breathe, to use in their future, are courting me back to my life as a warrior. Some offer me their bodies, some their enduring patience, some a separate fire, and still others, only a naked need whose face is all too familiar. It is the need to give voice to the complexities of living with cancer, outside of the tissue-thin assurance that they "got it all," or that the changes we have wrought in our lives will insure that cancer never reoccurs. And it is a need to give voice to living with cancer outside of that numbing acceptance of death as a resignation waiting after fury and before despair.

There is nothing I cannot use somehow in my living and my work, even if I would never have chosen it on my own, even if I am livid with fury at having to choose. Not only did nobody ever say it would be easy, nobody ever said what faces the challenges would wear. The point is to do as much as I can of what I came to do before they nickel and dime me to death.

Racism. Cancer. In both cases, to win the aggressor must conquer, but the resisters need only survive. How do I define that survival and on whose terms?

So I feel a sense of triumph as I pick up my pen and say yes I am going to write again from the world of cancer and with a different perspective—that of living with cancer in an intimate daily relationship. Yes, I'm going to say plainly, six years after my mastectomy, in spite of drastically altered patterns of eating and living, and in spite of my self-conscious living and increased self-empowerment, and in spite of my deepening commitment to using myself in the service of what I believe, and in spite of all my positive expectations to the contrary, I have been diagnosed as having cancer of the liver, metastasized from breast cancer.

This fact does not make my last six years of work any less vital or important or necessary. The accuracy of that diagnosis has become less important than how I use the life I have.

November 8, 1986
New York City

If I am to put this all down in a way that is useful, I should start with the beginning of the story.

Sizable tumor in the right lobe of the liver, the doctors said. Lots of blood vessels in it means it's most likely malignant. Let's cut you open right now and see what we can do about it. Wait a minute, I said. I need to feel this thing out and see what's going on inside myself first, I said, needing some time to absorb the shock, time to assay the situation and not act out of panic. Not one of them said, I can respect that, but don't take too long about it.

Instead, that simple claim to my body's own processes elicited such an attack response from a reputable Specialist In Liver Tumors that my deepest—if not necessarily most useful—suspicions were totally aroused.

What that doctor could have said to me that I would have heard was, "You have a serious condition going on in your body and whatever you do about it you must not ignore it or delay deciding how you are going to deal with it because it will not go away no matter what you think it is." Acknowledging my responsibility for my own body. Instead, what he said to me was, "If you do not do exactly what I tell you to do right now without questions you are going to die a horrible death." In exactly those words.

I felt the battle lines being drawn up within my own body.

I saw this specialist in liver tumors at a leading cancer hospital in New York City, where I had been referred as an outpatient by my own doctor.

The first people who interviewed me in white coats from behind a computer were only interested in my health-care benefits and proposed method of payment. Those crucial facts determined what kind of plastic ID card I would be given, and without a plastic ID card, no one at all was allowed upstairs to see any doctor, as I was told by the uniformed, pistoled guards at all the stairwells.

From the moment I was ushered into the doctor's office and he saw my x-rays, he proceeded to infantilize me with an obviously well-practiced technique. When I told him I was having second thoughts about a liver biopsy, he glanced at my chart. Racism and sexism joined hands across his table as he saw I taught at a university. "Well, you look like an *intelligent girl*," he said, staring at my one breast all the time he was speaking. "Not to have this biopsy immediately is like sticking your head in the sand." Then he went on to say that he would not be responsible when I wound up one day screaming in agony in the corner of his office!

I asked this specialist in liver tumors about the dangers of a liver biopsy spreading an existing malignancy, or even encouraging it in a borderline tumor. He dismissed my concerns with a wave of his hand, saying, instead of answering, that I really did not have any other sensible choice.

I would like to think that this doctor was sincerely motivated by a desire for me to seek what he truly believed to be the only remedy for my sickening body, but my faith in that scenario is considerably diminished by his $250 consultation fee and his subsequent medical report to my own doctor containing numerous supposedly clinical observations of *obese abdomen and remaining pendulous breast.*

In any event, I can thank him for the fierce shard lancing through my terror that shrieked there must be some other way, this doesn't feel right to me. If this is cancer and they cut me open to find out, what is stopping that intrusive action from spreading the cancer, or turning a questionable mass into an active malignancy? All I was asking for was the reassurance of a realistic answer to my real questions, and that was not forthcoming. I made up my mind that if I was going to die in agony on somebody's office floor, it certainly wasn't going to be his! I needed information, and pored over books on the liver in Barnes & Noble's medical textbook section on Fifth Avenue for hours. I learned, among other things, that the liver is the largest, most complex, and most generous organ in the human body. But that did not help me very much.

In this period of physical weakness and psychic turmoil, I found myself going through an intricate inventory of rage. First of all at my breast surgeon—had he perhaps done something wrong? How could such a small breast tumor have metastasized? Hadn't he assured me he'd gotten it all, and what was this now anyway about micro-metastases? Could this tumor in my liver have been seeded at the same time as my breast cancer? There were so many unanswered questions, and too much that I just did not understand.

But my worst rage was the rage at myself. For a brief time I felt like a total failure. What had I been busting my ass doing these past six years if it wasn't living and loving and working to my utmost potential? And wasn't that all a guarantee supposed to keep exactly this kind of thing from ever happening again? So what had I done wrong and what was I going to have to pay for it and WHY ME?

But finally a little voice inside me said sharply, "Now really, is there any other way you would have preferred living the past six years that would have been more satisfying? And be that as it may, *should or shouldn't* isn't even the question. How do you want to live the rest of your life from now on and what are you going to do about it?" Time's a-wasting!

Gradually, in those hours in the stacks of Barnes & Noble, I felt myself shifting into another gear. My resolve strengthened as my panic lessened. Deep breathing, regularly. I'm not going to let them cut into my body again until I'm convinced there is no other alternative. And this time, the burden of proof rests with the doctors because their record of success with liver cancer is not so good that it would make me jump at a surgical solution. And scare tactics are not going to work. I have been scared now for six years and that hasn't stopped me. I've given myself plenty of practice in doing whatever I need to do, scared or not, so scare tactics are just not going to work. Or I hoped they were not going to work. At any rate, thank the goddess, they were not working yet. One step at a time.

But some of my nightmares were pure hell, and I started having trouble sleeping.

In writing this I have discovered how important some things are that I thought were unimportant. I discovered this by the high price they exact for scrutiny. At first I did not want to look again at how I slowly came to terms with my own mortality on a level deeper than before, nor with the inevitable strength that gave me as I started to get on with my life in actual time. Medical textbooks on the liver were fine, but there were appointments to be kept, and bills to pay, and decisions about my upcoming trip to europe to be made. And what do I say to my children? Honesty has always been the bottom line between us, but did I really need them going through this with me during their final difficult years at college? On the other hand, how could I shut them out of this most important decision of my life?

I made a visit to my breast surgeon, a doctor with whom I have always been able to talk frankly, and it was from him that I got my first trustworthy and objective sense of timing. It was from him that I learned that the conventional forms of treatment for liver metastases made little more than one year's difference in the survival rate. I heard my old friend Clem's voice coming back to me through the dimness of thirty years: "I see you coming here trying to make sense where there is no sense. Try just living in it. Respond, alter, see what happens." I thought of the African way of perceiving life, as experience to be lived rather than as problem to be solved.

Homeopathic medicine calls cancer the cold disease. I understand that down to my bones that quake sometimes in their need for heat, for the sun, even for just a hot bath. Part of the way in which I am saving my own life is to refuse to submit my body to cold whenever possible.

In general, I fight hard to keep my treatment scene together in some coherent and serviceable way, integrated into my daily living and absolute. Forgetting is no excuse. It's as simple as one missed shot could make the difference between a quiescent malignancy and one that is growing again. This not only keeps me in an intimate, positive relationship to my own health, but it also underlines the fact that I have the responsibility for attending my own health. I cannot simply hand over that responsibility to anybody else.

Which does not mean I give in to the belief, arrogant or naive, that I know everything I need to know in order to make informed decisions about my body. But attending my own health, gaining enough information to help me understand and participate in the decisions made about my body by people who know more medicine than I do, are all crucial strategies in my battle for living. They also provide me with important prototypes for doing battle in all other arenas of my life.

Battling racism and battling heterosexism and battling apartheid share the same urgency inside me as battling cancer. None of these struggles are ever easy, and even the smallest victory is never to be taken for granted. Each victory must be applauded, because it is so easy not to battle at all, to just accept and call that acceptance inevitable.

And all power is relative. Recognizing the existence as well as the limitations of my own power, and accepting the responsibility for using it in my own behalf, involve me in direct and daily actions that preclude denial as a possible refuge. Simone de Beauvoir's words echo in my head: "It is in the recognition of the genuine conditions of our lives that we gain the strength to act and our motivation for change."

November 10, 1986
New York City

Building into my living—without succumbing to it—an awareness of this reality of my life, that I have a condition within my body of which I will eventually die, comes in waves, like a rising tide. It exists side by side with another force inside me that says no you don't, not you, and the x-rays are wrong and the tests are wrong and the doctors are wrong.

There is a different kind of energy inherent within each one of these feelings, and I try to reconcile and use these different energies whenever I need them. The energy generated by the first awareness serves to urge me always to get on with living my life and doing my work with an intensity and purpose of the urgent now. Throw the toys overboard, we're headed into rougher waters.

The energies generated by the second force fuel a feisty determination to continue doing what I am doing forever. The tensions created inside me by the contradictions is another source of energy and learning. I have always known I learn my most lasting lessons about difference by closely attending the ways in which the differences inside me lie down together.

November 11, 1986
New York City

I keep observing how other people die, comparing, learning, critiquing the process inside of me, matching it up to how I would like to do it. And I think about this scrutiny of myself in the context of its usefulness to other Black women living with cancer, born and unborn.

I have a privileged life or else I would be dead by now. It is two and a half years since the first tumor in my liver was discovered. When I needed to know, there was no one around to tell me that there were alternatives to turning myself over to doctors who are terrified of not knowing everything. There was no one around to remind me that I have a right to decide what happens to my own body, not because I know more than anybody else, but simply because it is my body. And I have a right to acquire the information that can help me make those crucial decisions.

It was an accident of circumstance that brought me to Germany at a critical moment in my health, and another which introduced me to one holistic/homeopathic approach to the treatment of certain cancers. Not all homeopathic alternatives work for every patient. Time is a crucial element in the treatment of cancer, and I had to decide which chances I would take, and why.

I think of what this means to other Black women living with cancer, to all women in general. Most of all I think of how important it is for us to share with each other the powers buried within the breaking of silence about our bodies and our health, even though we have been schooled to be secret and stoical about pain and disease. But that stoicism and silence does not serve us nor our communities, only the forces of things as they are.

November 12, 1986
New York City

When I write my own Book of the Dead, my own Book of Life, I want to celebrate being alive to do it even while I acknowledge the painful savor uncertainty lends to my living. I use the energy of dreams that are now impossible, not totally believing in them nor their power to become real, but recognizing them as templates for a future within which my labors can play a part. I am freer to choose what I will devote my energies toward and what I will leave for another lifetime, thanking the goddess for the strength to perceive that I can choose, despite obstacles.

So when I do a SISSA reading to raise funds for the women's collectives in Soweto, or to raise money for Kitchen Table: Women of Color Press, I am choosing to use myself for things in which I passionately believe. When I speak to rally support in the urgent war against apartheid in South Africa and the racial slaughter that is even now spreading across the U.S., when I demand justice in the police shotgun killing of a Black grandmother and lynchings in northern California and in Central Park in New York City, I am making a choice of how I wish to use my power. This work gives me a tremendous amount of energy back in satisfaction and in belief, as well as in a vision of how I want this earth to be for the people who come after me.

When I work with young poets who are reaching for the power of their poetry within themselves and the lives they choose to live, I feel I am working to capacity, and this gives me deep joy, a reservoir of strength I draw upon for the next venture. Right now. This makes it far less important that it will not be forever. It never was.

The energies I gain from my work help me neutralize those implanted forces of negativity and self-destructiveness that is white america's way of making sure I keep whatever is powerful and creative within me unavailable, ineffective, and nonthreatening.

But there is a terrible clarity that comes from living with cancer that can be empowering if we do not turn aside from it. What more can they do to me? My time is limited, and this is so for each one of us. So how will the opposition reward me for my silences? For the pretense that this is in fact the best of all possible worlds? What will they give me for lying? A lifelong Safe Conduct Pass for everyone I love? Another lifetime for me? The end to racism? Sexism? Homophobia? Cruelty? The common cold?

November 13, 1986
New York City

I do not find it useful any longer to speculate upon cancer as a political weapon. But I'm not being paranoid when I say my cancer is as political as if some CIA agent brushed past me in the A train on March 15, 1965, and air-injected me with a long-fused cancer virus. Or even if it is only that I stood in their wind to do my work and the billows flayed me. What possible choices do most of us have in the air we breathe and the water we must drink?

Sometimes we are blessed with being able to choose the time and the arena and the manner of our revolution, but more usually we must do battle wherever we are standing. It does not matter too much if it is in the radiation lab or a doctor's office or the telephone company, the streets, the welfare department, or the classroom. The real blessing is to be able to use whoever I am wherever I am, in concert with as many others as possible, or alone if needs be.

This is no longer a time of waiting. It is a time for the real work's urgencies. It is a time enhanced by an iron reclamation of what I call the burst of light—that inescapable knowledge, in the bone, of my own physical limitation. Metabolized and integrated into the fabric of my days, that knowledge makes the particulars of what is coming seem less important. When I speak of wanting as much good time as possible, I mean time over which I maintain some relative measure of control.

November 14, 1986
New York City

One reason I watch the death process so acutely is to rob it of some of its power over my consciousness. I have overcome my earlier need to ignore or turn away from films and books that deal with cancer or dying. It is ever so much more important now for me to fill the psyches of all the people I love and who love me with a sense of outrageous beauty and strength of purpose.

But it is also true that sometimes we cannot heal ourselves close to the very people from whom we draw strength and light, because they are also closest to the places and tastes and smells that go along with a pattern of living we are trying to rearrange. After my mastectomy, changing the ways I ate and struggled and slept and meditated also required that I change the external environment within which I was deciding what direction I would have to take.

I am on the cusp of change and the curve is shifting fast. If any of my decisions have been in error, I must stand—not prepared, for that is impossible—but open to dealing with the consequences of those errors.

Inside and outside, change is not easy nor quick, and I find myself always on guard against what is oversimplified, or merely cosmetic.

November 15, 1986
New York City

In my office at home I have created a space that is very special to me. It is simple and quiet, with beautiful things about, and a ray of sunlight cascading through a low window on the best of days. It is here that I write whenever I am home, and where I retreat to center myself, to rest and recharge at regular intervals. It is here that I do my morning visualizations and my eurhythmics.

It is a tiny alcove with an air mattress half-covered with bright pillows, and a low narrow table with a Nigerian tie-dye throw. Against one wall and central to this space is a painting by a young Guyanese woman called *The Yard.* It is a place of water and fire and flowers and trees, filled with Caribbean women and children working and playing and being.

When the sun lances through my small window and touches the painting, the yard comes alive. The red spirit who lives at the center of the painting flames. Children laugh, a woman nurses her baby, a little naked boy cuts the grass. One woman is building a fire outside for cooking; inside a house another woman is fixing a light. In a slat-house up the hill, windows are glowing under the red-tiled roof.

I keep company with the women of this place.

Yesterday, I sat in this space with a sharp Black woman, discussing the focus of a proposed piece for a Black women's magazine. We talked about whether it should be about the role of art and spirituality in Black women's lives, or about my survival struggles with current bouts of cancer. As we talked, I gradually realized that both articles were grounded in the same place within me, and required the same focus. I require the nourishment of art and spirituality in my life, and they lend strength and insight to all the endeavors that give substance to my living. It is the bread of art and the water of my spiritual life that remind me always to reach for what is highest within my capacities and in my demands of myself and others. Not for what is perfect but for what is the best possible. And I orchestrate my daily anticancer campaign with an intensity intrinsic to who I am, the intensity of making a poem. It is the same intensity with which I experience poetry, a student's first breakthrough, the loving energy of women I do not even know, the posted photograph of a sunrise taken from my winter dawn window, the intensity of loving.

I revel in the beauty of the faces of Black women at labor and at rest. I make, demand, translate satisfactions out of every ray of sunlight, scrap of bright cloth, beautiful sound, delicious smell that comes my way, out of every sincere smile and good wish. They are discreet bits of ammunition in my arsenal against despair. They all contribute to the strengthening of my determination to persevere when the greyness overwhelms, or Reaganomics wears me down. They whisper to me of joy when the light is dim, when I falter, when another Black child is gunned down from behind in Crossroads or Newark or lynched from a tree in Memphis, and when the health orchestration gets boring or depressing or just plain too much.

November 16, 1986
New York City

For Black women, learning to consciously extend ourselves to each other and to call upon each other's strengths is a life-saving strategy. In the

From *Sister Outsider* and *A Burst of Light*

best of circumstances surrounding our lives, it requires an enormous amount of mutual, consistent support for us to be emotionally able to look straight into the face of the powers aligned against us and still do our work with joy.

It takes determination and practice.

Black women who survive have a head start in learning how to be open and self-protective at the same time. One secret is to ask as many people as possible for help, depending on all of them and on none of them at the same time. Some will help, others cannot. For the time being.

Another secret is to find some particular thing your soul craves for nourishment—a different religion, a quiet spot, a dance class—and satisfy it. That satisfaction does not have to be costly or difficult. Only a need that is recognized, articulated, and answered.

There is an important difference between openness and naiveté. Not everyone has good intentions nor means me well. I remind myself I do not need to change these people, only recognize who they are.

November 17, 1986
New York City

How has everyday living changed for me with the advent of a second cancer? I move through a terrible and invigorating savor of now—a visceral awareness of the passage of time, with its nightmare and its energy. No more long-term loans, extended payments, twenty-year plans. Pay my debts. Call the tickets in, the charges, the emotional IOUs. Now is the time, if ever, once and for all, to alter the patterns of isolation. Remember that nice lady down the street whose son you used to cross at the light and who was always saying, "Now if there's ever anything I can do for you, just let me know." Well, her boy's got strong muscles and the lawn needs mowing.

I am not ashamed to let my friends know I need their collective spirit—not to make me live forever, but rather to help me move through the life I have. But I refuse to spend the rest of that life mourning what I do not have.

If living as a poet—living on the front lines—has ever had meaning, it has meaning now. Living a self-conscious life, vulnerability as armor.

I spend time every day meditating upon my physical self in battle, visualizing the actual war going on inside my body. As I move through the other parts of each day, that battle often merges with particular external campaigns, both political and personal. The devastations of apartheid in South Africa and racial murder in Howard Beach feel as critical to me as cancer.

Among my other daily activities I incorporate brief periods of physical self-monitoring without hysteria. I attend the changes within my body, anointing myself with healing light. Sometimes I have to do it while sitting on the Staten Island Ferry on my way home, surrounded by snapping gum and dirty rubber boots, all of which I banish from my consciousness.

I am learning to reduce stress in my practical everyday living. It's nonsense, however, to believe that any Black woman who is living an informed life in america can possibly abolish stress totally from her life without becoming psychically deaf, mute, and blind. (*News item: Unidentified Black man found hanging from a tree in Central Park with hands and feet bound. New York City police call it a suicide.*) I am learning to balance stress with periods of rest and restoration.

I juggle the technologies of eastern medicine with the holistic approach of anthroposophy with the richness of my psychic life, beautifully and womanfully nourished by people I love and who love me. Balancing them all. Knowing over and over again how blessed I am in my life, my loves, my children; how blessed I am in being able to give myself to work in which I passionately believe. And yes, some days I wish to heaven to Mawu to Seboulisa to Tiamat daughter of chaos that it could all have been easier.

But I wake in an early morning to see the sun rise over the tenements of Brooklyn across the bay, fingering through the wintered arms of the raintree Frances and I planted as a thin stick seventeen years ago, and I cannot possibly imagine trading my life for anyone else's, no matter how near termination that life may be. Living fully—how long is not the point. How and why take total precedence.

November 18, 1986
New York City

Despair and isolation are my greatest internal enemies. I need to remember I am not alone, even when it feels that way. Now more than ever it is time to put my solitary ways behind me, even while protecting my solitude. "Help is on the way," Margareta said, her fingers moving over the Tarot deck in a farewell gesture.

I need to identify that help and use it whenever I can.

Five million people in the U.S.—or 2 percent of the population of this country—are actively living with cancer. If you apply that percentage to the Black community—where it is probably higher because of the rising incidence of cancers without a corresponding rise in the cure rate—if we take that percentage into the Black population of 22 million, then every single day there are at least half a million Black people in the U.S. shopping in supermarkets, catching subways, grooming mules, objecting in PTA meetings, standing in a welfare line, teaching Sunday school, walking in the streets at noon looking for work, scrubbing a kitchen floor, all carrying within our bodies the seeds of a destruction not of our own choosing. It is a destruction we can keep from defining our living for as long as possible, if not our dying. Each one of us must define for ourselves what substance and shape we wish to give the life we have left.

November 19, 1986
New York City

Evil never appears in its own face to bargain, nor does impotence, nor does despair. After all, who believes any more in the devil buying up souls, anyway? But I warn myself, don't even pretend not to say no, loudly and often, no matter how symbolically. Because the choices presented in our lives are never simple or fable-clear. Survival never presents itself as "do this particular thing precisely as directed and you will go on living. Don't do that and no question about it you will surely die." Despite what the doctor said, it just doesn't happen that way.

Probably in some ideal world we would be offered distinct choices, where we make our decisions from a clearly typed and annotated menu. But no life for any Black woman I know is that simple or that banal. There are as many crucial, untimed decisions to be made as there are dots in a newspaper photo of great contrast, and as we get close enough to examine them within their own terrain, the whole picture becomes distorted and obscure.

I do not think about my death as being imminent, but I live my days against a background noise of mortality and constant uncertainty. Learning not to crumple before these uncertainties fuels my resolve to print myself upon the texture of each day fully rather than forever.

December 1, 1986
New York City

Cancer survivors are expected to be silent out of misguided concerns for others' feelings of guilt or despair, or out of a belief in the myth that there can be self-protection through secrecy. By and large, outside the radiation lab or the doctor's office, we are invisible to each other, and we begin to be invisible to ourselves. We begin to doubt whatever power we once knew we had, and once we doubt our power, we stop using it. We rob our comrades, our lovers, our friends, and our selves of ourselves.

I have periods of persistent and distracting visceral discomfort that are totally intrusive and energy-consuming. I say this rather than simply use the word *pain*, because there are too many gradations of effect and response that are not covered by that one word. Self-hypnosis seemed a workable possibility for maintaining some control over the processes going on inside my body. With trial and inquiry, I found a reliable person to train me in the techniques of self-hypnosis. It's certainly cheaper than codeine.

Self-hypnosis requires a concentration so intense I put myself into a waking trance. But we go into those states more often than we realize. Have you ever been wide awake on the subway and missed your station because you were thinking about something else? It's a question of recognizing this state and learning to use it to manipulate my consciousness of pain.

One of the worst things about intrusive pain is that it makes me feel impotent, unable to move against it and therefore against anything else, as if the pain swallows up all ability to act. Self-hypnosis has been useful to me not only for refocusing physical discomfort, it has also been useful to me in helping effect other bargains with my unconscious self. I've been able to use it to help me remember my dreams, raise a subnormal body temperature, and bring myself to complete a difficult article.

I respect the time I spend each day treating my body, and I consider it part of my political work. It is possible to have some conscious input into our physical processes—not expecting the impossible, but allowing for the unexpected—a kind of training in self-love and physical resistance.

December 7, 1986
New York City

I'm glad I don't have to turn away any more from movies about people dying of cancer. I no longer have to deny cancer as a reality in my life. As I wept over *Terms of Endearment* last night, I also laughed. It's hard to believe I avoided this movie for over two years.

Yet while I was watching it, involved in the situation of a young mother dying of breast cancer, I was also very aware of that standard of living, taken for granted in the film, that made the expression of her tragedy possible. Her mother's maid and the manicured garden, the unremarked but very tangible money so evident through its effects. Daughter's philandering husband is an unsuccessful English professor, but they still live in a white-shingled house with trees, not in some rack-ass tenement on the Lower East Side or in Harlem for which they pay too much rent.

Her private room in Lincoln Memorial Hospital has her mama's Renoir on the wall. There are never any Black people at all visible in that hospital in Lincoln, Nebraska, not even in the background. Now this may not make her death scenes any less touching, but it did strengthen my resolve to talk about my experiences with cancer as a Black woman.

December 14, 1986
New York City

It is exactly one year since I went to Switzerland and found the air cold and still. Yet what I found at the Lukas Klinik has helped me save my life.

[Its manifestation is not only therapeutic. It is vital. Underlining what is joyful and life-affirming in my living becomes crucial.

What have I had to leave behind? Old life habits, outgrown defenses put aside lest they siphon off energies to no useful purpose?

One of the hardest things to accept is learning to live within uncertainty and neither deny it nor hide behind it. Most of all, to listen to the messages of uncertainty without allowing them to immobilize me, nor keep me from the certainties of those truths in which I believe. I turn away from any need to justify the future—to live in what has not yet been. Believing, working for what has not yet been while living fully in the present now.

This is my life. Each hour is a possibility not to be banked. These days are not a preparation for living, some necessary but essentially extraneous divergence from the main course of my living. They are my life. The feeling of the bedsheet against my heels as I wake to the sound of crickets and bananaquits in Judith's Fancy. I am living my life every particular day no matter where I am, nor in what pursuit. It is the consciousness of this that gives a marvelous breadth to everything I do consciously. My most deeply held convictions and beliefs can be equally expressed in how I deal with chemotherapy as well as in how I scrutinize a poem. It's about trying to know who I am wherever I am. It's not as if I'm in struggle over here while someplace else, over there, real life is waiting for me to begin living it again.

I visualize daily winning the battles going on inside my body, and this is an important part of fighting for my life. In those visualizations, the cancer at times takes on the face and shape of my most implacable enemies, those I fight and resist most fiercely. Sometimes the wanton cells in my liver become Bull Connor and his police dogs completely smothered, rendered impotent in Birmingham, Alabama, by a mighty avalanche of young, determined Black marchers moving across him toward their future. P. W. Botha's bloated face of apartheid squashed into the earth beneath an onslaught of the slow rhythmic advance of furious Blackness. Black South African women moving through my blood destroying passbooks. Fireburn Mary sweeping over the Cruzan countryside, axe and torch in hand. Images from a Calypso singer:

The big black boot of freedom
Is mashing down your doorstep.

I train myself for triumph by knowing it is mine, no matter what. In fact, I am surrounded within my external living by ample examples of the struggle for life going on inside me. Visualizing the disease process inside my body in political images is not a quixotic dream. When I speak out against the cynical U.S. intervention in Central America, I am working to save my life in every sense. Government research grants to the National Cancer Institute were cut in 1986 by the exact amount illegally turned over to the contras in Nicaragua. One hundred and five million dollars. It gives yet another meaning to the personal as the political.

Cancer itself has an anonymous face. When we are visibly dying of cancer, it is sometimes easier to turn away from the particular experience into the sadness of loss, and when we are surviving, it is sometimes easier to deny that experience. But those of us who live our battles in the flesh must know ourselves as our strongest weapon in the most gallant struggle of our lives.

Living with cancer has forced me to consciously jettison the myth of omnipotence, of believing—or loosely asserting—that I can do anything, along with any dangerous illusion of immortality. Neither of these unscrutinized defenses is a solid base for either political activism or personal struggle. But in their place, another kind of power is growing, tempered and enduring, grounded within the realities of what I am in fact doing. An open-eyed assessment and appreciation of what I can and do accomplish, using who I am and who I most wish myself to be. To stretch as far as I can go and relish what is satisfying rather than what is sad. Building a strong and elegant pathway toward transition.

I work, I love, I rest, I see and learn. And I report. These are my givens. Not sureties, but a firm belief that whether or not living them with joy prolongs my life, it certainly enables me to pursue the objectives of that life with a deeper and more effective clarity.

August 1987
Carriacou, Grenada
Anguilla, British West Indies
St. Croix, Virgin Islands

MY WORDS WILL BE THERE

EVA'S MAN BY GAYL JONES

A Review

Eva Medina Canada, Black woman victim, poisons her lover of three days and then bites off his penis.

If this story needs to be told, it needs to be out of a pain that, unless examined and scrutinized, will be ever present and corrupting because it is never lessened nor resolved. But *Eva's Man* attempts no such emotional scrutiny. From Eva's childhood encounter with eight-year-old Freddy Smoot who examines her vaginally with a popsicle stick, to her connection with prison cellmate Elvira, *Eva's Man* presents a patchwork of sexual brutalizations that depersonalize and deprave at the same time as they bind victim to victim.

But it is a tragedy of oppression, that standing in the emotional and physical rubble of enemies, real or imagined, and of selves, loved or despised, still does not posit any different tomorrow. Repeated like a depraved slide-show rather than the terrible acts of brutalized people, the human destructiveness within *Eva's Man* erupts without feeling nor understanding, without context. And so it can exist safely separate from ourselves and our own angers.

In the author's first novel, *Corregidora*, Ursa gropes, however falteringly, for some definition of herself, different from that one which history and ancestry have forced upon her. But Eva Canada has no quest nor self, only unsatisfied hunger, hurt, and mute revenge. The lie has already been told too often, that what Black women best know how to do is suffer and castrate. Eva's final act upon Davis is not monstrous because it is ugly, but rather because it pretends to meaning.

Yet this book deserves attention. The talent behind its almost-insights should be encouraged to shed the safety of phantasmagoria. There are real Black girls being groped in stairwells and raped on rooftops, who have no voice, and who do not grow up to bite off Black men's penises.

When little Freddy of the dirty popsicle stick gives the child Eva his pocketknife as a parting gift, what the children cannot say to each other then remains unsaid throughout the book. Its unspoken presence fills us with question[s], as the grown Eva drifts from stabbing through marriage to murder. Does Eva submit for fear, stab for protection, marry for safety, kill for desire, or love? Are these encounters only more of the random violence that is so depressingly often served up to women as acceptable alternatives to the understanding of human suffering and oppression? We don't know, because we have only the emotionally provocative outlines of these encounters, redolent with the old female staples of blood, despair, and madness. Again, the twin myths of Black woman as victim and queen bee.

This absence of human insight seems to say to my brutalized sisters that if we participate in our own destruction it won't hurt so much. By this distortion of presenting occurrence rather than experience—happenings without feelings—*Eva's Man* suggests that biting off a penis might possibly fill that terrible emptiness of heart, or some other loveless hollow.

Any possible meeting of woman to woman is treated without warmth or with the bleakest contempt. On her visit south, Eva walks in the woods with Charlotte, the daughter of her mother's old friend. Charlotte's tentative gestures toward some closeness are quickly rejected by the suspicious Eva, in favor of the safety in speculation about "doing it" with boys. Later, in prison, her cellmate, Elvira, offers a harshly persistent refuge from Eva's sexual fantasies of the man she has killed. "I'll do it for you." The words represent the level of connection between the two women.

Incest, sexual abuse, and oral castration may be titillating to fantasize about, and so is revenge. But they are terrible realities just beneath the surface of some women's lives, and deserve to be treated with serious insights. Most of all, they are subjects that need to be treated with an emotional honesty that is lacking here. In *Eva's Man* we find not exploration but a cartoon-like flatness.

I read *Eva's Man* the same day I read a news article in the back pages of the *New York Times* which told of three teenaged sisters, two of whom had already borne children by their natural father. The three girls had been placed in a foster home, but had begged to be returned to their parents' house. And they were, by court order.

Beside that tragic nugget of female lovelessness and human waste, *Eva's Man* is an inhuman little book, however well-written.

9

SELF-DEFINITION AND MY POETRY

No poet worth salt writes out of anything other than those various entities she or he defines as self. How aware I am of those selves, and how much I accept those many parts of me will determine how my living appears within my poetry. How my living becomes available, in its strengths and its weaknesses, through my work, to each one of you.

In other words, time, more than anything else, shows me what I need. I know however, that if I, Audre Lorde, do not define myself, the outer world certainly will, and, as each one of you will discover, probably will define each one of us to our detriment, singly or in groups.

So I cannot separate my life and my poetry. I write my living and I live my work. And I find in my life truths which I hope can reach across, bring richness, to other women beyond the differences in our lives, beyond the differences in our loves, beyond the differences in our work. For it is within the sharing of these differences that we find growth. It is within these differences that I find growth, or can, if I am honest enough to speak out of my many selves, my loves, my hates, my mistakes, as well as my strengths.

I feel, and stake my life and my living upon it, that we become strong by doing whatever it is we need to be strong for.

Solstice.

And I feel that my words here now are part of what I pay, and repay, for whatever strengths are bred here between us as we speak.

I am constantly defining my selves, for I am, as we all are, made up of so many different parts. But when those selves war within me, I am immobilized, and when they move in harmony, or allowance, I am enriched, made strong. Yet I know there are Black women who do not use my work in their classes because I am a lesbian. There are lesbians who cannot hear me nor my work because I have two children, one of whom is a boy, both of whom I love dearly. There are women, maybe in this room, who cannot deal with me nor my vision because I am Black, and their racism becomes a blindness that separates us. And by us I mean all those who truly believe we can work for a world in which we can all live and define ourselves.

And I tell you this. My friends, there will always be someone seeking to use one part of your selves, and at the same time urging you to forget or destroy all of the other selves. And I warn you, this is death. Death to you as a woman, death to you as a poet, death to you as a human being.

When the desire for definition, self or otherwise, comes out of a desire for limitation rather than a desire for expansion, no true face can emerge. Because any ratification from the outside can only augment my self-definition, not provide it. Nobody telling me I am worthy, or that a poem is good, can possibly match that sense within my self of worthiness, or of having done what I set out to do. And those of us who are Black, those of us who are women, those of us who are lesbians, all know what I mean. Black is beautiful but currently going out of style, yet I am still Black. The women's movement may be going out of style soon too, because that is the american way. But I am not going to stop being a woman.

And just wait. Women loving women will come into and go out of style again too, but that does not alter the focus of my loving.

So remember. When they come after you or me, it won't matter particularly whether you are or I am a Black poet lesbian mother lover feeler doer woman, it will only matter that we shared in the rise of that most real and threatening human movement, the right to love, to work, and to define each of us, ourselves.

10

INTRODUCTION

Movement in Black by Pat Parker

On the last night of my first trip to the West Coast in 1969, I walked into a room and met a young Black poet with fire in her eyes, a beer in her hand, and a smile/scowl on her face. There were poems in her mouth, on the tables, in the refrigerator, under the bed, and in the way she cast about the apartment, searching for—not answers—but rather, unexpressible questions. We were both Black; we were Lesbians; we were both poets, in a very white, straight, male world, and we sat up all night trading poems. The next day the continent divided us, and during the next few years I read Pat Parker's two earlier books with appreciation, sometimes worrying about whether or not she'd/we'd survive (which for Black/Poet/Women is synonymous with grow).

Now, with love and admiration, I introduce Pat Parker and this new collection of her poetry. These poems would not need any introduction except for the racism and heterosexism of a poetry establishment which has whited out Parker from the recognition deserved by a dynamic and original voice in our poetry today.

> I am a child of America
> a step child
> raised in a back room

Even when a line falters, Parker's poetry maintains, reaches out, and does not let go. It is clean and sharp without ever being neat. Yet her images are precise, and the plain accuracy of her visions encourages an honesty that may be uncomfortable as it is compelling. Her words are womanly and uncompromising.

SISTER! your foot's smaller
but it's still on my neck.

Her tenderness is very direct:

A woman's body must be taught to
speak bearing a lifetime of keys, a patient soul

and her directness can be equally tender:

My hands are big
and rough and callous
like my mother's—

Her Black Woman's voice rings true and deep and gentle, with an iron echo. It is merciless and vulnerable and far ranging. In her poems Parker owns her weaknesses and she owns her strengths, and she does not give up. Even when she weeps, her words evoke that real power which is core-born.

A pit is an abyss
let's drink to my shame

For as a Black Lesbian poet, Parker knows, that for all women, the most enduring conflicts are far from simple.

And for the Sisters who still think that fear is a reason to be silent, Parker's poetry says loudly and clearly: I HAVE SURVIVED! I SEE, AND I SPEAK!

I have a duty to speak the truth as I see it and to share not
just my triumphs, not just the things that felt good, but the
pain, the intense, often unmitigating pain. . . . IF what I
have to say is wrong, then there will be some woman who
will stand up and say Audre Lorde was in error. But my
words will be there.

11

MY WORDS WILL BE THERE

I looked around when I was a young woman and there was no one saying what I wanted and needed to hear. I felt totally alienated, disoriented,
crazy. I thought that there's got to be somebody else who feels as I do.

I was very inarticulate as a youngster. I couldn't speak. I didn't speak
until I was five, in fact, not really, until I started reading and writing
poetry. I used to speak in poetry. I would read poems, and I would mem-
orize them. People would say, well what do you think, Audre? What happened to you yesterday? And I would recite a poem and somewhere in
that poem there would be a line or a feeling I would be sharing. In other
words, I literally communicated through poetry. And when I couldn't
find the poems to express the things I was feeling, that's what started me
writing poetry, and that was when I was twelve or thirteen.

My critics have always wanted to cast me in a particular role, from
the time my first poem was published when I was fifteen years old. My
English teachers at Hunter High School said that this particular poem
was much too romantic (it was a love poem about my first love affair
with a boy), and they didn't want to print it in the school paper, which is
why I sent it to *Seventeen* magazine, and, of course, *Seventeen* printed it.

My critics have always wanted to cast me in a particular light. People
do. It's easier to deal with a poet, certainly with a Black woman poet, when

you categorize her, narrow her so that she can fulfill your expectations. But I have always felt that I cannot be categorized. That has been both my weakness and my strength. It has been my weakness because my independence has cost me a lot of support. But you see, it has also been my strength because it has given me the power to go on. I don't know how I would have lived through the different things I have survived and continued to produce if I had not felt that all of who I am is what fulfills me and what fulfills the vision I have of a world.

I've only had one writer-in-residence position, and that was at Tougaloo College in Mississippi eleven years ago. It was pivotal for me. Pivotal, because in 1968 my first book had just been published; it was my first trip into the deep South; it was the first time I had been away from the children. It was the first time I dealt with young Black students in a workshop situation. I came to realize that this was my work, that teaching and writing were inextricably combined, and it was there that I knew what I wanted to do for the rest of my life.

I had been "the librarian who wrote." After my experience at Tougaloo, I realized that my writing was central to my life and that the library, although I loved books, was not enough. Combined with the circumstances that followed my stay at Tougaloo—King's death, Kennedy's death, Martha's accident—all of these things really made me see that life is very short, and what we have to do must be done in the now.

I have never had another writer-in-residence position. The poem "Touring" from *The Black Unicorn* represents very much how I feel about that. I go to read my poetry occasionally. I drop my little seeds, and then I leave. I hope they spring into something. Sometimes I find out they do; sometimes I never find out. I just have to have faith.

Primarily, I write for those women who do not speak, who do not have verbalization because they, we, are so terrified, because we are taught to respect fear more than ourselves. We've been taught to respect our fears but we *must* learn to respect ourselves and our needs.

In the forties and fifties my lifestyle and the rumors about my lesbianism made me persona non grata in Black literary circles.

I feel not to be open about who I am in all respects places a certain kind of expectation on me I'm just not into meeting any more. I hope that as many people as possible can deal with my work and with who I am, that they will find something in my work which can be of use to them in their lives. But if they do not, cannot, then we are all the losers. But then, perhaps their children will. But for myself, it has been very necessary and very generative for me to deal with all the aspects of who I am, and I've been saying this for a long time. I am not one piece of myself. I cannot be simply a Black person and not be a woman too, nor can I be a woman without being a lesbian. . . . Of course, there'll always be people, and there have always been people in my life, who will come to me and say, "Well, here, define yourself as such and such," to the exclusion of the other pieces of myself. There is an injustice to self in doing this, it is an injustice to the women for whom I write. In fact, it is an injustice to everyone. What happens when you narrow your definition to what is convenient, or what is fashionable, or what is expected, is dishonesty by silence.

Now, when you have a literary community oppressed by silence from the outside, as Black writers are in america, and you have this kind of tacit insistence upon some unilateral definition of what "Blackness" is or requires, then you are painfully and effectively silencing some of our most dynamic and creative talent, for all change and progress from within comes about from the recognition and use of difference between ourselves.

I consider myself to have been a victim of this silencing in the Black literary community for years, and I am certainly not the only one. For instance, there is no question about the *quality* of my work at this point. Then why do you think my last book, *The Black Unicorn*, has not been reviewed, nor even mentioned, in any Black newspaper or Black magazine within the thirteen months since it appeared?

I feel I have a duty to speak the truth as I see it and to share not just my triumphs, not just the things that felt good, but the pain, the intense, often unmitigating pain.

I never thought I would live to be forty and I'm forty-five! I feel like hey, I really did it! I am very pleased about really confronting the whole issue of breast cancer, of mortality, of dying. It was hard but very strengthening to remember that I could be silent my whole life long and then be dead, flat out, and never have said or done what I wanted to do, what I needed to do, because of pain, fear. . . . If I waited to be right before I spoke, I would be sending little cryptic messages on the Ouija board, complaints from the other side.

I really feel if what I have to say is wrong, then there will be some woman who will stand up and say Audre Lorde was in error. But my words will be there, something for her to bounce off, something to incite thought, activity.

Black male writers tend to cry out in rage as a means of convincing their readers that they too feel, whereas Black women writers tend to dramatize the pain, the love. They don't seem to need to intellectualize this capacity to feel; they focus on describing the feeling itself. And love often is pain. But I think what is really necessary is to see how much of this pain I can feel, how much of this truth I can see and still live un-blinded. And finally, it is necessary to determine how much of this pain I can use. That is the essential question that we must all ask ourselves. There is some point where pain becomes an end in itself, and then we must let it go. On the one hand, we must not be afraid of pain, but on the other we must not subject ourselves to pain as an end in itself. We must not celebrate victimization, because there are other ways of being Black.

There is a very thin but very definite line between these two re-sponses to pain. And I would like to see this line more carefully drawn in some of the works by Black women writers. I am particularly aware of the two responses in my own work. And I find I must remember that the pain is not its own reason for being. It is a part of living. And the only kind of pain that is intolerable is pain that is wasteful, pain from which we do not learn. And I think that we must learn to distinguish between the two.

I see protest as a genuine means of encouraging someone to feel the inconsistencies, the horror, of the lives we are living. Social protest is to say that we do not have to live this way. If we feel deeply, as we encour-age ourselves and others to feel deeply, we will, within that feeling, once we recognize we can feel deeply, we can love deeply, we can feel joy, then we will demand that all parts of our lives produce that kind of joy. And when they do not, we will ask, "Why don't they?" And it is the asking that will lead us inevitably toward change.

So the question of social protest and art is inseparable for me. I can't say it is an either/or proposition. Art for art's sake doesn't really exist for me, but then it never did. What I saw was wrong, and I had to speak up. I loved poetry and I loved words. But what was beautiful had to serve the purpose of changing my life, or I would have died. If I cannot air this pain and alter it, I will surely die of it. That's the beginning of social protest.

So much for pain; what about love? When you've been writing love poems for thirty years, those later poems are the ones that really hit the "nitty-gritty," that walk your boundaries. They witness what you've been through. Those are the real love poems. And I love those later love poems because they say, Hey! We define ourselves as lovers, as people who love each other all over again; we become new again. These poems insist that you can't separate loving from fighting, from dying, from hurting, but love is triumphant. It is powerful and strong, and I feel I grow a great deal in all of my emotions, especially in the capacity to love.

The love expressed between women is particular and powerful, because we have had to love in order to live; love has been our survival.

We're supposed to see "universal love" as heterosexual. And what I insist upon in my work is that there is no such thing as universal love in literature. There is this love, in this poem. The poem happened when I, Audre Lorde, poet, dealt with the particular instead of the "UNIVERSAL." My power as a person, as a poet, comes from who I am. I am a particular person. The relationships I have had, where people kept me alive, helped sustain me, people whom I've sustained give me my particular identity which is the source of my energy. Not to deal with my life in my art is to cut out the fount of my strength.

I love to write love poems; I love loving. And to put it into another framework, that is other than poetry, I wrote a paper, entitled "Uses of the Erotic," where I examine the whole question of loving, as a manifestation. Love is very important because it is a source of tremendous power.

Women have not been taught to respect the erotic urge, the place that is uniquely female. So, just as some Black people tend to reject Blackness because it has been termed inferior, we, as women, tend to reject our capacity for feeling, our ability to love, to touch the erotic, because it has been devalued. But it is within this that lies so much of our power, our ability to posit, to vision. Because once we know how deeply we can feel, we begin to demand from all of our life pursuits that they be in accordance with these feelings. And when they don't, we must perforce raise the question why . . . why . . . why do I feel constantly suicidal, for instance? What's wrong? Is it me? Or is it what I am doing? And we begin to need to answer such questions. But we cannot do this when we have no vision of joy, when we have no vision of what we are capable of. When you live always in darkness, when you live without the sunlight, you don't know what it is to relish the bright light or even to have too much of it. Once you have light, then you can measure its degree. So too with joy.

I keep a journal; I write in my journal fairly regularly. I get a lot of my poems out of it. It is the raw material for my poems. Sometimes I'm blessed with a poem that comes in the form of a poem, but sometimes I work for two years on a poem.

For me, there are two very basic and different processes for revising my poetry. One is recognizing that a poem has not yet become itself. In other words I mean that the feeling, the truth that the poem is anchored in is somehow not clearly clarified inside of me, and as a result the poem lacks something. Then the poem has to be refelt. Then there's the other process, which is easier. The poem is itself, but it has rough edges that need to be refined. That kind of revision involves picking the image that is more potent or tailoring it so that it carries the feeling. That's an easier kind of rewriting than refeeling.

My journal entries focus on things I feel. Feelings that sometimes have no place, no beginning, no end. Phrases I hear in passing. Something that looks good to me, delights me. Sometimes just observations of the world.

I went through a period when I felt like I was dying. It was during 1975. I wasn't writing any poetry, and I felt that if I couldn't write it, I would split. I was recording things in my journal, but no poems came. I know now that this period was a transition in my life and I wasn't dealing with it.

Later the next year, I went back to my journal, and there were these incredible poems that I could almost lift out of the journal; many of them are in *The Black Unicorn*. "Harriet" is one of them; "Sequelae" is another. "A Litany for Survival" is another. These poems were right out of the journal. But I didn't see them as poems prior to that.

"Power"* was in the journal too. It is a poem written about Clifford Glover, the ten-year-old Black child shot by a cop who was acquitted by a jury on which a Black woman sat. In fact, the day I heard on the radio that [Thomas] O'Shea had been acquitted, I was going across town on Eighty-eighth Street and I had to pull over. A kind of fury rose up in me; the sky turned red. I felt so sick. I felt as if I would drive this car into a wall, into the next person I saw. So I pulled over. I took out my journal just to air some of my fury, to get it out of my fingertips. Those expressed feelings are that poem. That was just how "Power" was written. There is an incredible gap occurring between the journal and my poetry, however; I write this stuff in my journals, and sometimes I can't even read my journals because there is so much pain, rage, in them. I'll put them away in a drawer, and six months, a year or so later, I'll pick up the journal, and there will be poems. The journal entries somehow have to be assimilated into my living, and only then can I deal with what I have written down.

Art is not living. It is a use of living. The artist has the ability to take that living and use it in a certain way, and produce art.

Afro-American literature is certainly part of an African tradition that deals with life as an experience to be lived. In many respects, it is much like the Eastern philosophies in that we see ourselves as a part of a life force; we are joined, for instance, to the air, to the earth. We are part of the whole life process. We live in accordance with, in a kind of correspondence with, the rest of the world as a whole. And therefore, living becomes an experience, rather than a problem, no matter how bad or how painful it may be. Change will rise endemically from the experience fully lived and responded to.

I feel this very much in African writing. And as a consequence, I have learned a great deal from [Chinua] Achebe, [Amos] Tutuola, [Cyprian] Ekwensi, from Flora Nwapa and Ama Ata Aidoo. Leslie Lacy, a Black

---

* Published in *Between Ourselves* (Point Reyes, CA: Eidolon Editions, 1976).

american who resided temporarily in Ghana, writes about experiencing this transcendence in his book *The Rise and Fall of a Proper Negro*. It's not a turning away from pain, from error, but seeing these things as part of living and learning from them. This characteristic is particularly African and it is transposed into the best of Afro-American literature.

This transcendence appears in [Ralph] Ellison, a little bit in [James] Baldwin, not as much as I would like. And very, very much so in Toni Morrison's *Sula*, which is the *most wonderful* piece of fiction I have recently read. And I don't care if she won a prize for *The Song of Solomon*. *Sula* is a totally incredible book. It made me light up inside like a Christmas tree. I particularly identified with the book because of the outsider idea. Toni laid that book to rest. Laid it to rest. That book is like one long poem. Sula is the ultimate Black female of our time, trapped in her power and her pain.

It's important that we share experiences and insights. *The Cancer Journals* is very important to me. It is a three-part prose monologue. It comes out of my experiences with my mastectomy and the aftermath: the rage, the terror, the fear, and the power that comes with dealing with my mortality. And since so little is being written about mastectomies, except the statistics, how do you do it, or do you pretend that it didn't happen? I thought we needed a new feminist outlook for Black women on the whole process. And that is the origin of *The Cancer Journals.*

Recent writing by many Black women seems to explore human concerns somewhat differently than do the men. These women refuse to blame racism entirely for every negative aspect of Black life. In fact, at times they hold Black men accountable. The men tend to respond defensively by labeling these women writers the darlings of the literary establishment.

It is not the destiny of Black america to repeat white america's mistakes. But we will, if we mistake the trappings of success in a sick society for the signs of a meaningful life. If Black men continue to do so, while defining "femininity" in its archaic european terms, this augurs ill for our survival as a people, let alone our survival as individuals. Freedom and future for Blacks does not mean absorbing the dominant white male disease.

As Black people, we cannot begin our dialogue by denying the oppressive nature of *male privilege*. And if Black males choose to assume that privilege, for whatever reason, raping, brutalizing, and killing women, then we cannot ignore Black male oppression. One oppression does not justify another.

As a people, we should most certainly work together to end our common oppression, and toward a future which is viable for us all. In that context, it is shortsighted to believe that Black men alone are to blame for the above situations, in a society dominated by white male privilege. But the Black male consciousness must be raised so that he realizes that sexism and woman-hating are critically dysfunctional to his liberation as a Black man because they arise out of the same constellation that engenders racism and homophobia, a constellation of intolerance for difference. Until this is done, he will view sexism and the destruction of Black women only as tangential to the cause of Black liberation rather than as central to that struggle, and as long as this occurs, we will never be able to embark upon that dialogue between Black women and Black men that is so essential to our survival as a people. And this continued blindness between us can only serve the oppressive system within which we live.

I write for myself. I write for myself and my children and for as many people as possible who can read me. When I say myself, I mean not only the Audre who inhabits my body but all those *feisty, incorrigible, beautiful Black women* who insist on standing up and saying *I am* and you can't wipe me out, no matter how irritating I am.

I feel a responsibility for myself, for those people who can now read and feel and need what I have to say, and for women and men who come after me. But primarily I think of my responsibility in terms of women because there are many voices for men. There are very few voices for women and particularly very few voices for Black women, speaking from the center of consciousness, for the *I am* out to the *we are*.

What can I share with the younger generation of Black women writers, writers in general? What can they learn from my experience? I can tell them not to be afraid to feel and not to be afraid to write about it. Even if you are afraid, do it anyway. We learn to work when we are tired, so we can learn to work when we are afraid.

12

FOREWORD TO THE ENGLISH EDITION OF *FARBE BEKENNEN: AFRO-DEUTSCHE FRAUEN AUF DEN SPUREN IHRER GESCHICHTE*

In the spring of 1984, I spent three months at the Free University in Berlin teaching a course in Black american women poets and a poetry workshop in English, for German students. One of my goals on this trip was to meet Black German women, for I had been told there were quite a few in Berlin.

Who are they, these German women of the diaspora? Beyond the details of our particular oppressions—although certainly not outside the reference of those details—where do our paths intersect as women of Color? And where do our paths diverge? Most important, what can we learn from our connected differences that will be useful to us both, Afro-German and Afro-American?

Afro-German. The women say they've never heard that term used before.

I asked one of my Black students how she'd thought about herself growing up. "The nicest thing they ever called us was 'warbaby,'" she said. But the existence of most Black Germans has nothing to do with the Second World War, and, in fact, predates it by many decades. I have Black

---

Except for the first paragraph, the opening section of this text was first published as a diary entry of May 23, 1984, in *A Burst of Light*. In the 1986 German edition of *Farbe bekennen*, Lorde's contribution is listed as an introduction; in the 1992 English-language edition of *Showing Our Colors*, this expanded contribution is listed as a foreword.

German women in my class who trace their Afro-German heritage back to the 1890s.

For me, Afro-German means the shining faces of May and Katharina in animated conversation about their fathers' homelands, the comparisons, joys, disappointments. It means my pleasure at seeing another Black woman walk into my classroom, her reticence slowly giving way as she explores a new self-awareness, gains a new way of thinking about herself in relation to other Black women.

"I've never thought of Afro-German as a positive concept before," she said, speaking out of the pain of having to live a difference that has no name, speaking out of the growing power self-scrutiny has forged from that difference.

I am excited by these women, by their blossoming sense of identity as they say, "Let us be ourselves now as we define us. We are not a figment of your imagination or an exotic answer to your desires. We are not some button on the pocket of your longings." I see these women as a growing force for international change, in concert with other Afro-Europeans, Afro-Asians, Afro-Americans.

We are the hyphenated people of the diaspora whose self-defined identities are no longer shameful secrets in the countries of our origin, but rather declarations of strength and solidarity. We are an increasingly united front from which the world has not yet heard.

Despite the terror and isolation some of these Black women have known from childhood, they are freer of the emotional dilemma facing many white feminists in Germany today. Too often, I have met an immobilizing national guilt in white German women which serves to keep them from acting upon what they profess to believe. Their energies, however well intentioned, are not being used, they are unavailable in the battles against racism, anti-Semitism, heterosexism, xenophobia. Because they seem unable to accept who they are, these women too often fail to examine and pursue the power relative to their identity. They waste that power, or worse, turn it over to their enemies. Four decades after National Socialism, the question still lingers for many white German women: how can I draw strength from my roots when those roots are entwined in such a terrible history? That terror of self-scrutiny is sometimes disguised as an unbearable arrogance, impotent and wasteful.

The words of these Black German women document their rejection of despair, of blindness, of silence. Once an oppression is expressed, it can be successfully fought.

FARBE BEKENNEN, "INTRODUCTION," 1984

It has been six years since I wrote the above. The appearance of this English translation of *Farbe bekennen* fulfills the dream I had as I wrote these words—of making the stories of our Black German sisters—and Afro-German history as a whole—available to the English-speaking diaspora.

Farbe bekennen tellingly presents the particular effects of racism in the lives of thirteen contemporary Black German women. And with the research of May Opitz, it also provides us with the little-known history of white racism in Germany and its influence upon Black German men and women, from the first African arrival to the present. It may come as a surprise to many that this period spans several hundred years.

The first book to be published in Germany dealing with Afro-Germans as a national entity, *Farbe bekennen* resulted in the formation of the Initiative Schwarze Deutsche (ISD), the first national organization of Black Germans. There are now ISD groups in several German cities, both East and West. The material in *Farbe bekennen* gains new importance now at this juncture in German history, when impending reunification raises critical questions about definitions of German identity.

Those of us who trace our roots back to the continent of Africa are spread across every country on earth. As we proceed upon the specific and difficult tasks of survival in the twenty-first century, we of the African diaspora need to recognize our differences as well as our similarities. We approach our living influenced by an African mode; life as experiences to be learned from rather than merely problems to be solved. We seek what is most fruitful for all people, and less hunger for our children. But we are not the same. Particular histories have fashioned our particular weapons, our particular insights. To successfully battle the many faces of institutionalized racial oppression, we must share the strengths of each other's vision as well as the weaponries born of particular experience.

First, we must recognize each other.

Some of these women have sustained and nurturing relationships with their African relatives. Others have grown into Blackness in the almost total absence of a Black community. What does it mean to be defined negatively from birth in one's own country because of a father who one may never see or know? How do you come to define a cultural identity when you have seen no other Black person throughout your childhood?*

Yet the presence of Africa in europe goes back before the Roman Empire. A Neanderthal skull, discovered in Dusseldorf, Germany, dates back to the Old Stone Age and is the earliest African type found in europe. Julius Caesar brought Black legions to Germany, and many never returned. The historical presence of Black Africans in the courts, universities, monasteries, and bedrooms of seventeenth-, eighteenth-, and nineteenth-century europe comes as a surprise only to those scholars pseudoeducated in europeanized bastions of institutional ethnocentricity. At the University of Wittenberg in the early 1700s, William Anthony Amo, a Guinean who later became a state counselor in Berlin, obtained his doctoral degree for a philosophical work entitled "The Want of Feeling."**

Two Black German elders who tell their stories here represent the second generation of a four-generation African-German family. One of their granddaughters is also a contributor.

Racism cuts a wide and corrosive swath across each of our lives. The overt climate that racism takes can alter according to society and our national situations. But our connections are real. In addition to shaping

---

* With thanks to Ike Hugel for our conversation of July 10, 1990.
** See May Optiz, "Racism, Sexism, and Precolonial Images of Africa in Germany," in *Showing Our Colors: Afro-German Women Speak Out*, ed. May Optiz, Katharina Oguntoye, and Dagmar Schultz, trans. Anne V. Adams (Amherst: University of Massachusetts Press, 1992); also Ivan Van Sertina, ed., *African Presence in Early Europe* (New Brunswick, N.J.: Transaction, 1985).

our individual national identities within the diaspora, the question pertains for African Americans and African Europeans and African Asians alike: what is our relationship to Africa as a whole? What should be our input into and expectation from strong and independent African states? What is our role as nationals in the liberation struggles of southern Africa? What is our responsibility?

As members of an international community of people of Color, how do we strengthen and support each other in our battles against the rising international tide of racism?

I walk into a shiny tourist sweetshop in the newly accessible East Berlin of 1990. The young white German saleswoman looks at me with aversion, snaps an outraged answer to my first question, then turns her back upon me and my companion until we leave the shop. Once outside, I look back. She turns also. Through the glass door, our eyes meet. That look of hatred she hurls against the glass in my direction is prolonged, intense, and very familiar. I have survived such looks in Jackson, Mississippi, San Francisco, Staten Island, and countless other North American cities.

I read the pages of *Farbe bekennen* and there is no question our war is the same.

I write these words at a time when West Berlin, like all of Germany, is becoming a very different place from the insulated, internationally flavored city of six years ago. The grim wall that once enclosed this city kept it at an equal distance from West Germany and the rest of europe. At the same time, it provided a veil of international glamour. Now the wall is down.

Geographically and politically, Germany stands at the center of europe. Reunified, it will once again represent a powerful force in european affairs. Historically, this force has not been a peaceful one. A new Germany's potential power and the relative part they will play in influencing the direction of that power are part of the destiny of African Germans, just as the political positions of the United States are a part of the destiny of African Americans.

Without a vision, every social change feels like death. Today, there are passions of violent hatred being loosened in East and West Germany, stoked by furies of bewilderment, displaced aggression at chaotic change, and despair at the collapsing textures of daily living. But these passions are not new in German history. Six million dead Jews and hundreds of thousands of dead, tortured, and castrated homosexuals, so-called Gypsies, Poles, and people of Color attest to what can happen when such passions are unleashed and directed into an ideology.

In East Germany after World War II, communism suppressed fascism but it did not destroy it. Racism, anti-Semitism, and xenophobia were severely legislated against in the East, but never admitted nor examined as a national reality. They remain an unaltered psychic time bomb in the national consciousness. These forces are now finding their physical expression in the sharp increase of attacks upon all people of Color, foreign guest workers as well as Black Germans.

Such attacks are also increasing in West Germany, encouraged by the same dormant neo-nazi element and stimulated by the prospect of a unification that will provide an economic and political climate within which to express this element. West Berlin children squirt water guns at a Black woman on the Kurfürstendamm. They use "Jew" as a curse word against any white neighbor their parents dislike, and do not even know what the word means. And this aggressive racism and anti-Semitism in Germany have been further nurtured by the spread of a worldwide reactionary conservatism whose chief spokespeople for the past ten years have been Britain's prime minister, Margaret Thatcher, and the United States' president, Ronald Reagan.

Communities of the African diaspora are national minorities in the countries of their birth, but considered together with the populations of the African continent, the balance changes. Globally, the rising tide of reactionary conservatism can be seen as a case of the white superpowers, East and West, deciding to come together despite their ideological differences, because, with the imminent liberation of southern Africa, even they can see the handwriting on the wall.

In West Germany within the last two months of the summer of 1990, young Turkish boys were stoned to death. A Pakistani student was fatally beaten on the steps of a university in West Berlin. Afro-German women were verbally accosted on the daytime subway in Berlin by skinheads, while the white passengers looked on silently. In Dresden, East Germany, a Turkish woman was beaten and her teeth kicked in by a gang of male sports fans while local police watched.

Two nights after the occurrence, at a poetry reading in Dresden, I speak about the need to organize against such happenings. The audience is mostly white women, and young Afro-German men and women. Black and white women from East and West Berlin guard the door. Through the glass door as I speak, I can see large young white men outside bending down and peering in, laughing and drinking beer. I feel myself assume a fighting stance as I read. For the first time in six years I am afraid as I read my poetry in Germany. I ask our Afro-German brothers to walk with us back to our car as we leave for Berlin. The beer drinkers lining the staircase as we leave do not know one of our Afro-German sisters is a black belt in Tai-kwan-do [*sic*].

Black Germans are not passively accepting this state of affairs. East and West, Afro-Germans are coming together for support and action, often in coalition with other groups. They are learning to identify and use their power, however relative, for their own survival and toward the redefinition of a national German consciousness.

Members of the African diaspora are connected by heritage although separated by birth. We can draw strength from that connectedness. African-Americans and Afro-Europeans incorporate within our consciousness certain splits and alienations of identity. At the same time we concentrate within our being the possibility of fusing the best of all our heritages. We are the hyphenated people, spread across every continent of the globe, members of that international community of people of Color who make up seven-eighths of the world's population.

The essence of a truly global feminism is the recognition of connection. Women in Micronesia bear babies who have no bones because of our history of nuclear testing in the South Pacific. In 1964 the CIA fingered Nelson Mandela for the South African police, resulting in his twenty-seven-year imprisonment. With the connivance of such senators as Jesse Helms, the United States sends millions in aid to the South African–backed UNITA forces in Angola, but less than 2 percent of U.S. aid goes to all the countries of the Caribbean. Women farm workers in

Foreword to the English Edition of *Farbe bekennen*   175

Jamaica are some of the lowest paid in the world. Yet at the beginning of 1990, while aid to eastern europe ballooned, aid to Jamaica was cut by 80 percent.

American women of whatever color cannot afford to indulge ourselves in the parochial attitudes that often blind us to the rest of the world. The Black German women included in this book offer some insights into the complexities of a future global feminism.

This book serves to remind African-American women that we are not alone in our world situation. In the face of new international alignments, vital connections and differences exist that need to be examined between African-European, African-Asian, African-American women, as well as between us and our African sisters. The first steps in examining these connections are to identify ourselves, to recognize each other, and to listen carefully to each other's stories.

In the interest of all our survivals and the survival of our children, these Black German women claim their color and their voices.

Audre Lorde
St. Croix, USVI
July 30, 1990

13

PREFACE TO A NEW EDITION OF *NEED: A CHORALE FOR BLACK WOMAN VOICES*

This revised version of *Need: A Chorale for Black Woman Voices* is created for particular use in classes, small community meetings, families, churches, and discussion groups, to open a dialogue between and among Black women and Black men on the subject of violence against women within our communities. Alterations in the text since the poem was originally published are a result of hearing the poem read aloud several times by groups of women.

Need was first written in 1979 after twelve Black women were killed in the Boston area within four months. In a grassroots movement spearheaded by Black and Latina Lesbians, Women of Color in the area rallied: Lesbian and straight, in coalitions and churches and c.r. [consciousness-raising] groups. Coming together with each other and their families and their friends, and their enemies, too—wherever—they launched a support outrage/information campaign. My lasting image of that spring, beyond the sick sadness and anger and worry, was of women whom I knew, loved, and trembled for: Barbara Smith, Demita Frazier, Margo Okazawa-Rey, and women whose names were unknown to me, leading a march through the streets of Boston behind a broad banner stitched with a line from Barbara Deming: "WE CANNOT LIVE WITHOUT OUR LIVES."

I wrote *Need: A Chorale for Black Woman Voices* because I felt I had to use the intensity of fury, frustration, and fear I was feeling to create something that could help alter the reasons for what I felt. Someone had to speak, beyond these events and this time, yet out of their terrible immediacy, to the repeated fact of the blood of Black women flowing through the streets of our communities—so often shed by our brothers, and so often without comment or note. Or worse, having that blood justified or explained away by those horrific effects of racism which we share as Black people.

When last have you seen an article on the front page—on any page—of your daily newspaper about the Black woman found dead, raped, beaten, stomped, burned, or poisoned around the corner from where you live?

As I began writing the poem, there flooded through me all the pain and waste of the Black women's deaths that I had read and heard about in the previous months during my travels and how if we were to progress as Black people, we could no longer hide this womanslaughter behind the smoke screen of nation-building. For we cannot build a Black nation upon the blood of Black women and children, without all of us, men and women, being the losers as Black people. It is as simple and as complex and as terrible as that.

And of course I was terrified. Of attack from my sisters and brothers for telling tales out of school. Of my sisters, who, out of their own fear and vulnerability, might betray me. Terrified of my brothers' anger, of being called traitor, of being accused of giving weapons to the enemy. But I knew that no weapon is so terrible as the ones we use against each other, and that Black women and men had to start speaking to each other and to our children about this wasteful expression of violence, or we would all be lost.

I wrote this poem in 1979 as an organizing tool, as a jump-off point for other pieces on the theme, and for discussion among and between Black women and men. I wrote this poem for each one of the twelve women dead in Boston that cold, bleak January. I wrote it for every face in that march, those I knew and those I did not know. I wrote it for Patricia Cowan, murdered in Detroit four months before. I wrote it for Marta, my neighbors' sweet-faced daughter, first one in her family to graduate high school, shot to death in her own bed.

I wrote it for the three little girls, victims in the Atlanta murders, whose names are never spoken.

I wrote it for every Black woman who has ever bled at the hands of a brother.

I wrote it for every brother who has ever hung his head and wept in stunned silence after the fact, wondering whatever had possessed him.

I wrote it for my son, and my daughter.

I wrote it because I wanted to talk about Black womanslaughter in a way that could not be unfelt or ignored by any Black person who heard it, with a hope perhaps of each one of us doing something within our immediate living to change this destruction.

I wrote it for every Black woman to read aloud whenever she needed. I wrote it for me.

I also wrote *Need: A Chorale for Black Woman Voices* for the Black man who came up to me in Rutgers, New Jersey, after the first time I read it, with tears in his eyes, saying how glad he was to have heard it. And I wrote it for the young brother who shook his fist at me as he walked out of my reading that same year in Detroit yelling, "You're a dangerous woman!"

Not enough has changed since then.

In 1985 I had a dialogue with James Baldwin at Hampshire College in Massachusetts, not far from Boston. One of the most heated discussions was around the issue of the twelve murdered Black women, and sexual violence and assault against Black women in general within our Black communities. There were present two other Black women, two other Black men, one white man, and a young Black male student.

Jimmy and one of the older Black men were in agreement that under the tremendous pressures of racism, Black men could not be held responsible for their violence against Black women, since it was a response to an unjust system, and Black women were only incidental victims. One of the Black men went so far as to say:

"The Black male is not attacking a Black female; it would be a sheep if that's what was there . . ." To this I replied, and still reply:

"Yes, but I'm not a sheep, I'm your sister . . . who is learning to use a gun. If we wind up having to kill each other instead of our enemies, what a terrible waste for us all."

And at this point it was the young Black male student in the room who spoke up to the older men, in defense of his mother and sisters and their right to defend themselves in the street. I want that young man to know he was a genuine affirmation for me, and that I wrote *Need: A Chorale for Black Woman Voices* for him, too.

As aggressive acts of white racist violence intensify around us, aimed primarily but not exclusively at Black males (remember Eleanor Bumpurs and Yvonne Smallwood),[1] violence against Black women, both reported and unreported, intensifies within our communities. It is time to pump up the volume again around this wasteful secret and not hide from it under a cloak of false unity, not turn away from it, believing it will be solved by somebody else.

Black women will no longer accept being slaughtered like sheep on the altars of Black male frustration. On the other hand, we do not want to have to blow away Black men in our own self-defense. So Black women and men must devise ways of working together as a people to end this slaughter. We need each other too much to be destroying each other. We need each other too much, genuinely, as Black people unafraid of each other.

Each one of us can have some input into the lives of young Black boys who are part of our future. Each one of us has a voice that can be heard, and that voice must be used. Every Black person in this country is responsible in some way for teaching our sons that their manhood cannot lie within a pool of Black women's blood.

And increasingly, there are Black male voices being raised with this lesson. In an extremely thorough and considered study of rape in Black communities, Kalamu ya Salaam noted, "[Black] women revolting and [Black] men made conscious of their responsibility to fight sexism will collectively stop rape."[2]

We need to talk about what we do to each other, no matter what pain and anger may be mined within those conversations. This poem is as good a place as any to begin. We are too important to each other to waste ourselves in silence.

"WE CANNOT LIVE WITHOUT OUR LIVES."

Audre Lorde
St. Croix
August 31, 1989

Notes

1. Eleanor Bumpurs, sixty-seven-year-old Black grandmother, [was] murdered in 1984 in her own apartment by New York City housing policemen with a shotgun, during eviction for being one month behind on her rent in public housing. Yvonne Smallwood [was] beaten to death by New York City policemen on a Manhattan street corner over a traffic ticket given to her boyfriend.

2. Kalamu ya Salaam, "Rape: A Radical Analysis from an African-American Perspective," in *Our Women Keep Our Skies from Falling* (Nkombo, 1980), 25–41.

14

POET AS TEACHER—HUMAN AS POET—TEACHER AS HUMAN

When ever I speak to this point I'm always torn between saying all right this is how I ran this particular class this particular day, it was raining, the class worked—it didn't work. . . . On the other hand, to deal with what I consider to be far more basic than any technique I use—because technique varies according to so many different factors—the exercise I choose for a rainy day with the same group is different from that which I'd have chosen had the day been bright, or the day after a police slaughter of a Black child, for make no mistake, these emotional climates are absorbed and metabolized by our children with frightening thoroughness—So more than technique, I consider as basic my total perception. The poet as teacher, human as poet, teacher as human. They all feel the same to me.

A writer by definition is a teacher. Whether or not I ever teach another class, every poem I create is an attempt at a piece of truth formed from the images of my experience and shared with as many people as can or will hear me. In this way, every poem I write is, in addition to everything else it is, also a learning device. There is something to be learned from the sharing of true feeling between two or more people; co-communicating is teaching—touching—really touching another human being is teaching—writing real poems is teaching—digging good ditches is teaching—living is teaching. I feel the only human state which is not teaching is sleeping, and that is a property which sleep shares with death.

I am a human being. I am a Black woman, a poet, mother, lover, teacher, friend, fat, shy, generous, loyal, crotchety. If I do not bring all of who I am to whatever I do, then I bring nothing, or nothing of lasting worth, for I have withheld my essence. If I do not bring all of who I am to you here tonight, speaking of what I feel, of what I know, then I do you an injustice. What you can use you will take away, what you cannot use you will leave behind.

So you see, I do not teach anyone how to create poetry. I can help children recognize and respect their own poetry; I can show a student how to improve what is already written—and by improve I mean specifically how to bring the poem closer to the feeling the poet wishes to evoke. And I can encourage a student to recognize, cherish, and set down those feelings and experiences out of which poetry is forged. But the only way I can teach another human being anything else about creating poetry is to teach that person about myself, about feeling herself or himself.

And I can only do that by being willing to share my feelings, my selves, with whatever selves, whatever feelings a student chooses to find in the pursuit of her or his poetry. The experience of poetry is an intimate one. It is neither easy nor casual, but it is real.

I hope I have not lost you nor frightened you merely because I am speaking of the intimate exchange that takes place when true learning—teaching—occurs, of feeling myself and the perception of and reaction to the feelings of other human beings. Because of course we all must realize that it is this exchange which is the most strongly prohibited, or discouraged, human exercise of our time.

The puritan ethic today is approaching its logical conclusion, and young people can now have sexual contact without batting an eyelash, but they cannot bear the intimacy of scrutiny, or of a shared feeling. Yet it is this intimacy which is necessary in order to truly teach, in order to write, in order to live.

You have asked me to speak my feelings about the poet as teacher. I present to you myself. I present to you each of your selves; learn to love your poet, learn to use it. As you feel, as you live, as you share your feelings, so do you teach.

15

POETRY MAKES SOMETHING
HAPPEN

Poetry makes something happen, indeed. It makes you happen. It makes your living happen, whether or not you deal with it. A poet is by definition a teacher also. If I never teach another class, every poem I create is an attempt at a piece of truth formed from the images of my experience, and share[d] with as many others as can or will hear me. This is something poetry shares with other hard work. Making real poems is teaching, digging good ditches is teaching, survival is teaching. The only human state I know of that is not teaching is sleep, and that is a property which sleep shares with death.

I cannot separate my life and my poetry. I write my living, and I live my work. I am a Black Woman Poet Lesbian Mother Lover Teacher Friend Warrior, and I am shy, strong, fat, generous, loyal, and crotchety, among other things. If I do not bring all of who I am to whatever I do, then I bring nothing of lasting worth, because I have withheld some piece of the essential. If I do not bring all of who I am to you here, speaking of what I feel, of what I know, then I do you all an injustice. Whatever you find here of use you will take away with you, whatever you cannot use you will leave behind.

My poetry is not separate from my living, nor is yours. The only way we can teach another person to create poetry is to teach that person how to feel herself or himself. The experience of poetry is intimate, and it is crucial. For that reason, of course, it is often resented or resisted. The pursuit of one's own poetry is basically a subversive activity, because the pursuit of one's feelings colors one's total existence, and we are paid well for refusing to feel ourselves. It is hard to feel anger and fury and frustration and grief. It is so much easier to remain emotionally aloof or to indulge in the quick emotional jerk-off that passes as sentiment so often. It is hard to accept the tragedy of children shot in the streets of Soweto as our tragedy. We are paid very well to refuse to feel. We are paid in poisonous creature comforts, we are paid in false securities, in the spurious belief that tenure might mean survival, that the knock at midnight will always be on somebody else's door. As we sit here now, Black children and university students are being imprisoned and tortured and killed on the streets and in the prisons of South Africa. We are not separate from that horror. It has happened before in New York, it has happened in Chicago, it has happened in Jackson, Mississippi, it has happened in Ohio, and it will happen again. How many of us feel these tragedies as our own? Yet we are intimately and vitally involved with them. How many of us recognize that they will continue to re-occur until we act, until we use our power, whoever and wherever we are, against these horrors? There is no separate survival.

The teaching of poetry then is teaching the recognition of feeling, is the teaching of survival. It is neither easy nor casual, but it is necessary and fruitful. The role of the poet as teacher is to encourage the intimacy of scrutiny. As we learn to bear that intimacy, those fears which rule our lives and form our silences begin to lose their power over us. We will probably always be afraid, because we have been socialized to fear; [fear] of being revealed, of being ridiculed, of being different, of being hurt. But as our poetry becomes stronger, being afraid becomes less important, the way being tired becomes less important. And we are used to working when we are tired.

Poetry is not a luxury. For the quality of light by which we scrutinize our lives has direct bearing upon the product which we live, and upon those changes which we hope to bring about through those lives. This is poetry as illumination, for it is through poetry that we give name to those ideas which are, until the poem, nameless and formless, about to be birthed, but already felt. That distillation of experience from which true poetry springs births thought as dreams birth concepts, as feeling births ideas, as knowledge births or precedes understanding.

When we view our living in the european mode, only as a problem to be solved, we rely solely upon our ideas to make us free, for the white fathers told us it was our ideas alone which were precious. But as we become more and more in touch with our own ancient and original non-european view of living as a situation to be experienced and interacted with, we learn to cherish our feelings, and to respect those hidden and deep sources of our power from whence true knowledge and therefore lasting action come. It is the fusion of these two approaches which is the keystone to our survival as a race, and we come closest to this combination in our poetry.

Poetry is the way we help give name to the nameless so it can be thought. The farthest external horizons of our hopes and fears are cobbled by our poems, carved from the rock experiences of our daily lives, honestly felt. For our feelings are the sanctuaries and spawning grounds for the most radical and daring of our ideas. Right now I could mention at least ten ideas I might have once found intolerable or frightening except as they came after dreams or poems. For poetry is not only dream and vision, it is the skeleton architect of our lives.

The white fathers have told us: I think, therefore I am. But the Black mother within each of us, the poet within each of us, whispers in our dreams: I feel, therefore I can be free. Poetry coins the language to express and charter the implementation of that freedom. Agostinho Neto knew this, the poet who led his people of Angola to freedom.

But sometimes we drug ourselves with the dream of new ideas. The head will save us. The brain alone will make us free. But there are no new ideas and forgotten ones, new combinations and recognitions within ourselves, together with the renewed courage to try them out, to dare to live as those dreams which some of our ideas disparage. And in the forefront of our move toward change, there is only our poetry to hint at possibility made real. There are no new ideas, only new ways of making them felt, of making them real. For within these structures which we live beneath, defined by profit, by flat linear power, by institutional dehumanization, our feelings were not meant to survive. They were meant to be kept around as unavoidable adjuncts or pleasant pastimes. Our feelings were meant to kneel to thought as women were meant to kneel to men. But women have survived, and our feelings have survived. As poetry. And there are no new pains. We have felt them all already. We have hidden that fact in the same place where we have hidden our power. They lie in our dreams, they lie in our poems, and it is our dreams and our poems that point the way to our freedom.

You have come here tonight to share my feelings on the poet as teacher. I present to you myself. I present to you each of your selves. Learn to love the power of your feelings, and to use that power for your good.

MY MOTHER'S MORTAR

When I was growing up in my mother's house, there were spices you grated and spices you pounded, and whenever you pounded spice and garlic or other herbs, you used a mortar. Every West Indian woman worth her salt had her own mortar. Now if you lost or broke your mortar, of course, you could buy another one in the market over on Park Avenue, under the bridge, but those were usually Puerto Rican mortars, and even though they were made out of wood and worked exactly the same way, somehow they were never really as good as West Indian mortar[s]. Now where the best mortars came from I was never really sure, but I knew it must be in the vicinity of that amorphous and mystically perfect place called "home." "Home" was the West Indies, Grenada or Barbados to be exact, and whatever came from "home" was bound to be special.

My mother's mortar was a beautiful affair, quite at variance with most of her other possessions, and certainly with her projected public view of herself. It had stood, solid and elegant, on a shelf in the kitchen cabinet for as long as I can remember, and I loved it dearly.

The mortar was of a foreign fragrant wood, too dark for cherry and too red for walnut. To my child's eyes, the outside was carved in an intricate and most enticing manner. There were rounded plums and oval indeterminate fruit, some long and fluted like a banana, others ovular and end-swollen like a ripe alligator pear. In between these were smaller rounded shapes like cherries, lying in batches against and around each other.

I loved to finger the hard roundness of the carved fruit, and the always surprising termination of the shapes as the carvings stopped at the rim and the bowl sloped abruptly downward, smoothly oval but suddenly businesslike. The heavy sturdiness of this useful wooden object always made me feel secure and somehow full; as if it conjured up from all the many different flavors pounded into the inside wall, visions of delicious feasts both once enjoyed and still to come.

The pestle was a slender tapering wand, fashioned from the same mysterious rose-deep wood, and fitted into the hand almost casually, familiarly. The actual shape reminded me of a summer crook-necked squash uncurled and slightly twisted. It could also have been an avocado, with the neck of the alligator pear elongated and the whole made businesslike and efficient for pounding, without ever losing the apparent soft firmness and the character of the fruit, which the wood suggested. It was slightly bigger at the grinding end than most pestles, and the widened curved end fitted into the bowl of the mortar easily. Long use and years of impact and grinding within the bowl's worn hollow had softened the very surface of the wooden pestle until a thin layer of split fibers coated the rounded end like a layer of velvet. A layer of the same velvety mashed wood lined the bottom inside the sloping bowl.

My mother did not particularly like to pound spice, and she looked upon the advent of powdered everything as a cook's boon. But there were some certain dishes that called for a particular savory blending of garlic, raw onion, and pepper, and souse was one of them.

For our mother's souse, it didn't matter what kind of meat was used. You could have hearts, or beef ends, or even chicken backs and gizzards when we were really poor. It was the pounded up saucy blend of herb[s] and spice[s] rubbed into the meat before it was left to stand so for a few hours before cooking that made that dish so special and unforgettable. But my mother had some very firm ideas about what she liked best to cook and about which were her favorite dishes, and souse was definitely not one of either.

On the very infrequent occasions that my mother would allow one of us three girls to choose a meal—as opposed to helping to prepare it, which was a daily routine—on those occasions my sisters would usually choose one of those proscribed dishes so dear to our hearts remembered from our relatives' tables, contraband, and so very rare in our house. They might ask for hot-doss, perhaps, smothered in ketchup sauce, or with crusty Boston-baked beans; or american chicken, breaded first and fried crispy the way the southern people did it; or creamed some-thing-or-other that one of my sisters had tasted at school; what-have-you croquettes or anything fritters; or once even a daring outrageous request for slices of fresh watermelon, hawked from the back of a rickety wooden pickup truck with the southern road dust still on her slatted sides, from which a young bony Black man with a turned-around ballcap on his head would hang and half-yell, half-yodel—"Wahr—deeeeeee—mayyyyyyyy—lawnnnnnnnnn."

There were many american dishes I longed for too, but on the one or two occasions a year that I got to choose a meal, I would always ask for souse. That way, I knew that I would get to use my mother's mortar, and this in itself was more treat for me than any of the forbidden foods. Besides, if I really wanted hot dogs or anything croquettes badly enough, I could steal some money from my father's pocket and buy them in the school lunch[room].

"Mother, let's have souse," I'd say, and never even stop to think about it. The anticipated taste of the soft spicy meat had become inseparable in my mind from the tactile pleasures of using my mother's mortar.

"But what makes you think anybody can find time to mash up all that stuff?" my mother would cut her hawk-grey eyes at me from be-neath their heavy black brows. "Among you children never stop to think, you know," and she'd turn back to whatever it was she had been doing. If she had just come from the office with my father, she might be checking the day's receipts, or she might be washing the endless piles of dirty linen that always seemed to issue from the rooming houses they managed.

"Oh, I'll pound the garlic, Mommy!" would be my next line in the script written by some ancient and secret hand, and off I'd go to the cabinet to get down the heavy wooden mortar and pestle.

I would get a head of garlic out from the garlic bottle in the ice-box, and breaking off ten or twelve cloves from the head, I would care-fully peel away the tissue lavender skin, slicing each stripped peg in half lengthwise. Then I would drop them piece by piece into the capacious waiting bowl of the mortar. Taking a slice from a small onion, I would put the rest aside, to be used later on over the meat, and cutting the slice into quarters, I would toss it into the mortar also. Next came the coarsely ground fresh black pepper, and then a lavish blanketing cover of salt over the whole. Last, if we had any, a few leaves from the top of a head of celery would be thrown in. My mother would sometimes add a slice of green pepper to be mashed in also, but I did not like the textures of the pepper skin under the pestle, and preferred to add it along with the sliced onion later on, leaving it all to sit over the seasoned and resting meat.

After all the ingredients were in the bowl of the mortar, I would fetch the pestle and placing it into the bowl, slowly rotate the shaft a few times, working it gently down through all the ingredients to mix them. Only then would I lift the pestle, and with one hand firmly pressed around the carved side of the mortar caressing the wooden fruit with my aromatic fingers, I would thrust sharply downward, feeling the shifting salt and the hard little pellets of garlic right up through the shaft of the wooden pestle. Up again, down, around, and up, so the rhythm would begin. The thud push rub rotate and up, repeated over and over; the muted thump of the pestle on the bed of grinding spice, as the salt and pepper absorbed the slowly yielded juices of the garlic and celery leaves and became moist; the mingling fragrances rising from the bowl of the mortar; the feeling of the pestle held between my fingers and the rounded fruit of the mortar's outside against my palm and curving fingers as I steadied it against my body; all these transported me into a world of scent and rhythm and movement and sound that grew more and more exciting as the ingredients liquefied.

Sometimes my mother would look over at me with that amused annoyance which passed for tenderness with her, and which was always such a welcome change for me from the furious annoyance which was so much more usual.

"What you think you making there, garlic soup? Enough, go get the meat now." And I would fetch the lamb hearts, for instance, from the icebox and begin to prepare them. Cutting away the hardened veins at the top of the smooth firm muscles, I would divide each oval heart into four wedge-shaped pieces, and taking a bit of the spicy mash from the mortar with my fingertips, I would rub each piece with the savory mix. The pungent smell of garlic and onion and celery would envelop the kitchen.

The last day I ever pounded seasoning for souse was in the summer of my fourteenth year. It had been a fairly unpleasant summer, for me.

My Mother's Mortar

I had just finished my first year in high school. Instead of being able to visit my newly found friends, all of whom lived in other parts of the city, I had had to accompany my mother on a round of doctors with whom she would have long whispered conversations that I was not supposed to listen to. Only a matter of the utmost importance could have kept her away from the office for so many mornings in a row. But my mother was concerned because I was fourteen and a half years old and had not yet menstruated. I had breasts but no period, and she was afraid there was "something wrong" with me. Yet, since she had never discussed this mysterious business of menstruation with me, I was certainly not supposed to know what all this whispering was about, even though it concerned my own body.

Of course, I knew as much as I could have possibly found out in those days from the hard-to-get books on the closed shelf behind the librarian's desk at the public library, where I had brought a forged note from home in order to be allowed to read them, sitting under the watchful eye of the librarian at a special desk reserved for that purpose.

Although not terribly informative, they were fascinating books, and used words like menses and ovulation and vagina.

But four years before, I had had to find out if I was going to become pregnant, because a boy from school much bigger than me had invited me up to the roof on my way home from the library and then threatened to break my glasses if I didn't let him stick his thing between my legs. And at that time I knew only that being pregnant had something to do with sex, and sex had something to do with that thin pencil-like thing and was in general nasty and not to be talked about by nice people, and I was afraid my mother might find out and what would she do to me then? I was not supposed to be looking at the mailboxes in the hallway of that house anyway, even though Doris was a girl in my class at St. Mark's who lived in that house and I was always so lonely in the summer, particularly that summer when I was ten.

So after I got home I washed myself up and lied about why I was late getting home from the library and got a whipping for being late. That must have been a hard summer for my parents at the office too, because that was the summer that I got a whipping for something or other almost every day between the 4th of July and Labor Day.

When I wasn't getting whippings, I hid out at the library on 135th Street and forged notes from my mother to get books from the closed shelf and read about sex and having babies and waited to become pregnant. None of the books were very clear to me about the relationship between having your period and having a baby, but they were all very clear about the relationship between penises and getting pregnant. Or maybe the confusion was all in my own mind, because I had always been a very fast but not a very careful reader.

So four years later, in my fourteenth year, I was a very scared little girl, still half-afraid that one of that endless stream of doctors would look up into my body and discover my four-year-old shame and say to my mother, "Aha! So that's what's wrong! Your daughter is about to become pregnant!"

On the other hand, if I let my mother know that I knew what was happening and what these medical safaris were all about, I would have to answer her questions about how and wherefore I knew, since she hadn't told me, divulging in the process the whole horrible and self-incriminating story of forbidden books and forged library notes and rooftops and stairwell conversations.

A year after the rooftop incident, we moved farther uptown and I was transferred to a different school. The kids there seemed to know a lot more about sex than at St. Mark's, and in the eighth grade, I had stolen money and bought Adeline a pack of cigarettes and she had confirmed my bookish suspicions about how babies were made. My response to her graphic descriptions had been to think to myself—there obviously must be another way that Adeline doesn't know about, because my parents have children and I know they never did anything like that. But the basic principles were all there, and sure enough they were the same as I had gathered from *The Young People's Family Book*.

So in my fourteenth summer, on examining table after examining table, I kept my legs open and my mouth shut, and when I saw blood on my pants one hot July afternoon, I rinsed them out secretly in the bathroom and put them back on wet because I didn't know how to break the news to my mother that both her worries and mine were finally over. (All this time I had at least understood that having your period was a sign you were not pregnant.)

What then happened felt like a piece of an old and elaborate dance between my mother and me. She discovers finally, through a stain on the toilet seat left there on purpose by me as a mute announcement, what has taken place; she scolds, "Why didn't you tell me about all of this, now? It's nothing to get upset over, now you are a woman, not a child any more. Now you go over to the drugstore and ask the man for . . ."

I was just relieved the whole damn thing was over with. It's difficult to talk about double messages without having a twin tongue. But meanwhile all these nightmarish evocations and restrictions were being verbalized by my mother:

"Now this means from now on you better watch your step and not be so friendly with every Tom Dick and Harry . . ." (which must have meant my staying late after school to talk with my girlfriends, because I did not even know any boys); and,

"Now remember too, don't leave your soiled napkins wrapped up in newspaper hanging around on the bathroom floor where your father has to see them, not that it's anything shameful but all the same remember . . ."

Along with all of these admonitions, there was something else coming from my mother that I almost could not define. It was the lurking of that amused/annoyed brow-furrowed half-smile that passed as an intimate moment between my mother and me, and I really felt—all her nagging words to the contrary, or the more confusing—that something very good and satisfactory and pleasing to her had just happened, and that we were both pretending otherwise for some very wise and secret reasons which I would come to understand later as a reward if I handled myself properly. And then at the end of it all, my mother thrust the box of Kotex in its plain wrapper which I had fetched back from the drugstore with a sanitary belt at me, and said,

"But look now what time it is already, I wonder what we're going to eat for supper tonight?" She waited. At first I didn't understand, but

I quickly picked up the cue. I had seen the beef ends in the icebox that morning.

"Mommy, please let's have some souse—I'll pound the garlic." I dropped the box onto a kitchen chair and started to wash my hands in anticipation.

"Well, go put your business away first. What did I tell you about leaving that lying around?" She wiped her hands from the washtub where she had been working and handed the plain wrapped box of Kotex back to me.

"I have to go out, I forgot to pick up tea at the store. Now make sure you rub the meat good."

When I came back into the kitchen, my mother had left. I moved toward the kitchen cabinet to fetch down the mortar and pestle. My body felt new and special and unfamiliar and suspect all at the same time.

I could feel bands of tension sweeping across my body back and forth like lunar winds across the moon's face. I felt the slight rubbing bulge of the cotton pad between my legs, and I smelled the warm delicate breadfruit smell rising up from the front of my print blouse that was my own womansmell, erotic, shameful, but secretly utterly delicious.

(Years afterward when I was grown, whenever I thought about the way I smelled that day, I would have a fantasy of my mother, her hands wiped dry from the washing, and her apron untied and laid neatly away, looking down upon me lying on the couch, and then slowly, thoroughly, our making love to each other.)

I took the mortar down, and smashed the cloves of garlic with the edge of its underside, to loosen the thin papery skins in a hurry. I sliced them and flung them into the mortar's bowl along with some black pepper and celery leaves. The white salt poured in, covering the garlic and black pepper and pale chartreuse celery fronds like a snowfall. I tossed in the onion and some bits of green pepper and reached for the pestle.

It slipped through my fingers and clattered to the floor, rolling around in a semicircle back and forth, until I bent to retrieve it. I grabbed the head of the wooden stick and straightened up, my ears ringing faintly. Without even wiping it, I plunged the pestle into the bowl, feeling the blanket of salt give way, and the broken cloves of garlic just beneath.

The downward thrust of the avocado-shaped wooden pestle slowed upon contact, rotated back and forth slowly, and then gently altered its rhythm to include an up and down beat. Back and forth, round, up and down, back, forth, round, round, up and down . . . There was a heavy fullness at the root of me that was exciting and dangerous.

As I continued to pound the spice, a vital connection seemed to establish itself between the muscles of my fingers curved tightly around the smooth pestle in its insistent downward motion, and the molten core of my body whose source emanated from a new ripe fullness just beneath the pit of my stomach. That invisible thread, taut and sensitive as a clitoris exposed, stretched through my curled fingers up my rounded brown arm into the moist reality of my armpits, whose warm sharp odor with a strange new overlay mixed with the ripe garlic smells from the mortar and the general sweat-heavy aromas of high summer.

The thread ran over my ribs and along my spine, tingling and singing, into a basin that was poised between my hips, now pressed against the low kitchen counter before which I stood, pounding spice. And within that basin was a tiding ocean of blood beginning to be made real and available to me for strength and information.

The jarring shocks of the velvet-lined pestle, striking the bed of spice, traveled up an invisible pathway along the thread into the center of me, and the harshness of the repeated impacts became increasingly more unbearable. The tidal basin suspended between my hips shuddered at each repetition of the strokes which now felt like assaults. Without my volition my downward thrusts of the pestle grew gentler and gentler until its velvety surface seemed almost to caress the liquefying mash at the bottom of the mortar.

The whole rhythm of my movements softened and elongated until, dreamlike, I stood, one hand tightly curved around the carved mortar, steadying it against the middle of my body; while my other hand, around the pestle, rubbed and pressed the moistening spice into readiness with a sweeping circular movement.

I hummed tunelessly to myself as I worked in the warm kitchen, thinking with relief about how simple my life had become now that I was a woman. The catalog of dire menstruation warnings from my mother passed out of my head. My body felt strong and full and open, yet captivated by the gentle motions of the pestle, and the rich smells filling the kitchen, and the fullness of the young summer heat.

I heard my mother's key in the lock.

She swept into the kitchen briskly, like a ship under full sail. There were tiny beads of sweat over her upper lip, and vertical creases between her brows.

"You mean to tell me no meat is ready?" My mother dropped her parcel of tea onto the table, and looking over my shoulder, sucked her teeth loudly in weary disgust. "What do you call yourself doing, now? You have all night to stand up there playing with the food? I go all the way to the store and back already and still you can't mash up a few pieces of garlic to season some meat? But you know how to do the thing better than this! Why you vex me so?"

She took the mortar and pestle out of my hands and started to grind vigorously. And there were still bits of garlic left at the bottom of the bowl.

"Now you do, so!" She brought the pestle down inside the bowl of the mortar with dispatch, crushing the last of the garlic. I heard the thump of wood brought down heavily upon wood, and I felt the harsh impact throughout my body, as if something had broken inside of me. Thump, thump, went the pestle, purposefully, up and down in the old familiar way.

"It was getting mashed, Mother," I dared to protest, turning away to the icebox. "I'll fetch the meat." I was surprised at my own brazenness in answering back.

But something in my voice interrupted my mother's efficient motions. She ignored my implied contradiction, itself an act of rebellion strictly forbidden in our house. The thumping stopped.

"What's wrong with you, now? Are you sick? You want to go to your bed?"

"No, I'm all right, Mother."

But I felt her strong fingers on my upper arm, turning me around, her other hand under my chin as she peered into my face. Her voice softened.

"Is it your period making you so slow-down today?" She gave my chin a little shake, as I looked up into her hooded grey eyes, now becoming almost gentle. The kitchen felt suddenly oppressively hot and still, and I felt myself beginning to shake all over.

Tears I did not understand started from my eyes, as I realized that my old enjoyment of the bone-jarring way I had been taught to pound spice would feel different to me from now on, and also that in my mother's kitchen, there was only one right way to do anything. Perhaps my life had not become so simple, after all.

My mother stepped away from the counter and put her heavy arm around my shoulders. I could smell the warm herness rising from between her arm and her body, mixed with the smell of glycerine and rosewater, and the scent of her thick bun of hair.

"I'll finish up the food for supper." She smiled at me, and there was a tenderness in her voice and an absence of annoyance that was welcome, although unfamiliar.

"You come inside now and lie down on the couch and I'll make you a hot cup of tea."

Her arm across my shoulders was warm and slightly damp. I rested my head upon her shoulder, and realized with a shock of pleasure and surprise that I was almost as tall as my mother, as she led me into the cool darkened parlor.

III

DIFFERENCE AND SURVIVAL

DIFFERENCE AND SURVIVAL

An Address at Hunter College

To those of you who sit here a little bemused and I hope very proud, I speak to you as a poet whose role is always to encourage the intimacy of scrutiny. For I believe that as each one of us learns to bear that intimacy those worse fears which rule our lives and shape our silences begin to lose their power over us.

Last week I asked a number of you if you felt different in any way and each one of you said very quickly and in a similar tone, "Oh no, of course not, I don't consider myself different from anybody else." I think it is not by accident that each of you heard my question as "Are you better than . . ." Yet each of you is sitting here now because in some particular way and time, in some particular place and for whatever reason, you dared to excel, to set yourself apart. And that makes you in this particular place and time, different. It is that difference that I urge you to affirm and to explore lest it someday be used against you and against me. It is within our differences that we are both most powerful and most vulnerable, and some of the most difficult tasks of our lives are the claiming of differences and learning to use those differences for bridges rather than as barriers between us.

In a profit economy which needs groups of outsiders as surplus people, we are programmed to respond to difference in one of three ways: to ignore it by denying the testament of our own senses, "Oh, I never noticed." Or if that is not possible, then we try to neutralize it in one of two ways. If the difference has been defined for us in our introductory courses as good, meaning useful in preserving the status quo, in perpetuating the myth of sameness, then we try to copy it. If the difference is defined as bad, that is revolutionary or threatening, then we try to destroy it. But we have few patterns for relating across differences as equals. And unclaimed, our differences are used against us in the service of separation and confusion, for we view them only in opposition to each other, dominant/subordinate, good/bad, superior/inferior. And of course, so long as the existence of human differences means one must be inferior, the recognition of those differences will be fraught with guilt and danger.

Which differences are positive and which negative are determined for us by a society that has been already established, and so must seek to perpetuate itself, faults as well as virtues.

To excel is considered a positive difference, and so you will be encouraged to think of yourselves as the elite. To be poor, or of Color, or female, or homosexual, or old is considered negative, and so these people are encouraged to think of themselves as surplus. Each of these imposed definitions has a place not in human growth and progress, but in human separation, for they represent the dehumanization of difference.

And certainly there are very real differences between us, of race, sex, age, sexuality, class, vision. But it is not the differences between us that tear us apart, destroying the commonalities we share. Rather, it is our refusal to examine the distortions which arise from their misnaming, and from the illegitimate usage of those differences which can be made when we do not claim them nor define them for ourselves.

Racism. The belief in the inherent superiority of one race over all others and thereby the right to dominance. Ageism. Heterosexism. Elitism. These are some of the distortions created around human differences, all serving the purpose of further separation. It is a lifetime pursuit for each one of us to extract these distortions from our living at the same time as we recognize, reclaim, and define the differences upon which they are imposed, and explore what these differences can teach us about the future we must all share. And we do not have forever. The distortions are endemic in our society, and so we pour energy needed for exposing difference into pretending these differences do not exist, thereby encouraging false and treacherous connections. Or we pretend the differences are insurmountable barriers, which encourages a voluntary isolation. Either way, we do not develop tools for using our differences as springboards for creative change within our lives.

Often, we do not even speak of human difference, which is a comparison of attributes best evaluated by their possible effect and illumination within our lives. Instead, we speak of deviance, which is a judgment upon the relationship between the attribute and some long-fixed and established construct. Somewhere on the edge of all our consciousness there is what I call the mythical norm, which each of us knows within our hearts is "not me." In this society, that norm is usually defined as white, thin, male, young, heterosexual, Christian, and financially secure. It is within this mythical norm that the trappings of power reside. Those of us who stand outside that power, for any reason, often identify one way in which we are different, and we assume that quality to be the primary reason for all oppression. We forget those other distortions around difference, some of which we ourselves may be acting out within our daily lives. For unacknowledged difference robs all of us of each other's energy and creative insight, and creates a false hierarchy.

What does this mean for each one of us? I think it means that I must choose to define my difference as you must choose to define yours, to claim it and to use it as creative before it is defined for you and used to eradicate any future, any change.

You must decide what it means to excel and to persevere beyond competence and why you do it. Or else this ability, this difference defined as good right now because it appears to promise a continuation of safety and sameness, this difference will be used to testify against your creativity, it will be used to cordon off those other differences defined/regarded as bad, improper, or threatening, those differences of race, sex, class, gender, and age, all those ways in which a profit economy defines its excess (different) people. And ultimately, it will be used to truncate your future and mine.

The house of your difference is the longing for your greatest power and your deepest vulnerability. It is an indelible part of your life's arsenal. If you allow your difference, whatever it might be, to be defined for you by imposed externals, then it will be defined to your detriment, always, for that definition must [be] dictated by the need of your society, rather than by a merging between the needs of that society and the human needs of self. But as you acknowledge your difference and examine how you wish to use it and for what—the creative power of difference explored—then you can focus it toward a future which we must each commit ourselves to in some particular way if it is to come to pass at all.

This is not a theoretical discussion. I am talking here about the very fabric of your lives, your dreams, your hopes, your visions, your place upon the earth. All of these will help to determine the shape of your future as they themselves are born from your efforts and pains and triumphs of the past. Cherish them. Learn from them. Our differences are polarities between which can spark possibilities for a future we cannot even now imagine, when we acknowledge that we share a unifying vision, no matter how differently expressed; a vision which supposes a future where we may all flourish, as well as a living earth upon which to support our choices. We must define our differences so that we may someday live beyond them, rather than change them.

So this is a call for each of you to remember herself and himself, to reach for new definitions of that self, and to live intensely. To not settle for the safety of pretended sameness and the false security that sameness seems to offer. To feel the consequences of who you wish to be, lest you bring nothing of lasting worth because you have withheld some piece of the essential, which is you.

And make no mistake; you will be paid well not to feel, not to scrutinize the function of your differences and their meaning, until it will be too late to feel at all. You will be paid in insularity, in poisonous creature comforts, false securities, in the spurious belief that the midnight knock will always be upon somebody else's door. But there is no separate survival.

18

THE FIRST BLACK FEMINIST RETREAT

July 6, 1977

Important work is being done here, and I urge each of us as Black Feminists not to limit our examinations, our plans, our dreams, merely to reactive remedies. By this I mean that at the same time as we organize behind specific and urgent issues, we must also develop and maintain an ongoing vision, and the theory following upon that vision, of why we struggle—of the shape and taste and philosophy of what we wish to see.

If we restrict ourselves only to the use of those dominant power games which we have been taught to fear, but which we still respect because they have worked within an antihuman context, then we risk defining our work simply as shifting our own roles within the same oppressive power relationships, rather than as seeking to alter and redefine the nature of those relationships. This will result only in the eventual rise of yet another oppressed group, this time with us as overseer. But our unique position within this system is to constantly question its most cherished assumption and to radically change it, not merely to co-opt it and make it work for us.

It is true that we must use what we can to move through our days, to deal pragmatically with the fact that all around us, our sisters and our children are dying, unspoken. But while we organize around the specific issues of abortion, of sterilization, of health care, we must give some of our energies also consistently to defining the shape of the future toward which we are working, as well as to a constant examination of the nature of the people we wish ourselves to be. For this is the background vision against which all issues must be seen. In what way can we cease to contribute to our own oppression? What hidden assumptions of the enemy have we eaten and made our own?

Taking my attendance here very seriously, I have asked myself what is my function here. I am a poet, and can never be unaware that it is our visions which sustain us. Do not neglect nor shortchange them. Do not treat your dreams lightly. They point the way toward a future made possible by our belief in them and our labors in their name, which is also ours.

There is a world in which we all wish to live. That world is not attained lightly. We call it future. If, as Black Feminists, we do not begin talking, thinking, feeling ourselves for its shape, we will condemn ourselves and our children to a repetition of corruption and error. It is not our destiny to repeat white america's errors, but we will, if we mistake its symbols of success.

19

WHEN WILL THE IGNORANCE END?

Keynote Speech at the National Third World Gay and Lesbian Conference, October 13, 1979

I wish to applaud every single one of you sitting here tonight. It is a wonderful and profound experience to see the row upon row of us gathered here, for we are the proof of the power of vision.

The ignorance will end when each one of us begins to seek out and trust the knowledge deep inside of us, when we dare to go into that chaos which exists before understanding and come back with new tools for action and for change. For it is from within that deep knowledge that our visions are fueled, and it is our vision which lays the groundwork for our actions, and for our future.

This conference is an affirmation of the power of vision. It is a triumph of vision to say the words, even, National Conference of Third World Lesbians and Gays. Thirty years ago, that was only possible in our dreams of what might someday come to pass. And yet, as we know, we have always been everywhere, haven't we? The power of vision nourishes us, encourages us to grow and to change, and to work toward a future which is not yet.

So I stand here as a forty-six-year-old Black Lesbian Feminist warrior poet come to do my work as we have each come to do hers and his—the tasks of joyfulness, of struggle, of community, and the work of redefining our joint power and goals, so that our younger people need never suffer in the isolation that so many of us have known. And while we are here, I ask that each of you remember the ghosts of those who came before us, that we carry within ourselves—the memory of those lesbians and gay men within our communities whose power and knowledge we have been robbed of, those who will never be with us, and those who are not here now. Some of our sisters and brothers are not here because they did not survive our holocausts, nor live to see the day when there finally was a National Conference of Third World Lesbians and Gays.

Some are absent because they cannot be here because of external constraints, and for our sisters and brothers in prison, in mental institutions, in the grip of incapacitating handicaps and illnesses, I ask your attention and your concern, which is another word for love.

But others are not here because they have lived a life so full of fear and isolation that they are no longer even able to reach out. They have lost their vision, they have lost their hope. And for every one of us here tonight, as we all know, there are many lesbians and gay men trapped by their fear into silence and invisibility, and they exist in a dim valley of terror wearing nooses of conformity. And for them, also, I ask your understanding. For as we also know, conformity is very seductive as it is destructive, and can also be a terrible and painful prison.

So while we party tonight, let a little drop fall, call it a libation, which is an ancient African custom, for all our sisters and brothers who did not survive. For it is within the contexts of our past as well as our present and our future that we must redefine community.

In the affirmation of our coming together and the potential power of our numbers, remember also how much work there is still to be done in our communities. In the present, vision must point the way toward action upon every level of our varied existences: the way we vote, the way we eat, the way we relate to each other, the way we raise our children, the way we work for change. This weekend we are here not only to share experience and connection, not only to discuss the many aspects of freedom for all homosexual peoples. We are also here to examine our roles as powerful forces within our communities. For not one of us will be free until we are all free, and until all members of our communities are free. So we are here to help shape a world where all people can flourish, beyond sexism, beyond racism, beyond ageism, beyond classism, and beyond homophobia. In order to do this, we must see ourselves within the context of a civilization that has notorious disrespect and loathing for any human value, for any human creativity or genuine human difference. And it is upon our ability to look honestly upon our differences, to see them as creative rather than divisive, that our future success may lie.

We are here as a conference of Third World lesbians and gay men. That tells us what brings us together. There is a wonderful diversity of groups within this conference, and a wonderful diversity between us within those groups. That diversity can be a generative force, a source of energy fueling our visions of action for the future. We must not let diversity be used to tear us apart from each other, nor from our communities. That is the mistake they made about us. I do not want to us to make it about ourselves.

In this country, historically, all oppressed peoples have been taught to fear and despise any difference among ourselves, since difference has been used against us so cruelly. And we all know how particularly painful homophobia in our communities can be, since we also share a struggle with our homophobic sisters and brothers.

Therefore our moves for change should be illuminated by that knowledge, should implement those lessons which we have learned within the communities of which we are a part. And we must never forget those lessons: that we cannot separate our oppressions, nor yet are they the same. That not one of us is free until we are all free; and that any move for our dignity and freedom is a move also for our communities' sisters and brothers, whether or not they have the vision to see it. And between ourselves, difference must not be used to separate us, but to generate energy for social change at the same time as we preserve our individuality. And although we have been programmed to look upon each other with suspicion and with fear (the old divide-and-conquer routine), we can move beyond that fear by learning to respect our visions of the future more than we respect our terrors of the past. And this cannot be done without strenuous personal effort, and the sometimes painful scrutinies of change.

For make no mistake. Not only our straight sisters and brothers, but we too have been taught to react to any difference with the killer instinct: destroy. I call it jugular vein psychology: "I don't like the way you act, so I'm going to eliminate you immediately." Well, that is not going to work for us here. We are going to learn how to make our differences into power and fuel for vision and for change.

We have to ask ourselves some difficult questions here this weekend. For instance, what does real support mean in a consistently hostile environment? What does a genuinely nonsexist, nonracist culture require and imply? What does the responsibility of community mean? Does it mean only a trick handshake, the latest fashion in cruising clothes, the right only to hold hands in the street? Or does it mean building genuine networks of support for each other and our communities, so that wherever, however, whenever we are functioning within this system which cannibalizes our loves and our lives; whenever and however we function within this system, we work to bring about more humanity and more light for each other and for those who, like ourselves, have felt the keen edge of rejection. In this room now there is a significant amount of people-power for social change, and it must become conscious and useful power. That is the meaning of support and community.

As a Black woman and a lesbian, I have lived without that support for most of my life, and I know what it has cost me and what it has cost many of you. And for me, it was only the consciousness, the vision, of a community somewhere, someday—it was only my vision of the existence and possibility of what is, in fact, here tonight, that helped to keep me sane. And sometimes not even that did. Now we have a chance to make that support for each other real.

I think we are all here because we are seeking a new kind of power, a force for change beyond the old forms which did not serve us. We are here because each of us believes in a future for ourselves and for those who come after us. We are redefining our power for a reason, and that reason is a future, and that future lies in our children and our young people. I'm speaking here not only about those children we may have mothered and fathered ourselves, but about all our children together, for they are our joint responsibility and our joint hope. They have a right to grow, free from the diseases of racism, sexism, classism, homophobia, and the terror of any difference. These children will take what we do and carry it on through their visions, and their visions will be different in turn from ours. But they need us as role models, to know they are not alone in daring to define themselves outside the structures approved of. They need to know our triumphs, and our errors.

So this weekend, I ask that each of us make a commitment to those children within our communities, to a future for them which will be free from oppression and abuse as well as from starvation. I ask that in our planning and discussions we include the children in our future, and bring our insights and knowledge to bear so that they will not be tyrannized and ghettoized as we were. We must become actively involved with the ways in which the children of our communities are being socialized to accept the many forms of their own death, eating poison, reading poison, learning poison. For instance, where do our children learn the lessons of racism, sexism, classism, homophobia, and self-hate? What are our schools teaching our children?

What we dare to dream today we can work to make real tomorrow. Visions point the way to make the possible real. Thirty years ago, most of you sitting in this room could not eat a dish of ice cream in a drugstore in Washington, D.C., because you were not white. The idea of this conference was an impossible dream. Now the future is ours, with vision and with work. And that work will not be easy, for those who fear our visions will try to keep them silent and invisible. But the ignorance will end, when each one of us is prepared to put ourselves upon the line to end it, within ourselves, and within our communities. That is real love, that is real power.

We stand as the last bulwark of humanity in an increasingly depersonalized and antihuman world. A search for acceptance within that world must never blind us to the need for genuine and far-reaching change. We must always ask ourselves, what kind of a world do we really want to become part of?

As lesbians and gay men, we have been the most despised, the most oppressed, and the most spat-upon people within our communities. AND we have survived. That survival is a testament to our strength. We have survived, and we have come together now to use that strength to implement a future, hopefully, a future that shall be free from the mistakes of our oppressors, as well as from our own. What we are doing here this weekend can help shape our tomorrows and a world.

We are going to turn that beat totally around.

When Will the Ignorance End?

20

AN ADDRESS DELIVERED AS PART OF THE "LITANY OF COMMITMENT" AT THE MARCH ON WASHINGTON, AUGUST 27, 1983

I am Audre Lorde, speaking for the National Coalition of Black Lesbians and Gay Men. Today's march openly joins the Black civil rights movement and the gay civil rights movement in the struggles we have always shared, the struggles for jobs, for health, for peace, and for freedom. We marched in 1963 with Dr. Martin Luther King, and dared to dream that freedom would include us, because not one of us is free to choose the terms of our living until all of us are free to choose the terms of our living.

Today the Black civil rights movement has pledged its support for gay civil rights legislation. Today we march, lesbians and gay men and our children, standing in our own names together with all our struggling sisters and brothers here and around the world, in the Middle East, in Central America, in the Caribbean and South Africa, sharing our commitment to work for a joint livable future. We know we do not have to become copies of each other in order to be able to work together. We know that when we join hands across the table of our difference, our diversity gives us great power. When we can arm ourselves with the strength and vision from all of our diverse communities then we will in truth all be free at last.

Washington, D.C.
August 27, 1983

21

COMMENCEMENT ADDRESS

Oberlin College, May 29, 1989

I congratulate you all on this moment of your lives. Most people don't remember their commencement addresses. Next year, when someone asks you who spoke at graduation, I wonder what you will say. I remember she was a middle-aged Black woman. I remember she had a nice voice. I remember she was a poet. But what did she say? After all, there are no new ideas. Only new ways of making those ideas real and active through our lives. What you most of all do not need right now is more rhetoric. What you need are facts you don't ordinarily get to help you fashion weapons that matter for the war in which we are all engaged. A war for survival in the twenty-first century, the survival of this planet and all this planet's people.

Thanks to Jesse Jackson (Poem)

The US and the USSR
are the most powerful countries in the world
but only 1/8 of the world's population
African people are also 1/8 of the world's population.
1/2 of the world's population is Asian.
1/2 of that number is Chinese.
There are 22 nations in the Middle East.
Not three.

Most people in the world
are Yellow, Black, Brown, Poor, Female
Non-Christian
and do not speak english.

By the year 2000
the 20 largest cities in the world
will have two things in common
none of them will be in Europe
and none in the United States.

You are all so very beautiful. But I have seen special and beautiful before, and I ask myself where are they now? What makes you different? Well, to begin with, you are different because you have asked me to come and speak with you from my heart, on what is a very special day for each of you. So when they ask you, who spoke at your commencement, remember this: I am a Black feminist lesbian warrior poet doing my work, and a piece of my work is asking you, how are you doing yours? And when they ask you, what did she say, tell them I asked you the most fundamental question of your life—who are you, and how are you using the powers of that self in the service of what you believe?

You are inheriting a country that has grown hysterical with denial and contradiction. Last month in space five men released a satellite that is on its way to the planet Venus, and the infant mortality rate in the capital of this nation is higher than in Kuwait. We are citizens of the most powerful country on earth—we are also citizens of a country that stands upon the wrong side of every liberation struggle on earth. Feel what that means. It is a reality that haunts each of our lives and that can help inform our dreams. It's not about altruism, it's about self-preservation. Survival.

A twenty-eight-year-old white woman is beaten and raped in Central Park. Eight Black boys are arrested and accused of taking part in a rampage against joggers. That is a nightmare that affects each of our lives. I pray for the body and soul of every one of these young people trapped in this compound tragedy of violence and social reprisal. None of us escapes the brutalization of the other. Using who we are, testifying with our lives to what we believe is not altruism, it is a question of self-preservation. Black children did not declare war upon this system, it is the system which declared war upon Black children, both female and male.

Ricky Boden, eleven, Staten Island, killed by police, 1972. Clifford Glover, ten, Queens, New York, killed by police, 1975. Randy Evans, fourteen, Bronx, New York, killed by police, 1976. Andre Roland, seventh grader, found hanged in Columbia, Missouri, after being threatened for dating a white girl. The list goes on. You are strong and intelligent. Your beauty and your promise lie like a haze over your faces. I beg you, do not waste it. Translate that power and beauty into action wherever you find yourself to be, or you will participate in your own destruction.

I have no platitudes for you. Before most of you are thirty, 10 percent of you will be involved with space traffic and 10 percent of you will have contracted AIDS. This disease which may yet rival the plague of the Dark Ages is said to have originated in Africa, spontaneously and inexplicably jumping from the green monkey to man. Yet in 1969, twenty years ago, a book entitled *A Survey of Chemical and Biological Warfare*, written by John Cookson and Judith Nottingham, published by Monthly Review Press, discussed green monkey disease as a fatal blood, tissue, and venereally transmitted virus which is an example of a whole new class of disease-causing organisms, and of biological warfare interest. It also discussed the possibilities of this virus being genetically manipulated to produce "new" organisms.

But I do have hope. To face the realities of our lives is not a reason for despair—despair is a tool of your enemies. Facing the realities of our lives gives us motivation for action. For you are not powerless. This diploma is a piece of your power. You know why the hard questions must be asked. It is not altruism, it is self-preservation—survival.

Each one of us in this room is privileged. You have a bed, and you do not go to it hungry. We are not part of those millions of homeless people roaming america today. Your privilege is not a reason for guilt, it is part of your power, to be used in support of those things you say you believe. Because to absorb without use is the gravest error of privilege. The poorest one-fifth of this nation became 7 percent poorer in the last ten years, and the richest one-fifth of the nation became 11 percent richer. How much of your lives are you willing to spend merely protecting your privileged status? Is that more than you are prepared to spend putting your dreams and beliefs for a better world into action? That is what creativity and empowerment [are] all about. The rest is destruction. And it will have to be one or the other.

It is not enough to believe in justice. The median income for Black and Hispanic families has fallen in the last three years, while the median income of white families rose 1.5 percent. We are eleven years away from a new century, and a leader of the Ku Klux Klan can still be elected to Congress from the Republican party in Louisiana. Little fourteen-year-old Black boys in the seventh grade are still being lynched for dating a white girl. It is not enough to say we are against racism.

It is not enough to believe in everyone's right to her or his own sexual preference. Homophobic jokes are not just fraternity high jinks. Gay bashing is not just fooling around. Less than a year ago a white man shot two white women in their campsite in Pennsylvania, killing one of them. He pleaded innocent, saying he had been maddened by their making love inside their own tent. If you were sitting on that jury, what would you decide?

It is not enough to believe anti-Semitism is wrong, when the vandalism of synagogues is increasing, amid the homegrown fascism of hate groups like the Christian Identity and Tom Metzger's American Front. The current rise in jokes against Jewish women masks anti-Semitism as well as women hatred. What are you going to say the next time you hear a JAP story?

We do not need to become each other in order to work together. But we do need to recognize each other, our differences as well as the sameness of our goals. Not for altruism. For self-preservation—survival.

Every day of your lives is practice in becoming the person you want to be. No instantaneous miracle is suddenly going to occur and make you brave and courageous and true. And every day that you sit back silent, refusing to use your power, terrible things are being done in our name.

Our federal taxes contribute $3 billion yearly in military and economic aid to Israel. Over $200 million of that money is spent fighting the uprising of Palestinian people who are trying to end the military occupation of their homeland. Israeli solders fire tear gas canisters made in america into Palestinian homes and hospitals, killing babies, the sick, and the elderly. Thousands of Palestinians, some as young as twelve, are being detained without trial in barbed-wired detention camps, and even many Jews of conscience opposing these acts have also been arrested and detained.

Encouraging your congresspeople to press for a peaceful solution in the Middle East, and for recognition of the rights of the Palestinian people, is not altruism, it is survival.

In particular, my sisters and brothers, I urge you to remember, while we battle the many faces of racism in our daily lives as African Americans, that we are part of an international community of people of Color, and people of the African diaspora around the world are looking to us and asking, how are we using the power we have? Or are we allowing our power to be used against them, our brothers and sisters in struggle for their liberation?

Apartheid is a disease spreading out from South Africa across the whole southern tip of Africa. This genocidal system in South Africa is kept propped into place by the military and economic support of the U.S., Israel, and Japan. Let me say here that I support the existence of the state of Israel as I support the existence of the U.S.A., but this does not blind me to the grave injustices emanating from either. Israel and South Africa are intimately entwined, politically and economically. There are no diamonds in Israel, yet diamonds are Israel's major source of income. Meanwhile, Black people slave in the diamond mines of South Africa for less than thirty cents a day.

It is not enough to say we are against apartheid. Forty million of our tax dollars go as aid to the South Africa–backed UNITA forces to suppress an independent Angola. Our dollars pay for the land mines responsible for over 50,000 Angolan amputees. It appears that Washington is joining hands with South Africa to prevent [the] independence of Namibia. Now make no mistake. South Africa, Angola, Namibia will be free. But what will we say when our children ask us, what were you doing, mommy and daddy, while american-made bullets were murdering Black children in Soweto?

In this country, children of all colors are dying of neglect. Since 1980, poverty has increased 30 percent among white children in america. Fifty percent of African American children and 30 percent of Latino children grow up in poverty, and that percentage is even higher for the indigenous people of this land, American Indians. While the *Magellan* capsule speeds through space toward the planet Venus, thirty children on this planet earth die every minute from hunger and inadequate health care. And in each one of those minutes, $1,700,000 are spent on war.

The white fathers have told us: "I think, therefore I am." But the Black mother within each one of us—the poet inside—whispers in our dreams: "I feel, therefore I can be free." Learn to use what you feel to move you toward action. Change, personal and political, does not come about in a day, nor a year. But it is our day-to-day decisions, the way in which we testify with our lives to those things in which we say we believe, that empower us. Your power is relative, but it is real. And if you do not learn to use it, it will be used, against you, and me, and our children. Change did not begin with you, and it will not end with you, but what you do with your life is an absolutely vital piece of that chain. The testimony of your daily living is the missing remnant in the fabric of our future.

There are so many different parts to each of us. And there are so many of us. If we can envision the future we desire, we can work to bring it into being. We need all the different pieces of ourselves to be strong, as we need each other and each other's battles for empowerment.

That surge of power you feel inside you now does not belong to me, nor to your parents, nor to your professors. That power lives inside of you. It is yours, you own it, and you will carry it out of this room. And whether you use it or whether you waste it, you are responsible for it. Good luck to you all. Together, in the conscious recognition of our differences, we can win, and we will. A LUTA CONTINUA [The struggle continues].

22

THERE IS NO HIERARCHY OF OPPRESSION

I was born Black, and a woman. I am trying to become the strongest person I can become to live the life I have been given and to help effect change toward a livable future for this earth and for my children. As a Black, lesbian, feminist, socialist, poet, mother of two, including one boy, and a member of an interracial couple, I usually find myself part of some group in which the majority defines me as deviant, difficult, inferior, or just plain "wrong."

From my membership in all of these groups I have learned that oppression and the intolerance of difference come in all shapes and sizes and colors and sexualities; and that among those of us who share the goals of liberation and a workable future for our children, there can be no hierarchies of oppression. I have learned that sexism (a belief in the inherent superiority of one sex over all others and thereby its right to dominance) and heterosexism (a belief in the inherent superiority of one pattern of loving over all others and thereby its right to dominance) both arise from the same source as racism—a belief in the inherent superiority of one race over all others and thereby its right to dominance.

"Oh," says a voice from the Black community, "but being Black is NORMAL!" Well, I and many Black people of my age can remember grimly the days when it didn't used to be!

I simply do not believe that one aspect of myself can possibly profit from the oppression of any other part of my identity. I know that my people cannot possibly profit from the oppression of any other group which seeks the right to peaceful existence. Rather, we diminish ourselves by denying to others what we have shed blood to obtain for our children. And those children need to learn that they do not have to become like each other in order to work together for a future they will all share.

The increasing attacks upon lesbians and gay men are only an introduction to the increasing attacks upon all Black people, for wherever oppression manifests itself in this country, Black people are potential victims. And it is a standard of right-wing cynicism to encourage members of oppressed groups to act against each other, and so long as we are divided because of our particular identities we cannot join together in effective political action.

Within the lesbian community I am Black, and within the Black community I am a lesbian. Any attack against Black people is a lesbian and gay issue, because I and thousands of other Black women are part of the lesbian community. Any attack against lesbians and gays is a Black issue, because thousands of lesbians and gay men are Black. There is no hierarchy of oppression.

It is not accidental that the Family Protection Act,[1] which is virulently antiwoman and antiblack, is also antigay. As a Black person, I know who my enemies are, and when the Ku Klux Klan goes to court in Detroit to try and force the board of education to remove books the Klan believes "hint at homosexuality," then I know I cannot afford the luxury of fighting one form of oppression only. I cannot afford to believe that freedom from intolerance is the right of only one particular group. And I cannot afford to choose between the fronts upon which I must battle these forces of discrimination, wherever they appear to destroy me. And when they appear to destroy me, it will not be long before they appear to destroy you.

Note

1. A 1981 congressional bill repealing federal laws that promoted equal rights for women, including coeducational school-related activities and protection for battered wives, and providing tax incentives for married mothers to stay at home.

23

WHAT IS AT STAKE IN LESBIAN AND GAY PUBLISHING TODAY

The Bill Whitehead Award Ceremony, 1990

What is at stake in Lesbian and Gay publishing today basically is what has always been at stake—our survival—our future: for each one of us and collectively, the question—how do we define ourselves, and how do we put who we are behind what we say we believe?

We are Lesbians and Gay men helping to shape a future for ourselves and for those various communities of which we are a part, and within which we must define the meaning of being Lesbian and Gay. For without community, whatever we do can be only a temporary armistice between an individual and his or her particular situation.

Lesbian and Gay Publishing does not exist in a vacuum, however, and we are not one great vat of homogenized milk. We are Lesbian and Gay in a world growing increasingly hysterical with denial and contradiction—a world where the increasing disparity between the haves and the have-nots threatens to detonate in each one of our dooryards. Of course, you say, we all recognize the importance of a world view—we know the ozone layer is disappearing, nuclear proliferation is poisoning our planet. But to an increasing percentage of people upon this earth, watching their children starve to death in Lahore and the Sahel, lost to drugs in L.A. and New York, stomped to death in Leipzig and Berlin and Brooklyn because of the color of their skin, nuclear holocaust and ecological disaster is of little concern. What does Lesbian and Gay publishing have to offer them?

I am a Black Lesbian Feminist Warrior Poet Mother, stronger for all my identities, and I am indivisible. Out of the insights and power of those identities have come the work which you honor here tonight.

The increase in racist, anti-Semitic, heterosexist attacks here in North America is being mirrored throughout europe by the rise in neo-fascist activity against Afro-Europeans, Jews, homosexuals, and foreign workers.

There are Lesbian and Gay writers of Color in this country articulating in their work questions and positions which must be heard if we are to survive into the twenty-first century. How many of these Lesbian and Gay writers of Color are included in the Triangle Group, supported or encouraged by its individual members? There are Lesbian and Gay writers of Color across europe chronicling what the current political changes on that continent can mean for people of Color, that is, for the majority of people upon this earth. How many of these writers are known to you? How do you use your power when their manuscripts come across your desk, the modest announcements of their books appear in your mail?

What is at stake in Lesbian and Gay publishing in 1990, quite simply, is: how will you define yourselves in the twenty-first century in a world where seven-eighths of that world's population are people of Color? And how will you use the power that definition engenders?

I recognize the honor you do me with this award. But honors are most meaningful when they include peer decisions. How many Lesbians and Gay men of Color are included in your group? How many were polled for this award? Or even, how many writers of Color have you published, or encouraged, or helped to give voice in any way? At the National Lesbian and Gay March on Washington, D.C., the largest gathering of Lesbian and Gay men to date, the one book exhibit at the march ignored the works of gay people of Color. Lesbian and Gay writers of Color, our work and our concerns, are consistently invisible within the publishing and literary newsletters circulating in the Lesbian and Gay communities.

Kitchen Table: Women of Color Press was started, and is maintained, by Lesbians of Color. It is a first in the annals of Lesbian and Gay publishing, and [we are] now approaching our tenth year. Where are we represented at this gathering?

One award will not counterbalance a continuing invisibility of Lesbian and Gay writers of Color.

I believe the Bill Whitehead Memorial Award is being given to me in good faith. Therefore, I accept the recognition which comes with this award, but I will not accept any money from the Triangle Group. If this group wishes to truly honor my work, built upon the creative use of differences for all our survivals, then I charge you, as a group, in some way to include and further expose the work of new Lesbian and Gay writers of Color within the coming year, and to report on what has been done at next year's award ceremony.

That will be a truly bold and meaningful gesture, and one reflective of the growing vision and power of Lesbian and Gay publishing in the 1990s.

May 15, 1990

24

IS YOUR HAIR STILL POLITICAL?

My first trip to Virgin Gorda earlier this year had been an enjoyable, relaxing time. After coping with the devastations of Hurricane Hugo, three friends and I decided to meet somewhere in the Caribbean for a Christmas vacation. From my personal and professional travels, Virgin Gorda seemed the ideal spot. And less than an hour's flight time from my home.

My friend, another Black woman from St. Croix, and I deplaned in Tortola to clear BVI [British Virgin Islands] immigration at the Beef Island Airport. I was happy to be a tourist for a change, looking forward to a wonderful holiday, post-hurricane problems left behind for a few days. The morning was brilliant and sunny, and in our bags was a frozen turkey, along with decorations for the rented house.

The Black woman in a smartly pressed uniform behind the Immigration Control desk was younger than I, with heavily processed hair flawlessly styled. I handed her my completed entry card. She looked up at me, took it with a smile, and said, "Who does your hair?"

My friend and I were the only passengers going on to Virgin Gorda. As a Black woman writer who travels widely, I have recently been asked that question many times. Thinking we were about to embark on one of those conversations about hairstyle Black women so often have in passing, on supermarket lines, buses, in laundromats, I told her I had done it myself. Upon her further questioning, I described how.

I was not at all prepared when, still smiling, she suddenly said, "Well, you can't come in here with your hair like that you know." And reaching over she stamped "no admittance" across my visitor's card.

"Oh, I didn't know," I said, "then I'll cover it," and I pulled out my headkerchief.

"That won't make any difference," she said. "The next plane back to St. Croix is 5:00 p.m. this evening." By this time my friend, who wears her hair in braided extensions, tried to come to my aid. "What's wrong with her hair," she asked, "and what about mine?"

"Yours is all right," she was told. "That's just a hairstyle."

"But mine is just a hairstyle too," I protested, still not believing this was happening to me. I had traveled freely all over the world; now, in a Caribbean country, a Black woman was telling me I could not enter her land because of how I wore my hair?

"There is a law on our books," she said. "You can't come in here looking LIKE THAT."

I touched my natural locks, of which I was so proud. A year ago I had decided to stop cutting my hair and to grow locks as a personal style statement, much the same as I had worn a natural afro for most of my adult life. I remembered an *Essence* magazine cover story in the early 80s that had inspired one of my most popular poems—*Is Your Hair Still Political?*

"You can't be serious," I said. "Then why didn't I know about this before? Where is it written in any of your tourist information that Black women are only allowed to wear our hair in certain styles in your country? And why do we have to?"

Her smile was gone by now.

"It's been a law for over five years," she snapped. And I realized she was very serious when I saw our bags being taken off the plane, and it preparing to go on without us.

"But how was I supposed to know that?" I protested, visions of our holiday feast defrosting on the tarmac, our friends from New York wondering where we were, our hostess at the airport waiting in vain to drive us to our rented house by the sea.

"I've read I can't bring drugs into the British Virgin Islands. I've read I can't seek employment in the British Virgin Islands. I've read about everything else I can't do in the British Virgin Islands, but how are Black tourists supposed to know we can't wear locks if we visit the British Virgin Islands? Or don't you want Black tourists?"

By now I was outraged. Even with the hot sun outside and the dark face before me, I was confused for a moment as to where I was. Nazi

Germany? Fascist Spain? Racist South Africa? One of those places where for so many decades white people had excluded Black people because of how they LOOKED? But no, it was a Black woman, in the Caribbean, telling me I wasn't acceptable as a tourist in her country—not because of what I do, not even because of who I am, but because of how I wear my hair. I felt chilled to the bone.

By this time the young white pilot had come in to see why the flight was being delayed. "What do you mean, because of her HAIR?" Finally an immigration supervisor came, asking me to fill out another entry card.

"Why can't I go on to Virgin Gorda," I began. "I've been there before. And what's wrong with my hair? It's not unhealthy, it's not unsanitary, it's not immoral, and it certainly is not unnatural!"

The supervisor looked at my well-groomed ear-length locks. "Are you a Rasta?" he asked. And then it finally dawned on me what this was all about.

He didn't ask me if I was a murderer. He didn't ask me if I was a drug dealer, or a racist, or if I was a member of the Ku Klux Klan. Instead, he asked me if I was a follower of the Rastafarian religion.

Some see locks and they see revolution. Because Rastafarians smoke marijuana as a religious rite, some see locks and automatically see drug peddlers. But the people who are pushing drugs throughout the Caribbean do not wear locks; they wear three-piece suits, carry attaché cases and diplomatic pouches, and usually have no trouble at all passing through Immigration.

I stared at this earnest young Black man for a moment. Suddenly my hair became very political. Waves of horror washed over me. How many forms of religious persecution are we now going to visit upon each other as Black people in the name of our public safety? And suppose I was a Rastafarian? What then? Why did that automatically mean I could not vacation in Virgin Gorda? Did it make my tourist dollars unusable?

What if he had asked me if I were a Jew? A Quaker? A Protestant? A Catholic? What have we learned from the bloody pages of history and are we really doomed to repeat these mistakes?

There was an ache in my heart. I wanted to say, "What does it matter if I am a Rasta or not?" But I saw our bags sitting out in the sun, and the pilot walking slowly back to his plane. Deep in my heart I thought—*it is always the same question: where do we begin to take a stand?* But I turned away.

"No, I'm not a Rastafarian," I said. And true, I am not. But deep inside of me I felt I was being asked to deny some piece of myself, and I felt a solidarity with my Rastafarian brothers and sisters that I had never been conscious of before.

"Is your hair still political?"
Tell me, when it starts to burn.[1]

My immigration card was stamped admit, our bags were put back on the plane, and we continued our journey, twenty minutes overdue. As the plane taxied to the end of the runway, I looked back at the Beef Island Airport.

On this tiny island, I had found another example of Black people being used to testify against other Black people, using our enemies' weapons against each other, judging each other on the color of our skin, the cut of our clothes, the styling of our hair. How long will Black women allow ourselves to be used as instruments of oppression against each other?

On a Black Caribbean island, one Black woman had looked into another Black woman's face and found her unacceptable. Not because of what she did, not because of who she was, not even because of what she believed. But because of how she LOOKED. What does it mean, Black people practicing this kind of self-hatred with one another?

The sun was still shining, but somehow the day seemed less bright.

St. Croix, Virgin Islands
January 10, 1990

Note

1. From "A Question of ESSENCE," in Lorde, *Our Dead Behind Us* (New York: Norton, 1986).

IV

REFLECTIONS

25

AUDRE LORDE

My Shero, My Teacher, My Sister Friend

Johnnetta Betsch Cole

In countless ways, I remember, reflect upon, and cherish the privilege I enjoyed of knowing Audre Lorde. I knew of "the warrior poet" years before I met her, claimed her as one of my sheroes, learned from her, and respectfully called her my sister friend.

When I arrived at Hunter College, in the fall of 1982, to teach in the anthropology department and the women's studies program, I was told that I had to meet Audre Lorde, a dynamic poet and professor in the English department. I do not remember on which day I was introduced to her, nor can I recall the details of our first conversation. But this I do know: from that day forward, Audre Lorde had a profound effect on the way that I view the world and wish to have the world see me. Three years later, as I witnessed the dedication of the Audre Lorde Women's Poetry Center, I could proudly claim the warrior poet as my colleague and my friend. That same year, Dr. Gloria Joseph, feminist scholar and former professor at Cornell University and Hampshire College, extended an invitation to Audre Lorde and to me to participate in a conference on Caribbean women that would be held in St. Croix. As that conference drew to a close, it was clear that the sister outsider and I shared a commitment to finding the tools that would dismantle the master's house.

In 1984, Dr. Gloria Joseph convened a group of black feminist scholar/activists to form an organization that she would name SISSA— Sisters in Support of Sisters in South Africa. Zala Chandler, Gloria

Joseph, Audre Lorde, Andree McLaughlin, Barbara Riley, and I were the founding mothers. The goals of SISSA were to support black women in South Africa, relate to the women's self-help movement in South Africa, and develop a relationship with two South African grassroots organizations. Sharing membership in SISSA with Audre Lorde gave me an opportunity to witness how comfortable she was in being a writer/activist. How Audre related to SISSA was indicative of how generous she was to people and causes she believed in.

Every institution has lore about good and not so good things that transpired in their space, famous people who had passed their way, and a mystery or so that had not been solved. When I arrived at Spelman College in 1987 to serve as the president of that historically black college for women, I was told that Audre Lorde had visited the campus in 1978. But because she had been coldly received and was the target of homophobic barbs, she had vowed to never return to Spelman.

Drawing on our sisterly relationship, I invited Audre to come to Spelman to participate in a series that I called "Speaking at Spelman, Readings at Reynolds." At first, she would hear nothing of this invitation; but finally, perhaps as much to end my persistent asking, Audre agreed to visit the campus in 1988. This time, our sister, the warrior poet Audre Lorde was warmly and properly received.

In the community where I grew up in Jacksonville, Florida, it was said of someone who followed one request with a substantially larger one: you give some people an inch and they will take a mile. And so, I began to respectfully ask Audre Lorde for "a mile," namely, the donation of her papers to Spelman College. I shared with her that, from the extraordinary gift of $20 million to Spelman from Drs. Bill and Camille Cosby, the college had constructed an academic center in which there would be archival space that could house her literary legacy. I let Sister Audre know that her papers would be under the watchful care of Spelman alumna and seasoned archivist Brenda Banks; that Dr. Beverly Guy-Sheftall, the founding director of Spelman's Women's Research and Resource Center, was committed to acquiring for the archives the papers of other black feminists; and that her papers, the papers of the most prominent black lesbian feminist writer of the twentieth century, belonged at a historically black college for women. Each time I interacted with Sister Audre Lorde, I did my best to reinforce what I hoped was a compelling case for her to donate her written works to the Spelman Archives. In an extraordinary act of sisterhood, she finally agreed to leave to Spelman all of her written works that were not already at the Lesbian Herstory Archives in Brooklyn, New York. Three years after her death in 1992, Sister Audre Lorde's papers were brought to the Spelman archives.

> How important it is for us to recognize and
> celebrate our heroes and she-roes!
>
> —Maya Angelou

Our sister outsider became and will remain one of my sheroes. We were both grown women when I first met Audre Lorde, yet I found myself struggling not to give in to the starry-eyed posturing that a youngster can adopt when a grown-up takes on a presence that appears bigger than life.

We all need sheroes, and yes, we need heroes too. Not the distorted images of straight, white, able-bodied men who take up most of the time and space in grade B movies. And not the real-life version who, if we let them, take up most of the pages of textbooks and dominate whatever is taking place in every sector of a society. We all need the real kind of sheroes and heroes, people whose greatness *and* vulnerabilities convince us that we too can help to advance a just cause. If only through what we are told about them, we ordinary folks need to know women and men who are extraordinary because they stay the course when doing so has been declared a hopeless process. And we are all made better when we engage with the work of sheroes and heroes, whether in real time, through a story well told, or simply in our imagination. That work may be a poem, a painting or a song; a scientific discovery or an explanation of some aspect of human behavior; a proposal for relieving human suffering or bringing peace to some corner of our troubled world.

However we describe our sheroes and heroes, they are inevitably people of great courage. They stand against untruths no matter how popular those untruths are. As sister poet Gwendolyn Brooks reminds us: "Truthtellers are not always palatable. There is a preference for candy bars."

Audre Lorde was all that I have described here as the makings of a shero. She was all of that and more. Acknowledgment of her literary genius did not come soon enough for Lorde, but it did come. Far more today than when she wrote her poems, prose, and essays that now constitute her collected works, Audre Lorde has gained iconic status. Her name is now inextricably associated with a stance against the multiple forms of oppression. Lorde's written words, her calls to action, and her insistence on speaking truth to power earned her a presence in realms as wide apart as queer theory and mainstream literary circles.

Reaching the pinnacle of success as a warrior poet did not shield Lorde from the insecurities she first wrestled with as a child, especially her uneasiness over questions of her color and caste. Nothing was as painful to her as the possibility of rejection by black women who were at home with their darker hues. When Lorde felt she was not being acknowledged as a great writer, her responses ranged from sulking to diva-like outbursts.

Audre Lorde could be fierce, but she was rarely secure. The way that she moved through the world reminds us that greatness is not synonymous with perfection. Indeed, to be human is to be flawed.

In the protracted struggle she waged with cancer, and the aftermath of a modified radical mastectomy, Audre Lorde repeatedly used the power of human will to turn the improbable into a reality. As she valiantly fought the cancer that came, was conquered, and came yet again, winning months and years beyond what most would say she could have, her sheroic qualities were a sight to behold.

Audre Lorde had no shortage of courage—a defining attribute of those we admire and pledge to model our lives after—and the persistent challenges in her life offered ample opportunities for her to use it. For Audre Lorde, a young woman of conservative West Indian parents, to own her homosexuality was a courageous act. When she confronted and exposed people who had not owned their "isms," that took courage. At the time and in the places where she would present herself as a black, lesbian, mother, warrior poet: that took courage.

She who learns must teach
She who teaches must learn

—adapted from an African proverb

Audre Lorde was not only my shero, she was my teacher. In the classic image of a teacher and student, the teacher is always older than and knows far more than the student. Audre Lorde and I were bound in a different kind of relationship. I, the student, was two years younger than she; and at issue was not who knew the most about anything, but how she who teaches must learn, and she who learns must teach.

By the time I reached Hunter College, I thought I had rooted out my homophobia and heterosexism. To convince myself of this, I would reference an experience I had at the University of Massachusetts, Amherst, in the 1970s. During a discussion in a course that Dr. Esther Terry and I team taught on "The Black Woman," we were "called out" for being homophobic and heterosexist by one of our students, Arlene Avakian, who at that time was an administrative assistant in the women's studies program, and who some years later received her doctorate and now chairs the university's women's studies department.

I took Arlene Avakian's charge seriously and began to read about, think about, and talk about how I and so many others practiced heterosexism. By the time I arrived at Hunter College and met Audre Lorde in 1982, I assumed that I had put such bigotry and privilege aside. Audre Lorde challenged my homophobia not so much by what she said to me but by how she lived what she said. And it was her written works, her public lectures, and my conversations with her that led me to more fully confront the ways in which I enjoyed heterosexist privilege.

When I met Lorde at Hunter College in the early eighties, I had clocked countless hours in reading about, lecturing on, and indeed experiencing firsthand the stuff of racism and sexism. From my early days in the Jim Crow circumstances of Jacksonville, Florida, I knew that water fountains, toilets, schools, libraries, movie houses, and neighborhoods all came in a white and a colored version. And while I had grown up both black and female, I did not grow up poor. But the fact that no amount of money could buy my family out of the places reserved for

Black people taught me how solidly race trumped class in the American South.

My decision to study anthropology and to pioneer in founding one of the first Black Studies programs in a U.S. university spoke to my ongoing struggle against racism as an entrenched system of inequality. So entangled was I in the web of racism that my consciousness about sexism, although there in some form from my childhood, did not receive my serious attention until the 1970s, when I began to explore the arena of inquiry called Women's Studies.

It was not long after those explorations that I began to ask the fundamental questions: where are the women in Black Studies, and where are the black folks in Women's Studies? Because I continued to raise those questions at Hunter College, I was ripe for reading about and hearing about Audre Lorde's notions about the intersection of race, gender, class, and sexuality—and the importance of not privileging one form of oppression over another.

A third and ever so critical lesson that my teacher, Audre Lorde, brought into my world flows from the notion that each of us has multiple identities. Her dramatic rendition of this reality was announced each time she introduced herself as a black, woman, feminist, lesbian, mother, teacher, warrior poet. She would then warn her audience of the futility and indeed the danger of any attempt to deny her any of her multiple identities. The futility in asking one to choose between identities happens when a black woman is asked to choose if her race or her gender is more important to her; when a gay Latino is asked if his primary identity is as a Latino or a gay man.

I lift up here one more lesson that Audre Lorde brilliantly taught me and all who would dare to listen to her as she broke the silence in her readings and her writings. Being the victim of one form of oppression does not prevent one from oppressing someone else. Because a white woman is a victim of sexism does not block her ability to be a racist. Because an African American has been and continues to be a victim of institutionalized and individual forms of racism does not prevent that person from being homophobic and practicing heterosexism. This notion that each of us has some form of power and privilege—being a Christian in the United States, being able-bodied, being young—is not simply an important theoretical point. This reality requires each of us to confront the basis or bases around which we have the potential to harm others.

No one is your friend who demands your silence.

—Alice Walker

I have always valued friends. Indeed, I wouldn't want to try to do without them. The brilliant and at times irreverent sister anthropologist Zora Neale Hurston put it this way: "It seems to me that trying to do without friends is like milking a cow to get cream for your morning coffee. It is a whole lot of trouble, and then not worth much after you get it" (*Dust Tracks on a Road*, 1942). It was an honor and a joy to count Audre Lorde among my friends.

Audre and I did not regularly call each other, or set specific times each year when we would get together. But when we were in the same place, we always found a way to be in each other's company. There was always a kind of magic that floated between us, the source of which was our shared belief that each of us had a role to play in doing what Sister Sojourner Truth had commanded us women folks to do: to get the world right side up again. When our paths intersected at Hunter College or at an event in New York and most of all when we were in St. Croix at the home of Gloria Joseph, a dear friend each of us cherished, when we parted, I inevitably felt that I was more powerful than I had ever been before.

26

AUDRE'S VOICE

Alice Walker

The first time I heard Audre Lorde's voice was in the spring of 1973; I was living in Jackson, Mississippi. She called from New York to read a statement that she and Adrienne Rich were preparing for delivery on National Book Awards night. All three of us had been nominated: Audre and I suspected the winner would be Adrienne—no black woman poet had ever been selected before—but I realized as we talked that Adrienne and Audre were friends, and determined not to have something so extraneous as an award come between them. I firmly supported this attitude. Audre and I went over the statement, the gist of which was that whoever was selected by the National Book Award committee would accept the award in the names of the other two, as well as in the name of all women, those who would understand the significance of our statement and those who would not. Adrienne Rich did win, and she read our statement, in her strong and brilliant voice, and to this day I feel this means we all won.

Many years later, during a summer in the early eighties, I heard Audre's voice again, this time in my small living room in San Francisco. She had been brought by Adrienne Rich and her partner, Michelle Cliff, and while we chatted about the allure of the city and how I had come to live there, Audre impressed me by her quiet scrutiny and detailed identification of the numerous rocks my daughter, Rebecca, and I, had collected. What I didn't know at that time was that, like me, Audre had once taught at Tougaloo, the small black college in Mississippi. That we had both been interracially married and both had daughters. Audre had a son as well. I was to find this out later, from reading her books. These were similarities—and of course we were both black women poets who loved rocks and books—never claimed, and the possibility of a connection that was never explored. Was all this sheer coincidence, or was there a deeper kinship than either of us, at the time, could recognize?

The third time I heard Audre's voice was in the late eighties, I do not recall the season; I called her in St. Croix, where she was living after many years of treatment for cancer, to express my dismay at a comment she had made about me in an interview. She was questioning my use of the word "womanist," in lieu of "black feminist," saying that it appeared to be an attempt to disclaim being feminist, and saying, as well, that I had chosen to speak about the controversy surrounding the film *The Color Purple*—ongoing at the time—to a white audience, using a white medium. I pointed out to her that it is a necessary act of liberation to name oneself with words that fit; that this was a position her own work celebrated. As for *The Color Purple* event, I explained I had been interviewed by Barbara Christian, an African American critic, on a hookup to dozens of universities and colleges across North America, some black, some racially mixed, some white. We talked until Audre seemed to understand my point about using the word "womanist"; more room in it for changes, said I, sexual and otherwise. More reflective of black women's culture, especially southern culture. As a woman of Caribbean heritage, I think she appreciated this point. She hadn't actually seen *The Color Purple* broadcast herself, but had relied on someone else's report about it. We ended our conversation amicably.

The fourth time I heard Audre's voice, in the early summer of 1995, I was sitting beside Adrienne Rich at a screening in San Francisco of the wonderful and moving film about Audre's life *A Litany for Survival*. Adrienne and I had bumped into each other on the way to the theater, delighted and amazed that the three of us—Audre, Adrienne, and I—would be brought together once again. Audre's voice, rich and firm and true, filled the air. Her amazon beauty glowed from the screen. Seeing her with her partner, Dr. Gloria Joseph, as they lived the serene and simple life of black women close to the edge of many things, including the Caribbean sea and Audre's life, was an experience of infinite meaning. I felt Audre's strength, and Dr. Joseph's, flowing into me. There was something timeless about them, a rightness that could neither be overlooked nor ever denied. These were women who loved women, loved each other, fought Audre's cancer together, enjoyed happy meals with friends, shared a coconut. You could see in them the ancient tradition of woman-loving being humbly and proudly carried on.

And for the last two days, as I write this in the late summer of 1995, I have been listening to Audre's voice, again. As I listen, enthralled, I muse about why it might have bothered her that I prefer "womanist" to "black feminist." Or why she misunderstood my effort to reach out and connect with the many people who needed a dialogue around a film based on my book. I am glad I called immediately after reading her comments and that we talked, sister to sister. I feel this stronger than ever, listening to her now. For it is really an honor to feel accountable to Audre, to know that it matters deeply that we at least attempted to come to an understanding directly, between ourselves.

While I was meditating this morning, thinking of Audre's incredible legacy of courage and deep intelligence, I thought: she is clearly a fallen warrior. But immediately I thought: but how far can such a magnificent warrior fall? Not far, as we read in her books. Not far, as we hear in her voice on the numerous tapes she recorded. As she herself says about Malcolm X, I do not think I fully grasped her greatness while she lived, though I knew she was formidable. What I love about Audre Lorde is her political and emotional honesty, her passion for living life as herself, her understanding of what a privilege and joy this is. I love her patience, as she taught generations (by now) of women and men the sweet if dangerous fun of self-love. I love her cool stare back into the eyes of death, as cancer stalked her, and finally dragged her down.

I miss her. Listening to her voice makes me want to talk back to her. That is what I am doing here.

Audre, as I listen to you, and reread your books, I learn many new and endearing things about you: that until you were four, because your vision was poor and you didn't have glasses yet, you thought trees were green clouds. That the first woman with whom you made love didn't particularly appeal to you, until you'd actually kissed her. That you sometimes thought of your white, Jewish husband as your third child. You are actually so much yourself, as you ramble the fields and corridors of your own unique life, you make me laugh, as anything that is original and spontaneous might. Once, when I was praising you, someone referred to you as a professional lesbian, because you always implacably presented that inseparable part of yourself. I was saddened by this attempt to minimize your bravery. I always saw your behavior, hiding nothing of importance, as the ultimate expression of dignity, and it is that word, along with others—determined, spirited, powerful, loving, and grand—with which, it seems to me, you are still only partially characterized.

27

LORDE

The Imagination of Justice

bell hooks

In these times of extreme antifeminist backlash, of mounting fascism and its concomitant support of war and all things that are like war, it is vital that we celebrate the strength of a sustained feminist movement, the twenty-fifth anniversary of the Women's Research and Resource Center here at Spelman. Its very existence, its survival, its continued growth and development is a testament to the power of solidarity between progressive women and men, especially the solidarity of individual visionary black women who have had to work against the conservative history rooted in sexist biases that once were the absolute foundation of a Spelman education.

In the introduction to her new book, *We Are the Ones We Have Been Waiting For*, Alice Walker shares this insight:

> It is the worst of times because it feels as though the very earth is being stolen from us . . .: the land and air poisoned, the water polluted, the animals disappeared, humans degraded and misguided. War is everywhere. It is the best of times because we have entered a period . . . of great clarity as to cause and effect. A blessing when we consider how much suffering human beings have endured, in previous millennia, without a clue to its cause. . . . Because we can now see into every crevice of the globe and because we are free to explore previously unexplored

crevices in our own hearts and minds, it is inevitable that everything we have needed to comprehend in order to survive, everything we have needed to understand in the most basic ways will be illuminated now. . . . We live in a time of global enlightenment. This alone should make us shout for joy.

We are here at Spelman to shout for joy. And we are also here to arouse our collective will to continue the freedom struggle, to continue to use our intellect, our imaginations to forge new and liberatory ways of knowing, thinking, and being, to work for change. We are here to revitalize our critical consciousness, to rekindle the seeds of militant radicalism that are the roots of every women's studies, feminist studies, and women's research center in our nation. To do that, we must dare to make this occasion both a time to celebrate and a time to expand our consciousness. Let us honor the insight of Audre Lorde, who once asked all of us, in all our diversity and differences of race, class, nationality, religion, sexual practice, to "re-member what is dark and ancient and divine within ourselves" that it may aid our speaking, our dreaming, our way of life.

When we speak of the ancient dark divine, the intent is not to reinscribe some folksy image of us as all-knowing strong black female. Our intent is not re-mammification or the evocation of any racialized sexist thinking that would render exotic the bodies and beings of black women by suggesting that we are innately more in tune with the earth, more soulful, more nurturing, more caring, more ethical than other groups of women or that we represent a feminine alternative to patriarchy. Patriarchy has no gender.

When we speak radically of the dark divine, the invitation is for each and every one of us to transcend race and gender, to move beyond categories into the interior spaces of our psyches and encounter there the ground of our being, the place of mystery, creativity, and possibility, for it is there that we can construct the mind that can resist, that can revision, that can create the maps that when followed will liberate us. To embrace the ancient dark divine is to engage the political and the spiritual. Engaging the dark divine, we are all called to empathic identification with black females globally. We are called to see clearly that the fate of black females in the world is the mirror into which everyone can look and see all our destinies unfolding.

During the early stages of contemporary feminist movement, it was common to talk about black women as experiencing double jeopardy because we were likely to be victimized by both sexism and racism. Then, as the movement progressed, class was added to this equation and a discussion of triple jeopardy ensued. In actuality, black females are assailed on all sides, on so many fronts that words like double or triple jeopardy are simply inadequate descriptions. We face exploitation and/or oppression. We face dehumanization from so many locations that the feminist strategies for our continued survival envisioned so far are nowhere near as complex and as clearly defined as they must be if we are to thrive.

For black females globally and here in our nation, these are dangerous times. To create lives of optimal well-being and, most fundamentally, just to survive we require a feminist theory and practice that not only raises consciousness but offers new and different ways to think and be, activist strategies that can only be radical and/or revolutionary because there is no place in the existing structure of imperialist white supremacist capitalist patriarchy where we are truly safe, individually or collectively. Coming here to celebrate for some of us, those of us who were engaged with the women's center from its inception, we find that our shouts of joy must also make way for moments of mourning, or ritual remembrance. For in this unsafe world, we have witnessed the untimely loss, the deaths of so many powerful black female voices, writers, thinkers, activists, artists, visionary feminists. And for some of us, Spelman was the place where we all first gathered, met one another face to face, and made our voices heard. Here at Spelman, we experienced our first taste of a solidarity so sweet, so soul nurturing that we were indeed literally carried away, ecstatically transported by the power of silences broken, by the sound of our decolonized speech. This is what Audre Lorde describes in conversation with Adrienne Rich when she declares: "What understanding begins to do is to make knowledge available for use, and that's the urgency, that's the push, that's the drive." In those heady days, we were learning how to do just that. We needed the women's center, women's studies then and we need it now. Much vital feminist theory/ black feminist theory emerged in conversations and debates here.

In those days, Toni Cade Bambara was with us, leftist, social commentator, writer, leader of a black feminist vanguard, lover of blackness; it was her voice that told us in the anthology *The Black Woman* that we needed to

> set up a comparative study of the woman's role . . . in all the third world nations; to examine the public school and blueprint some viable alternatives; to explore ourselves and set the record straight on the matriarch and the Evil Black Bitch; to delve into history and pay tribute to all [black female] warriors . . .; to outline work that has been done and remains to be done in the area of consumer education and cooperative economics; [and] that we needed to get into the whole area of sensuality and sex.

These are just some of the insights we must remember and use.

Wisely, Bambara was telling us that we would need to move beyond simplistic categories like masculine and feminine because, she explains, "I have always found the either/or implicit in those definitions antithetical to what . . . revolution for self is all about—the whole person . . . that the usual notions of sexual differentiation in roles is an obstacle to political consciousness . . . that a revolutionary must be capable of, above all, total self-autonomy." Bambara [wrote] those words in 1970 and yet audiences still ask me and other black women engaged in feminist theory and practice, "are you black first or a woman?" We know that when we ask them what feminist thinkers do you read and study, the answer is almost always "none." This is why archives are important and why the continual study of our work is crucial. This is why it is important that work by visionary black thinkers be collected in archives. Ones that are first and foremost accessible to those who are engaged in the process of decolonization.

We know how easily, how quickly our words are forgotten, our histories buried. We all know that students, even our women's studies students, often show no hint of recognition when we talk about the works of Pat Parker, Lorraine Hansberry, Barbara Christian, Endesha Mae

Holland, June Jordan, Octavia Butler, and even Audre Lorde. We know that feminist thinker Michele Wallace has theorized the nature and substance of our continued invisibility because she has lived with the fear of erasure. In *Invisibility Blues*, she reminds us:

> I have come to see the difficulties black women writers encounter as structural and systemic. . . . Because black women are perceived as marginal to the production of knowledge, their judgment cannot be trusted. . . . As a consequence black women are not allowed (by themselves as well as by others) to make definitive statements about the character of power, agency, and resistance within and beyond the black community. If and when they persist in doing so, the discouragement is great.

Wallace's insight is yet another reminder of why it is important that our papers be gathered, respected, used. As we all know, there are a small number of individual black women writers who have managed to engage in the insurrection of subjugated knowledge in such a way that our work is read more broadly, studied in classrooms, and quoted in a variety of texts (I place my writing among this work). Yet this inclusion does not ensure lasting presence, continued visibility, or sustained recognition.

On one hand, it is awesome that the critique of race and racism women of color, many of us black women, brought to the feminist movement fundamentally altered the nature of feminist theory. Yet we can still all read celebrated theory by white women which builds on this work without any mention of the individual black women thinkers who laid the foundation. To resist this erasure, we must do all we can to document, to highlight, to study, to celebrate, and most important to create work that is cutting edge, that breaks through silences, the different walls that have been erected to block our vision of ourselves, of our futures.

Ironically, as more work by black women has received attention, much of that work has become more conservative, reformist, and not radical. We get gender without feminism. We are offered womanism as though it is the antidote to a powerful poison, that dangerous substance being feminism. When we connect Wallace's writing on invisibility with the constant demand Lorde makes in her work that silences be broken, that we claim our power to make ourselves visible, we have both a theory that enables us to understand what hems us in and a theory that conceptualizes our power to set ourselves and our words free. Lorde challenges us to not be trapped by fear. In "The Transformation of Silence," she declares:

> We can learn to work and speak when we are afraid in the same
> way we have learned to work and speak when we are tired.
> For we have been socialized to respect fear more than our own
> needs for language and definition, and while we wait in silence
> for that final luxury of fearlessness, the weight of that silence
> will choke us. . . . there are many silences to be broken.

At times, we want to be silent about how grave our circumstances are. We do not want to speak about how difficult it has become for black females of all classes to garner support in all areas of our lives. We want to be silent about how hard it is to raise consciousness, to critique, challenge, and change sexism, within and beyond black communities (particularly when the forms of black community that once placed us in meaningful solidarity with progressive black men are daily eroding). All black females, irrespective of class positionality, know how difficult it is to constructively change our lives so that we can have the necessary health and well-being to fuel revolutionary visions of social change.

Significantly, Toni Cade Bambara, Audre Lorde, and June Jordan were all critical thinkers who dared to be militant, to speak when silence would have afforded them greater comfort. They all wrote about the need for black females to claim the space of becoming whole. Speaking openly of her commitment to feminism in the essay "Where Is the Love," Jordan testifies: "I am a feminist, and what that means to me is much the same as the meaning of the fact that I am Black: it means that I must undertake to love myself and to respect myself as though my very life depends upon self-love and self-respect. It means that I must everlastingly seek to cleanse myself of the hatred and contempt that surrounds and permeates my identity. . . . It means that the achievement of self-love and self-respect will require inordinate, hourly vigilance, and that

I am entering my soul into a struggle that will most certainly transform the experience of all the peoples of the earth, as no other movement can, in fact hope to claim: because the movement into self-love, self-respect, and self-determination is the movement now galvanizing the true, the unarguable majority of human beings everywhere." It is essential to our struggle for self-determination that we speak of love. For love is the necessary foundation enabling us to survive the wars, the hardships, the sickness, and the dying with our spirits intact. It is love that allows us to survive whole.

When I began to write books on love for a more popular audience, I would often hear from readers that I was no longer as radical, as militant as I once was. To those who would limit and define black female intellect, imprison us in academies where our teaching cannot reach the masses of people who are seeking life-changing theory and practice, love has no meaning. Hence, they will not understand that it is the most militant, most radical intervention anyone can make to not only speak of love but to engage in the practice of love. For love as the foundation of all social movements for self-determination is the only way we create a world that domination and dominator thinking cannot destroy. Anytime we do the work of love, we are doing the work of ending domination.

We, black females globally, have a long history of struggling through brokenness, of enduring great pain and yet holding on. This is still the history of victimhood. The history visionary radical black women are making in our lives and in our work, and here today at the Center, is not a history that begins with brokenness. It is a history that begins with the recognition that the work of love is our revolutionary starting point, that to love ourselves no matter our circumstance is already to stand in the place of victory.

28

REMEMBERING AUDRE LORDE

Gloria I. Joseph

I think it was Billie Holiday, or perhaps another singer from the past, who sang this phrase in one of her songs: "The difficult, I'll do right now, the impossible may take a little while." The task of remembering Audre Lorde in a few pages is impossible. I don't have infinite space—I have the here and now. So the difficult, I'll do right now.

When Audre Lorde lived in St. Croix, her life was markedly different from her city life. She wasn't viewed as a world-renowned black lesbian, mother, activist, poet—an icon on a pedestal. She became what was dearest to her, part of a community. As Audre reminded us, "Without community, there is no liberation."

As soon as roads were navigable, after Hurricane Hugo in 1989, two male friends arrived in our yard with a small refrigerator to ensure the proper treatment of Audre's medical supplies for the treatment of her cancer. All the power lines were out, but we had a generator.

The name Gamba Adisa was given to her in St. Croix at a naming ceremony. The word "Audre-ism" began to emerge. Audre had a vivid, creative imagination and at times she embellished stories, and the Crucians would say, "Now is that factual or an Audre-ism?"

In St. Croix there was less fury and anger, which allowed Audre more space for contemplation and compassion. Audre was part of a bee collective and among them was concern for her health and well-being. Once Audre was insisting on lifting a ten-frame super, loaded with honey; supers are the frames where the bees store their honey, and they can be very heavy. I can still hear Curtis yelling, "Audre, NO!" Surprisingly, she did not lift the super.

St. Croix was a base for frequent travel and enjoyment and endless knowledge which often resulted in her writing more poems and essays. One Thanksgiving we planned to spend on Virgin Gorda with friends. As we were going through immigration, the young woman on duty stared at her hair and began asking Audre questions about her locks. Audre answered willingly, thinking the woman was personally interested. Not so. She indicated decisively, "You cannot enter this island with locks," and she firmly stamped "rejection" on the form. I decided to enter the conversation and proceeded to tell the woman all kinds of reasons why she was wrong to reject Audre's entry. In the meanwhile, our luggage was sitting on the runway, and it included our roasted Thanksgiving turkey, which was ready for eating. We finally asked to see the manager. He listened and reluctantly allowed us to board the plane. Audre's essay "Is Your Hair Still Political?" resulted from that unpleasant airport experience.

We visited Grenada and Carriacou, her mother's birthplace. Audre learned that she had half sisters, twins, in Grenada. She had a strong desire for restitution for the neglect suffered by her twin sisters because they had been unrecognized by their father. She arranged to meet the twin who lived in Grenada and it was an extremely emotional but satisfying experience for Audre. She continued having contact with this sister for as long as she could. We made a trip to Grenada shortly after the U.S. invasion and met with some of Audre's relatives who gave us detailed information about the situation.

Audre took yearly trips to Berlin, Germany, for her alternative cancer treatments. While in Germany, there were many memorable activities. One in particular was an invitation to the German Opera House in Berlin. During one of Audre's readings at the American House, we met Annabell Bernard, a black opera singer, and her husband, Karl, who held an administrative post at the opera house. They were very impressed and when Annabell was asked to sing the lead role in La Bohème, she invited us to attend. Following the invitation, I had to practically drag Audre to the opera. Once there, however, it was a spectacular night for her! After the performance, we waited while Anabell signed autographs; then we were escorted to Karl's brown Jaguar and driven to a restaurant.

The couple had arranged for dinner at an Italian restaurant, Salt and Pepper. Anabell and Karl had told the restaurant manager that they wanted them to cook something very special for their guests. When we arrived, the owner, Mario, presented each of us with a red rose. There were six of us: Collin, a black male opera singer; his girlfriend; Karl; and Anabell, Audre, and myself. The menu was pasta with shrimp and green peppers, Italian red wine, and Italian pastries for dessert.

There was also the trip to Hawaii to see the eclipse and visit Pele at the volcano crater. We went with Clare Coss and Blanche Cook. Audre was using a wheelchair at times, and we pushed her along the black volcanic ash with excitement and joy. It was here that she told me that some of her ashes were to be spread here at the appropriate time. Previously, during a trip to Carriacou, we were at a restaurant and Audre began talking about the many places she wanted her ashes spread. In a typical Gloria way, I said, "With all those places you keep naming, why don't you do like they do on Ash Wednesday—put a spot of ashes on everyone's forehead?" She looked at me with a half smile and responded seriously, "When the time comes, you will know what to do." *And she was right.*

Her ashes were spread at two places in Hawaii: at Pele's volcano center and at the Sacred Women's Place. At the latter, Dawn Wasson, a native Hawaiian *kupuna*, conducted the ceremony. We were a small group, which included Sonia Sanchez. We were attending a special gathering sponsored by Medgar Evers' International Cross-Cultural Black Women's Studies Institute, founded by Professor Andree McLaughlin. The setting was at the foot of a beautiful forest with a waterfall as backdrop. Dawn, Sonia, always committed, resourceful, and reliable, and I spoke as we individually spread her ashes. There would be two more special places that Audre's ashes were spread. One was in Berlin on Krumme Lanke, the lake where Audre rowed in her blown-up rubber boat with her Berlin friends Ika and Dagmar. And ashes were spread along the Buck Island underwater trail. Several of her Crucian friends chartered a boat, sang spirituals, and spread her ashes. Some of her ashes were also spread in New York City, but I'm not familiar with the specific locale.

I learned a lot about poetry from Audre. The major thing I learned was the necessity to *work* a poem—write it and rework it as many times as necessary until you finally are able to convey the intended meaning. Today, I hear folks proudly saying they wrote a poem and that was it—first writing and the poem is finished! I want to say to them, "That's like playing tennis without a net and declaring yourself a great tennis player." Audre's poetry and prose spoke to events, to the inner core of who we are and why we exist. They were political, spiritual, and topical.

Audre dealt with the here and now. She would frequently ask, "What are we going to do about the situation now?" At this juncture, with a George W. Bush administration, the question is, "What is the role of black feminism and how is it actualized in the daily realities of our lives?" Audre and I discussed this question back in the eighties and certain conclusions remain the same. I am tempted to go into a longer discussion, but I'm reminded of Audre's words. Recently, I listened to tapes of a meeting with Audre and Afro Germans, a meeting I attended. At one point, I was giving a lengthy political statement and Audre responded: "Keep it simple, Joseph."

So, I'll simply ask, what would it mean to take seriously strong black feminist voices—a community of scholars in the academy? As Audre would say, "without community, there is no liberation."

We are a people. A people do not throw their geniuses away.
And if they are thrown away, it is our duty as artists and as
witnesses for the future to collect them again for the sake of
our children, and if necessary, bone by bone. —Alice Walker

Generations of women of all colors blossomed on her
poems and grew stronger. . . . She was their heroine. They
quoted her as if her words would make them brave . . .
brave enough to speak. —Ruby Nell Sales

BEARING WITNESS

The Legacy of Audre Lorde

Beverly Guy-Sheftall

When the Women's Research and Resource Center at Spelman College celebrated its twenty-fifth anniversary in October 2006, the memory of perhaps the most revered, powerful, and influential African American feminist writer/activist of the twentieth century was invoked.[1] Scholars and activists from around the globe convened at Spelman to commemorate the Women's Center's twenty-five years of boldly transformative feminist scholarship, activism, and collaboration.[2] The celebratory symposium, "Remembering Audre Lorde: In Celebration of Black Women Writers, Scholars, Artists, and Activists," was dedicated to the extraordinary life and work of Audre Lorde (1934–1992), a radical lesbian writer, poet, and educator who taught women around the globe that "it is not difference which immobilizes us, but silence. And there are so many silences to be broken."[3] Audre was certainly a comrade in many struggles for freedom and justice and a sister/friend to countless women seeking wisdom and healing.[4] What is not well known, however, is her special bond with Spelman College, the oldest historically black college for women in the world.

Her connection with Spelman began in the spring of 1978 when she journeyed to the college to speak at the invitation of Ruby Sales, a member of the history department. I dare say this was a historic moment since she was the first *out* black lesbian to speak to students and faculty. June Jordan, her feminist comrade in the struggle for human rights, also came to Spelman at the invitation of Ruby. Even more striking and impactful would be Audre's return to Spelman at the invitation of her friend Dr. Johnnetta Cole not very long after Cole was inaugurated as its seventh president. When I reflect upon Lorde's perhaps unlikely sojourn to Spelman, I am reminded of the ways in which—whether she was present or not—she helped us envision a "beloved community" of sisters and brothers who are committed to positive change and a world free of racism, sexism, classism, heterosexism, ableism, poverty, religious intolerance, misogyny, war, and violence.

To be sure, Audre's most cherished gift to the college and future generations of scholars was her decision to give her personal papers and other artifacts to the Spelman Archives, a component of the Women's Center. Capturing the significance of this connection at the twenty-fifth anniversary, Leslie Feinberg, transgender writer/activist, asserted, "It is here at Spelman that the words and works of Audre Lorde have found a home. This historically black college has ensured that her fiery words will never be extinguished."[5] It was her long-time friendship with Johnnetta Cole and her subsequent visit to the Spelman campus that precipitated Audre's decision to deposit her papers here. Her will made provisions for this extraordinary gift, and three years after her death in 1992, Audre's archive came to Spelman. At the request of Lorde's estate, the collection was closed until an authorized biography was completed. *Warrior Poet*, written by Professor Alexis de Veaux, was published in 2004.

With a generous grant in 2006 from the Arcus Foundation, the Audre Lorde Papers were finally able to be processed by the Spelman Archives and will be opened to the public in 2009. The collection includes poems, manuscripts, journals, letters, and other artifacts; it also includes unpublished speeches and letters. Arcus is a Michigan-based philanthropy that funds groups that illuminate the presence and contributions of people in the gay, lesbian, bisexual, and transgender community and the issues which confront them. The Arcus grant also enabled the center to establish a groundbreaking ZAMI Project (named after Lorde's biomythography) whose purpose is to increase public awareness and understanding about African American gay and lesbian experiences; explore the marginalization of racial issues in the GLBT (gay, lesbian, bisexual, transgender) movement; initiate a series of student-driven workshops and other activities to combat homophobia in the Atlanta University Center community and other historically black colleges and universities; and contribute to the production of scholarship on Lorde. Urvashi Vaid, executive director of Arcus, indicated how proud they are "to partner with the flagship institution in terms of black women's education."[6] She indicated that this extraordinary collection "increases awareness and understanding about African American gay and lesbian experiences, and preserves the archives of an incredible writer who contributed so much to the GLBT and racial justice movements." The Women's Center began to explore issues related to sexual orientation over a decade ago, and it is the only historically black college or university (HBCU) with a serious commitment and funding dedicated to tackling these issues at the curricular and co-curricular levels, as well as explicitly exploring LGBT issues in the African diaspora.

The Audre Lorde Lesbian Feminist Project, its official designation, celebrates the work of Lorde and remembers the short and tragic life of Sakia Gunn, a fifteen-year-old black girl from Newark, New Jersey, whose murder on May 14, 2006, ignited a movement and led to New Jersey's first bias-murder prosecution. Gunn was stabbed to death when she and four friends were attacked by two men after they rejected the men's sexual advances and declared themselves to be lesbians. Violence against women and GLBT black people are issues that Audre Lorde foregrounded in her lifelong struggle for human rights, civil rights, and gender justice.

The Lorde papers are one of the most significant among the special collections in the Spelman Archives. They were the first acquisition in a broader strategy on the part of the Women's Center of becoming a major repository for the papers of prominent contemporary black feminist scholar/activist/writers. In 2005, the Toni Cade Bambara Papers were acquired as a result of the generosity of her daughter, Karma Bambara-Daniel. In 2001, the annual Toni Cade Bambara Scholar/Activism Conference was inaugurated on campus and Karma was its most special guest. Karma's daughter, Zoe, looking very much like her grandmother Toni, eventually attended the conference. Karma's decision to entrust her mother's papers to the Spelman Archives was certainly impacted by her bearing witness since 2001 to the annual student-led Toni Cade Bambara Conference during Women's History Month.

The personal papers of Johnnetta Cole were also given to the Spelman Archives in 2005. Her collection (1949–2007) documents her long career as a professor of anthropology, African American studies, Caribbean studies, and women's studies, and her work as a college administrator at several universities and as president of Spelman College and Bennett College for Women, the nation's two historically black women's colleges. The papers also document her service on the boards of corporations and her work with nonprofit and community-based organizations. These three pioneers in the development of black women's studies and feminist thought—Lorde, Bambara, and Cole—are linked in their lifelong struggles for social justice and human rights. They also have in common their individual bonds with Spelman College and now their permanent connection with an institution that has been dedicated to the education and empowerment of black women since 1881.

Scholar/activist Angela Davis, who had the privilege of knowing Audre, captures her far-reaching impact: "Through her life, she galvanized alliances among individuals and groups who were not expected to discover points of convergence. Thus her legacy is claimed by poets, writers, scholars and activists, by working-class people and women and men of all racial backgrounds."[7] In a tribute to Audre Lorde, three years after her death, poet Essex Hemphill wrote her a letter in which he thanked her for welcoming "your [gay] brothers to come into the circle you were creating. You never barred us from participating in envisioning a new world. You only asked that we be brave, we be strong, we be committed to working for a joint liberation for the oppressed, a joint liberation for us all."[8] Self-defined as a "white, anti-racist, working-class, transgender, lesbian woman socialist activist," Leslie Feinberg acknowledges her indebtedness to Audre for her "razor-sharp truths" and her "profound insights about difference."[9]

The Women's Center at Spelman has been a vibrant site for transnational feminist exchange and activist networking across difference, which Audre's life underscored. The center was represented at the United Nations' World Conferences on Women in Nairobi, Kenya, and Beijing, China (1995); the Women of Africa and the African Diaspora (WAAD) Conference in Madagascar (2001); the Eighth International Interdisciplinary Congress on Women in Uganda (2002); the Writing African Women Conference in Capetown, South Africa (2006); the international conference Feminism Without Borders at the Instituto de Estudios de la Mujer at the University of Granada, the first women's studies institute in Spain (2007); and the First International Congress on the Marginalization of Queer Theory in Latin American Studies at the Universidad Nacional Mayor de San Marcos in Lima, Peru (2007). The center has also hosted scholars and representatives of nongovernmental organizations from around the world, including Nigeria, Trinidad, Jamaica, South Africa, Zimbabwe, Tanzania, Nigeria, Swaziland, Canada, and India. In addition, the Women's Center and SisterLove, Inc., organized an invitational, international conference on Women, Girls and HIV/AIDS in Africa and the African Diaspora (2004).

Prior to the celebratory symposium, the center hosted a day-long planning meeting that recognized the signal contribution of Audre Lorde's vision in helping the center to craft the radical feminist site that we have become over the past quarter of a century.[10] We began this historic meeting of sister/feminists from around the world with Professor Gloria Wade-Gayles' poem "Sometimes as Women Only."[11] Center faculty members reflected upon our curriculum development workshops on global black feminisms and the impact of the scholarship we've produced about the complexities of the lives of women of African descent and other women of color. We pondered the importance of the numerous women's conferences and gatherings that we hosted or attended. We recalled the steady stream of sister scholar/activists we'd welcomed and organized among around a variety of social justice issues.

During the morning session, "Feminist Collaboration," Guy-Sheftall discussed how cross-cultural collaborations had underpinned and enhanced the identity and activism of the center as a subversive space, and how this essential feminist value had been critical to our endeavors to establish and sustain global feminist solidarities. The questions we explored together were: what types of radical feminist collaborations have you experienced/created in forging transnational black/African feminist networks and partnerships? How do you think the nature of feminist collaboration is changing and why? What do you envision might be the future for global radical feminist scholar/activism? We anticipated that such deliberations would enable us to clarify the meaning and value of feminist collaborations as a conceptual and activist notion and praxis. We also hoped to identify new ways of collaborating as feminists using the most cost-effective and the most politically effective strategies. We also hoped to identify the ways in which collaborative research/teaching/writing and activism can be deployed to strengthen the work of the center and our feminist partners.

In the afternoon's "Personal as Political" roundtable, all of us spoke candidly in response to the following questions: What have you been doing as a feminist activist/scholar that continues to shape your perspectives and vision of the spaces or communities you inhabit? What are the most intractable/difficult ideological and structural challenges facing you in your work as a feminist scholar/activist? In which areas/fields do you think you are having the most impact in relation to the global women's movement and women's studies? What are the most urgent emerging issues and debates in your region/location? And finally, we committed to crafting a new black feminist manifesto, like the Combahee River Collective document, that would provide a framework for our collective transnational struggles in the years ahead.[12]

Following the end of the symposium, we reconvened on Sunday morning to reflect upon the insights we had shared during the planning meeting in light of the symposium sessions. We began the process of envisioning as a collective the future of the Women's Center and how we might engage in even more productive collaborations. We named ourselves the Transnational Black Radical Feminist Think Circle and promised to meet the next time in Barbados. When our deliberations were over, we formed a circle, celebrated our remarkable journey together, and basked in the memory of Audre Lorde, who reminded us, "Without community, there is no liberation."

Notes

1. Audre Lorde's significance in the academy is underscored by numerous courses that include her writings and an endowed professorship at the University of Louisville, thanks to a $1 million gift by Carla Wallace in 2005. A sister lesbian and cancer survivor, Wallace consulted Angela Davis about her desire to endow a chair at the university. The Audre Lorde Chair in Race, Class, Gender, and Sexuality was filled for the first time in 2007 and is a joint appointment between the Women's Studies and Pan-African Studies Departments. Wallace's gift was matched by Kentucky's Bucks for Brains program, which will be used for scholarships and a second endowed professorship for the Pan-African Studies Department.

2. Excellent coverage of the symposium and twenty-fifth anniversary activities of the center appeared in *Southern Voice* (December 1, 2006), in an article by Ryan Lee, "Remembering the Warrior," 37.

3. Audre Lorde, "The Transformation of Silence into Language and Action," in *Sister Outsider: Essays and Speeches* (1984; reprint, Berkeley: Crossing Press, 2007), 44.

4. See Cassie Premo Steele, *We Heal from Memory: Sexton, Lorde, Anzaldua and the Poetry of Witness* (New York: Palgrave Macmillan, 2000).

5. Unpublished paper delivered at the symposium in celebration of the Women's Center's twenty-fifth anniversary, Spelman College, October 27, 2008.

6. Cited in Lee, "Remembering the Warrior," 37.

7. Quoted in Betty Winston Baye, "A Seat at the Table," *Black Issues Book Review* (November–December 2006), 45.

8. A special section of *Standards* 5, no. 1 (Fall 1995), includes "A Tribute to Audre Lorde," in which Hemphill's piece appears.

9. Unpublished paper, Women's Center's twenty-fifth anniversary symposium.

10. Patricia McFadden, Cosby Chair in the Social Sciences and radical African feminist from Zimbabwe, and M. Bahati Kuumba, associate director of the Women's Center, provided the conceptual framework, discussion questions, and agenda for the meeting, in collaboration with Guy-Sheftall.

11. The poem appears in *Sturdy Black Bridges: Visions of Black Women in Literature*, ed. Roseann P. Bell, Bettye J. Parker, and Beverly Guy-Sheftall (Garden City, N.Y.: Doubleday, 1979), 363–364.

12. Participants included faculty, staff, and students from the Women's Center, Beverly Guy-Sheftall, M. Bahati Kuumba, Yvonne Vinson, Malika Redmond, Sarah Thompson, Leana Cabral, Judy Willis; and guests Carole Boyce Davies (Trinidad); Eudine Barriteau (Barbados); M. Jacqui Alexander (Trinidad); Chandra Talpade Mohanty (India); Bernedette Muthien (South Africa); Linda Carty (Canada). I have not identified their institutional homes. We are indebted to Sarah Thompson, Spelman class of 2005, for her note taking and her synthesis of the planning meeting, "Repositioning Our Scholar-Activism: The Way Forward" (photocopy, Spelman Women's Center).

CONTRIBUTORS

RUDOLPH P. BYRD is Goodrich C. White Professor of American Studies in the Graduate Institute of the Liberal Arts and the Department of African American Studies and is the founding director of the James Weldon Johnson Institute for Advanced Interdisciplinary Studies at Emory University. He is the author of *Jean Toomer's Years with G. I. Gurdjieff* and *Charles Johnson's Novels: Writing the American Palimpsest*. He is the editor of *Generations in Black and White: Photographs from the James Weldon Johnson Collection of Negro Arts and Letters; I Call Myself an Artist: Writings by and about Charles Johnson; Traps: African American Men on Gender and Sexuality* (with Beverly Guy-Sheftall); and *The Essential Writings of James Weldon Johnson*. He is one of the founding officers of the Alice Walker Literary Society.

JOHNNETTA BETSCH COLE is president emerita of Spelman College and of Bennett College for Women. She is also professor emerita of Emory University from which she retired as Presidential Distinguished Professor of Anthropology, Women's Studies and African American Studies. She is the author of numerous publications for scholarly and general audiences, including a book coauthored with Beverly Guy-Sheftall: *Gender Talk: The Struggle for Women's Equality in African-American Communities*. Dr. Cole's work as a college professor and president, her published works, her speeches and community service consistently address issues of race, gender, and all other forms of discrimination. Much of her work in the interest of equality and social justice is now centered in her role as the chair of the board of the Johnnetta B. Cole Global Diversity and Inclusion Institute, founded at Bennett College for Women.

BEVERLY GUY-SHEFTALL is founding director of the Women's Research and Resource Center at Spelman College and is Anna Julia Cooper Professor of Women's Studies at Spelman. She also teaches graduate courses in black feminist studies at Emory University's Institute for Women's Studies. She has published a number of texts in African American and women's studies, including the first anthology on black women's literature, *Sturdy Black Bridges: Visions of Black Women in Literature*, which she coedited with Roseann P. Bell and Bettye Parker Smith; *Daughters of Sorrow: Attitudes Toward Black Women, 1880–1920; Words of Fire: An Anthology of African American Feminist Thought; Traps: African American Men on Gender and Sexuality* (with Rudolph P. Byrd); and *Gender Talk: The Struggle for Women's Equality in African-American Communities* (with Johnnetta Betsch Cole). She is also a founding coeditor of *Sage: A Scholarly Journal on Black Women*.

BELL HOOKS is professor of women's studies at Berea College in Berea, Kentucky. She is one of the foremost black intellectuals in America today and the most prolific, most anthologized black feminist theorist and cultural critic on the contemporary scene. hooks has described herself as a "Black woman intellectual, revolutionary activist." She has authored over twenty books, including *"Ain't I a Woman": Black Women and Feminism* and *Sisters of the Yam: Black Women and Self-Recovery*. hooks has been speaking as a guest of the Women's Center at Spelman College since the 1980s. She was a plenary speaker at the twenty-fifth anniversary celebration of the Women's Center, which paid tribute to the life and work of Audre Lorde.

GLORIA I. JOSEPH is a writer/activist who returned to her home in the Virgin Islands after retiring from the School of Social Science at Hampshire College in Amherst, Massachusetts. She coedited (with Jill Lewis) *Common Differences*, in which she wrote a compelling essay on mothers and daughters within African American communities. She has written a number of other important essays, including "The Incompatible Ménage à Trois: Marxism, Feminism, and Racism" and "Black Feminist Pedagogy and Schooling in Capitalist White America." Joseph was a speaker on the plenary panel during the Spelman College Women's Center's twenty-fifth anniversary celebration in October 2006.

ALICE WALKER is the author of twenty-three books spanning the genres of the essay, the short story, the novel, and poetry. These works are a permanent part of our national literature. Translated into the world's many languages, these works include *Once*, a volume of poems; *In Love and Trouble: Stories of Black Women; The Third Life of Grange Copeland*, her debut novel; *In Search of Our Mothers' Gardens*, her first collection of essays; and *The Color Purple*, a novel for which she was awarded the Pulitzer Prize and the American Book Award, a novel adapted for film and for the stage. Beyond these foundational works, which prominently feature her native Georgia and her special concern for the lived experience of black women, she is the author of works that further testify to the compassionate and integrative nature of her dialogic imagination, including *The Temple of My Familiar*, a novel; *Her Blue Body Everything We Know*, a collection of poetry; *Now Is the Time to Open Your Heart*, a novel; and *We Are the Ones We Have Been Waiting For*, a collection of essays.

SELECTED BIBLIOGRAPHY

Works by Audre Lorde

The First Cities. New York: Poets Press, 1968.

Cable to Rage. London: Paul Breman, 1970.

From a Land Where Other People Live. Detroit: Broadside Press, 1973.

New York Head Shop and Museum. Detroit: Broadside Press, 1973.

Coal. New York: W. W. Norton, 1976.

Between Our Selves. Point Reyes, CA: Eidolon Editions, 1976.

The Black Unicorn. New York: W. W. Norton, 1978.

The Cancer Journals. San Francisco: Spinsters Ink, 1980.

Zami: A New Spelling of My Name. Boston: Persephone Press, 1982.

Chosen Poems: Old and New. New York: W. W. Norton, 1982.

Sister Outsider: Essays and Speeches by Audre Lorde. Trumansburg, NY: Crossing Press, 1984.

I Am Your Sister: Black Women Organizing across Sexualities. New York: Kitchen Table: Women of Color Press, 1985.

Our Dead Behind Us: Poems. New York: W. W. Norton, 1986.

A Burst of Light: Essays by Audre Lorde. Ithaca, NY: Firebrand Books, 1988.

Undersong: Chosen Poems, Old and New. New York: W. W. Norton, 1992.

The Marvelous Arithmetic of Distance: Poems, 1987–1992. New York: W. W. Norton, 1993.

Scholarship on Audre Lorde

Alexander, Elizabeth. "Coming Out Blackened and Whole: Fragmentation and Reintegration in Audre Lorde's *Zami* and *The Cancer Journals*." *American Literary History* 6, no. 4 (1994): 695–715.

Braxton, Joanne M. *Black Women Writing Autobiography: A Tradition within a Tradition*. Philadelphia: Temple University Press, 1989.

Burr, Zofia. *Of Women, Poetry, and Power: Strategies of Address in Dickinson, Miles, Brooks, Lorde and Angelou*. Urbana: University of Illinois Press, 2002.

de Veaux, Alexis. *Warrior Poet: A Biography of Audre Lorde.* New York: W. W. Norton, 2004.

Ginzberg, Ruth. "Audre Lorde's (Nonessentialist) Lesbian Eros." *Hypatia* 7, no. 4 (Fall 1992): 73–90.

King, Katie. "Audre Lorde's Lacquered Layerings: The Lesbian Bar as a Site of Literary Production." In Sally Munt, ed., *New Lesbian Criticism: Literary and Cultural Readings.* New York: Columbia University Press, 1992.

Martin, Joan M. "The Notion of Difference for Emerging Womanist Ethics: The Writings of Audre Lorde and bell hooks." *Journal of Feminist Studies in Religion* 9, nos. 1–2 (Fall 1993): 39–51.

Shelly, Elaine. "Conceptualizing Images of Multiple Selves in the Poetry of Audre Lorde." *Lesbian Ethics* (Winter 1995): 88–98.

Steele, Cassie Premo. *We Heal From Memory: Sexton, Lorde, Anzaldua, and the Poetry of Witness.* New York: Palgrave, 2000.

Wilson, Anna. "Audre Lorde and the African-American Tradition." In Sally Munt, ed., *New Lesbian Criticism: Literary and Cultural Readings.* New York: Columbia University Press, 1992.

———. *Persuasive Fictions: Feminist Narrative and Critical Myth.* Lewisburg: Bucknell University Press; London; Cranbury, NJ: Associated University Presses, 2001.

CHRONOLOGY

1934   Audrey Geraldine Lorde born in Harlem, New York City

1951   Enters Hunter College

1959   Earns bachelor's degree

1961   Earns master's degree in library science from Columbia University

1962   Marries Edwin Rollins

1963   Daughter Elizabeth is born; Audre attends historic March on Washington

1964   Son Jonathan is born

1966   Becomes head librarian at Town School Library in New York City

1968   Writer-in-residence at Tougaloo College; publishes first book of poetry, *The First Cities*; begins relationship with Frances Clayton which lasts for nearly twenty years

1969   Begins teaching at Lehman College in New York City

1970   Publishes second book of poetry, *Cables to Rage*; joins English Department at John Jay College of Criminal Justice in New York City

1974   Combahee River Collective (originally the Boston chapter of the National Black Feminist Organization [1973]) founded in Boston

1975   Divorces Edwin Rollins

1977   Feminist journal *Chrysalis* launched in Los Angeles; Lorde becomes poetry editor; participates in first black feminist retreat of Combahee River Collective, in South Hadley, Massachusetts; receives breast cancer diagnosis

1978   Invited to speak at Spelman College; contributor to special issue of *Black Scholar* on "Blacks and the Sexual Revolution"

1979   Delivers keynote address at the National Third World Gay and Lesbian Conference in Washington, D.C., on October 13

1980   Co-founds Kitchen Table: Women of Color Press; publishes *The Cancer Journals*

1981   Joins Hunter College's English department (Creative Writing Program); meets Gloria Joseph (her companion until her death in 1992)

in St. Croix; Women Writers Symposium organized by Joseph held in St. Croix; Women's Coalition of St. Croix founded by Lorde; speaks at National Women's Studies Association Annual Conference at University of Connecticut, Storrs, on "The Uses of Anger: Women Responding to Racism"

1983 Delivers address at the March on Washington, August 27; publishes *Zami: A New Spelling of My Name*

1984 Receives liver cancer diagnosis; publishes *Sister Outsider: Essays and Speeches*; co-founds with Gloria Joseph and others Sisters in Support of Sisters in South Africa (SISSA) in St. Croix

1985 Dedication of the Audre Lorde Women's Poetry Center, Hunter College

1986 Moves to St. Croix

1988 Invited to speak at Spelman College by President Johnnetta B. Cole

1989 Hurricane Hugo devastates St. Croix

1991 Named New York State's Poet Laureate; held post till 1993.

1992 Dies in St. Croix after long struggle with cancer; memorial services in New York City's Cathedral of St. John the Divine, in St. Croix, and in Berlin, Germany

1995 Audre Lorde Papers arrive at Spelman College Archives

2004 Alexis de Veaux's biography of Lorde, *Warrior Poet*, published

2006 Spelman College receives grant from Arcus Foundation to process Lorde's papers; 25th anniversary of Women's Research and Resource Center at Spelman College celebrates life and work of Audre Lorde

2009 Audre Lorde Papers available to public in Spelman College Archives

INDEX

poetry (*continued*)
Lorde communicates through, 160
love and, 164
of Pat Parker, 158–159
reading in Zurich, 90
role of journals in, 165–166
self-definition and, 156–157
teaching, 182–185
police, 67
politics
the erotic and, 18
hair and, 224–227, 250
international Black community
and, 95–96
Lorde's contributions to, 21–23
role of African American women
in, 9–10
sadomasochism and, 55
poverty, children and, 217–218
Powell, Betty, 62
power
for social change, 218
taking back, 139–140
privilege, 215–216
protest, 163–164
publications, of Audre Lorde, 4
publishing, gay and lesbian, 221–223

quilts, 125, 126, 128

"race women," 7–8
racism
of aging cancer patient, 116–117
apartheid and, 68–72, 216–217
of Australian man at Lukas
Klinik, 112
difference and, 202–203
feminism and, 92–94, 244
fighting cancer and, 137

racism (*continued*)
in Germany, 171–176
heterosexism and, 221–223
hierarchy of oppression and,
219–220, 235–236
lesbianism and, 156–157
Lorde's efforts in fighting, 122–123
oppression and, 27–29
social movements and, 21–23
in United States and Australia,
98–100
rage
against Black women, 61–62
sexism and, 44–49
teaching children to control, 76–77
Rainey, Ma, 61
Rastafarians, 226–227
Reagan, Ronald, 174
Redmond, Malika, 260n12
Redmond, Sarah, 8
religion, 224–227
Rich, Adrienne, 238, 239, 244
Richardson, Allene, 67
Richardson, Marilyn, 6
Riley, Barbara, 232
Rios, Yolanda, 60, 104, 130
Rogers, Gwendolyn, 62
Roland, Andre, 215
Rollins, Edwin, 4, 267
Rollins, Elizabeth
attends poetry center
dedication, 104
birth of, 267
childhood of, 76–77, 79–80
graduation of, 96–97
on lesbian parents, 78
love for, 118
mentioned, 4
on remaining silent, 40–41

Lightning Source UK Ltd.
Milton Keynes UK
UKOW01f0357050417
298378UK00003B/18/P